W9-AZY-127

Critical Issues in Educational Leadership Series
Joseph Murphy, Series Editor

School Districts and Instructional Renewal

EDITED BY

Amy M. Hightower

Michael S. Knapp

Julie A. Marsh

Milbrey W. McLaughlin

Teachers College, Columbia University
New York and London

Published by Teachers College Press, 1234 Amsterdam Avenue, New York, NY 10027

Copyright © 2002 by Teachers College, Columbia University

All rights reserved. No part of this publication may be reproduced or transmitted in any form or by any means, electronic or mechanical, including photocopy, or any information storage and retrieval system, without permission from the publisher.

Library of Congress Cataloging-in-Publication Data

School districts and instructional renewal / edited by Amy M.
    Hightower . . . [et al.].
        p.   cm. — (Critical issues in educational leadership series)
    Includes bibliographical references and index.
    ISBN 0-8077-4267-8 (cloth : alk. paper) — ISBN 0-8077-4266-X (pbk. : alk. paper)
    1. School districts—United States.   2. Educational change—United States.
    I. Hightower, Amy M.   II. Series.

    LB2817.3 .S38 2002
    379.1'535'0973—dc21   2002020297

ISBN 0-8077-4266-X (paper)
ISBN 0-8077-4267-8 (cloth)

Printed on acid-free paper
Manufactured in the United States of America

09   08   07   06   05   04   03   02   8   7   6   5   4   3   2   1

Contents

The District Role in Instructional Renewal: Setting the Stage for Dialogue

In the last few years, school districts have moved from being perceived as a bureaucratic backwater of educational policy to being seen as potent sites and sources of educational reform. Many foundations, reform organizations, and policy makers have placed new confidence in the central role districts assume in improving teaching and learning. In addition, researchers have produced work on district efforts to support students and teachers, bring coherence to an easily fragmented policy environment, and promote equity across a system of schools.

This volume assembles emerging evidence and conceptual work on district policy and leadership as opportunities for supporting teaching and learning. Our goal is to open or expand conversation on what school districts are, what they do, and how they can enhance the quality of teaching and learning in America's schools. This volume also identifies puzzles and contradictions that arise when examining the district as a key unit of analysis and raises questions for future research and practice. This chapter sets the stage by first asking "What is a district?" and then detailing current initiatives that reassert the role of the district as change agent and unit of instructional renewal. Following this review, we present an overview of the empirical and conceptual work represented in the chapters that follow.

WHAT IS A DISTRICT?

Different conceptions of "district" underlie current research and policies. In definitional terms, districts are geographic entities representing a designated area and a set of schools contained within these boundaries. Districts are also legal entities, required by state law to provide education to all students—regardless of race, ethnicity, socioeconomic background, and disability—within the attendance boundaries. Additionally, school districts are organizational entities responsible for the development and enforcement of functions, including attendance, transportation, educational goals, instructional guidance, personnel, operation and maintenance of facilities, and teacher professional development. In general, while states set learn-

ing standards, offer curriculum guidance, and establish student assessment and graduation requirements, districts often retain discretion over
the purchase of textbooks and curricular materials, as well as hiring, firing, evaluating, compensating, and supporting teachers and school administrators. Finally, districts are also democratic institutions, guided by
laypersons either elected or appointed to represent the interests of local
communities.

How one conceives of a district and which of these definitions are
emphasized vary. In policy circles, districts are often equated with the central office. Accordingly, the role of the school district often centers on key
administrators and their actions. Some policy makers and researchers,
however, focus on the aggregate system of schools contained within the
district—examining conditions, programs, and outcomes across schools
and the extent to which they differ or are similar. Some policy makers,
historians, and political scientists emphasize the democratic purposes of
districts and, therefore, concentrate on the governance roles and functions
of school board members and broader community interests. All of these
perspectives emphasize different district actors.

The level of discretion afforded to district actors is also contested.
To some, districts are best understood as implementers of laws, regulations, and policies determined at higher state and federal levels. Such a
conception focuses on districts as recipients of policies and funds, legally
obligated to carry out the terms and requirements of the funding program
or policy. To others, districts are leaders and implementers, interpreters
and originators of educational policies. As active agents in a busy environment, districts make policies and exercise leadership while simultaneously mediating forces and conditions on the community, state, and
national scene. Some within this group further characterize districts
as nonmonolithic entities that yield policies and actions that often vary
and conflict across departments and individual administrators (Spillane,
1998b).

The authors included in this volume reflect a range of conceptions of
school districts. Given the volume's policy focus, most authors focus on
the central office and the discretionary roles professional staff play in implementing, interpreting, and initiating policies to improve teaching and learning. David Tyack's historical analysis of districts, in Chapter 1, however,
places emphasis on the role of school board members and their relationships to "expert" administrators over time. Several chapters also broaden
the examination of districts to include intermediary organizations, local
education foundations, unions, and citizens that play potentially important
formal and informal roles in supporting systemwide educational improvement. While Julie Marsh, in Chapter 2, raises questions about community

relationships to districts, Patricia Ellen Burch, in Chapter 7, explores the roles of professional development organizations in building district capacity to support teachers.

PROVOCATIVE POSSIBILITIES: THE DISTRICT
AS CATALYST AND CRITICAL SUPPORT

In recent years, renewed attention to districts and a new sense of possibilities have emerged from the work of reformers, administrators, foundations, and researchers, bringing evidence to bear on these questions, in both contemporary and historical perspectives.

In 2001, the Cross-City Campaign for Urban School Reform—a national network of reform leaders from Baltimore, Chicago, Denver, Houston, Los Angeles, New York, Oakland, Philadelphia, and Seattle—launched a new effort to identify district roles and central office configurations that enhance instruction and systemwide student performance. Reversing its 1995 call for dismantling central offices and shifting all funds and authority to schools, the Campaign now recognizes districts as potentially "important elements to improving low-performing schools" (Cross-City Campaign for Urban School Reform, 2001). Accordingly, the Campaign has undertaken a 3-year action-research project in Milwaukee, Seattle, and Chicago to identify district supports, policies, and practices that improve teaching and student learning.

The California Bay Area School Reform Collaborative (BASRC)—a regional reform organization funded by the Annenberg and Hewlett Foundations—has also recently identified the pivotal role of districts in supporting inquiry-based school reform. While BASRC focused on whole-school change to the exclusion of districts in the first 5-year phase of its work, it recently reversed this policy. BASRC's new funding guidelines require explicit involvement of districts in their schools' reform efforts and provide opportunities for districts themselves to rethink and revise central office strategies and structures.

Similarly, the Wallace–Reader's Digest Funds launched a district initiative aimed at improving educational leadership. According to the foundation, "Our investigations show that districts should be at the heart of any well-designed improvement plan" (Wallace–Reader's Digest Funds, 2001). With plans to award grants to up to 15 districts, the initiative intends to build district capacity to support improvements in student learning. The foundation is fostering university partnerships, developing a national academy of superintendents, and establishing an educational council of city leaders to further support district grantees.

Finally, Brown University's Annenberg Institute for School Reform has convened "School Communities That Work: A National Task Force on the Future of Urban Districts." Sponsored by the Carnegie Corporation of New York, the Pew Charitable Trusts, the Ford Foundation, and the Rockefeller Foundation, the task force involves leaders from the education, civic, business, and nonprofit communities, along with additional practitioners and researchers, in pursuit of one goal:

> To describe and help construct the systems and supports needed to create communities of successful schools for all children, and to promote a new coalition that will lead in testing and implementing these action plans. (Annenberg Institute for School Reform, 2001)

Design groups are developing action plans, in conjunction with on-the-ground work with partner districts, in three areas: capacity building for quality teaching and leadership; family and community support; and, organizing, managing, and governing schools.

In addition to action-oriented initiatives, an emerging body of research is providing evidence that districts can make a substantial difference in teaching and learning. Marsh, in Chapter 2, synthesizes much of this contemporary literature, examining two streams of research: studies of district–state relations and studies of district relations with schools and teachers.

Specific images of the possible can be found in single and comparative case-study research. The work in this volume concentrates on these kinds of studies because they offer more detailed pictures of district strategies as well as their dynamics, consequences, and interaction with local and state conditions. Therefore, these cases have much to teach the field. The limited number of cases also demonstrates that despite increased attention to and activity around districts, the majority of districts remain inexperienced with substantive reform.

One case in particular has gained wide notoriety as an example—in some views, an exemplar—of a fully developed district strategy in action: New York City Community District #2 (Elmore & Burney, 1997a). In Chapter 4, Mary Kay Stein and Laura D'Amico examine the professional development efforts of District #2 and identify striking parallels between the way teachers arrange successful learning environments for children and the way the schools and district arrange successful learning environments for adults. This case offers evidence that the district office can be purposeful and effective in addressing teaching quality under difficult conditions.

Cases elsewhere in the country provide provocative parallels or contrasts to the District #2 story. In Chapter 5, Amy M. Hightower examines

San Diego, California, a district guided by the same individual who orchestrated the District #2 strategy. This case illustrates the adaptation of principles at work in the New York City context in a different organizational culture and on a larger scale. Jon Snyder, in Chapter 6, details the reform efforts of New Haven, California, a low-wealth, diverse school district in the San Francisco Bay Area. New Haven addressed persistent problems in the quality of teaching and learning through a concerted investment in the quality of teachers, combined with high, explicit, *professional* standards and an elaborate system of teacher development, especially for beginning teachers. Its story illustrates a different strategy within a system of comparable size and conditions to District #2.

Other investigations in this volume provide additional perspectives on the possibilities and complexities of the district's role in a variety of settings. Diane Massell and Margaret E. Goertz (Chapter 3) and Patricia Ellen Burch (Chapter 7) explore district efforts to build capacity to support high-quality teaching and learning. Massell and Goertz's analysis of eight school districts identifies capacity-building strategies, including strategies to increase professional knowledge and skills, strengthen and align instructional guidance, and use data to guide instructional improvement. Burch's examination of instructional reform in Chicago highlights the important capacity-building and mediating role of professional development organizations working with complex districts.

BUILDING BETTER FRAMEWORKS
FOR UNDERSTANDING AND ACTION

The case accounts and the manner in which they have been investigated raise as many questions as they answer. We know, for example, what some of the ingredients of a coherent instructional improvement strategy might be. In District #2, New Haven, and San Diego, the central office projects a consistent and unwavering instructional vision for the district that places teachers and teacher learning at the center of the district's renewal strategy. Often over extended periods, these districts have invested heavily and in more than one way in the quality of the teachers and their continued development. The relatively small central office staffs in these settings have oriented their attention primarily to instructional supports of various kinds, and they intentionally have built a "thicker" infrastructure supporting teachers' work. Central office administrators have established many ways to expand and exercise their teachers' professional expertise among colleagues as well as in the classroom. The existence and basic features of these cases provide useful groundwork for framing what many districts might do to develop a more potent professional teaching force. But "existence proofs" of this kind raise a host of questions that other chapters address to some degree and that further research must explore. For one, are there particular conditions that permit these districts to thrive, but only at the expense of surrounding districts? How sustainable are these strategies, and what conditions help a district maintain a coherent strategy over time? How does a sudden change of conditions (e.g., leadership turnover, state policy directives) affect the strategy's viability over time? Are these strategies equally viable in other settings? Are there other strategic elements not envisioned that also show promise?

A larger task confronts educational leaders and scholars who wish to learn from these cases and imagine more powerful ways to guide teaching and learning from the district level. We need more powerful frameworks for conceptualizing what a district is and does, how thinking and action from the central office and school board can permeate the teaching environment, and thereby how the district can positively shape the work and careers of its teaching force. To that end, we have included chapters that focus on important dimensions of the conceptual problem.

In Chapter 8, Pam Grossman, Clarissa S. Thompson, and Sheila W. Valencia examine the channels of influence available to districts within particular subject areas. James P. Spillane, in Chapter 9, analyzes how district leaders come to understand instructional reforms and, in turn, "teach" the district's teacher force about these reforms. In Chapter 10, Lauren B. Resnick and Thomas K. Glennan, Jr., explore ways in which leaders, especially in urban districts, can develop coherent theories of action connecting their work with student and professional learning. Finally, Milbrey W. McLaughlin and Joan E. Talbert, in Chapter 11, investigate how the task of influencing instruction involves the reformation of the district itself.

These chapters represent a useful start in a conversation that has a long way to go—but much to offer a nation that is intensely concerned with the quality of public education. There are many participants in that conversation—not only scholars who frame long-term and systematic programs of study in this domain, but also practicing educational leaders whose everyday work demands continual experimentation with ways of enhancing student learning. Both can gain from a close reading of the research that has begun to emerge and from the framework-building task that begs to be done. We present this work in hopes that the dialogue will be joined fully.

PART I

Enduring Perceptions, Limited Research: The District's Place and Presence in Instructional Renewal

Any consideration of the school district's role in the renewal of instruction should rest on two sets of understandings—the first concerning how the district has evolved as an institutional feature of American public schooling, and the second regarding what research has established so far about the district's presence and place in educational reform. The two chapters in this part—by Tyack and Marsh, respectively—offer that foundation.

Chapter 1 puts the matter in historical perspective, by taking the reader back to the origins of the public school district more than a century ago. Moving forward in time, Chapter 2 demonstrates how the district came to assume essential functions that are often ignored or taken for granted. The second chapter systematically reviews the relatively limited body of research in the past two decades that has explicitly focused on the district in relation to other loci of reform activity—in the state, the school, and the community. Together, the two chapters clarify how the district has been understood and perceived—more often than not as an irrelevancy or obstacle to reform—and lay a foundation for building a richer understanding of possibilities.

CHAPTER 1

Forgotten Players: How Local School Districts Shaped American Education

DAVID TYACK

No other nation in the world has created such a decentralized system of public education as has the United States. Given Americans' distrust of distant government, this nation might never have created the most popular and comprehensive system of public education in the world if it had not been built on the principle of local control. The local school district with its elected trustees has been the chief form of representative democracy in education and has offered abundant opportunities to make collective decisions and to practice democratic governance. Indeed, in the 19th century school committee members were the most numerous class of public officials in the world (Blodgett, 1897).

Beyond their function as schools for citizenship, for both children and adults, school districts became major sites for innovation and models of systemic reform for the nation's schools during the first half of the 20th century. This was especially true of urban school districts, many of which were fairly free from external control. City systems competed with one another in reform and copied one another's successful experiments. Until the second half of the 20th century, the federal government was a minor player in shaping public education, with a few exceptions such as vocational education.

Today, local control, or "devolution," has become a Republican mantra in Congress and in state legislatures, though a century ago Democrats and Populists were the ones most loudly touting local self-rule. Local control has appealed to citizens of many political persuasions, both liberal and conservative. Repeatedly, citizens have shown in votes and in opinion polls that they trust and respect local control and local districts far more than distant governments and distant schools. In 1992, 57% of Americans said

School Districts and Instructional Renewal. Copyright © 2002 by Teachers College, Columbia University. All rights reserved. ISBN 0-8077-4266-X (pbk), ISBN 0-8077-4267-8 (cloth). Prior to photocopying items for classroom use, please contact the Copyright Clearance Center, Customer Service, 222 Rosewood Dr., Danvers, MA 01923, USA, tel. (508) 750-8400.

that they wanted local school boards to have more control; only 26% wanted more federal control. They showed far less confidence in educational leadership by Congress and state legislators than in decision making by local officials (Will, 1995). The same was true during the 19th century, when legislatures kept revising their state constitutions to hog-tie state officials so as to prevent them from misbehaving.

Despite the popularity of local control by elected trustees, elite policy makers in education have done their best to restrict or eliminate lay self-rule. During the first half of the 20th century, this leadership cadre in public education was composed chiefly of city and state superintendents, foundation officials, leaders in university schools of education, and professional and business allies. They radically reduced lay governance in rural districts and city systems. They wanted professionals to run things and called that "taking the schools out of politics." They consolidated schools in the countryside and abolished local ward boards in cities. Their escape from local democracy was breathtaking: They eliminated about nine out of ten rural districts, and in cities they created a "corporate model" of urban school systems that camouflaged the fact that these were democratic institutions based in a local polity, not businesses (Chancellor, 1915).

Since the 1950s, local school districts and their boards have faced continuing erosion of their powers. They have become, in Jacqueline Danzberger's (1987) phrase, "forgotten players on the education team." Reformers often bypassed local boards or regarded local control as more the problem than the solution. Remedy for faults lay up the chain of command, not down. The people elected to represent their communities in education—local school boards—faced an intense drumbeat of criticism.

Critics have periodically concluded—usually in times of social stress—that elected school boards and local districts are ineffective and obsolete and therefore should be abolished. Educator Charles Judd (1934) of the University of Chicago argued for the abolition of local school boards, claiming that local control of schools by elected school trustees was an inefficient anachronism. Instead, he said, expert superintendents should run the schools, unencumbered by school boards that meddled with matters—such as curriculum—that were best left to experts. Myron Lieberman (1960), another critic concerned about the issue of professionalism, wrote that local control of schools was the main source of "the dull parochialism and attenuated totalitarianism" of American schooling. In 1991, Chester E. Finn declared school boards and their districts to be dinosaurs. They no longer raised the bulk of the school funds, lagged behind in reforms, were irrelevant to national or state standards, and hassled school-site reform. People with different agendas, then, found local districts and school boards an apt target.

Federal activists have not seen much point in school districts, either. Architects of Great Society programs regarded local school board members mostly as obstacles to reform, not as partners in educational improvement. No members of local school boards were invited to the White House for the signing of the Elementary and Secondary Education Act (ESEA). Instead, the honored guests were the teacher unions, foundation officials, and scholars associated with new federal curricula in science and mathematics. In congressional hearings on helping poor children through ESEA, Senator Robert Kennedy asked "would you not agree . . . that one of the really great problems we have . . . is the school boards in some of these states?" (quoted in Exton, 1965, p. 8). Local district leaders were excluded from LBJ's party and scorned by some New Frontiersmen as supporting the status quo on racial segregation and insensitive to the needs of the poor. They were clearly out of the loop of federal policy formation.

At home, superintendents and school trustees saw their freedom of action constricted by powerful new forces. In the 1960s, militant teacher unions won collective bargaining. Federal and state laws mandated new categorical programs. Litigants took school boards to court on issues ranging from racial segregation to policies on student discipline. State legislatures required curricular changes, new tests, and higher standards for teachers. When reformers have discussed national standards, state frameworks, and school-site management, they have typically ignored local districts and their school boards (Danzberger, 1987). With some important exceptions (Fuhrman & Elmore, 1990; Purkey & Smith, 1985), policy analysts have recently focused attention on every level of governance *but* local districts.

Why is it that most citizens have trusted local control and local schools, but cosmopolitan policy analysts and reformers have generally weakened, ignored, or disparaged local control? Clues to this puzzle lie buried in the complex political history of the creation and evolution of public schools. To that history we now turn, ending with some implications for school districts today.

LOCAL CONTROL OF PUBLIC SCHOOLS IN THE 19TH CENTURY

Darwin Atwater was school trustee and clerk of the common school in Mantua Village, Ohio, in 1841. He waxed philosophical as he pondered the meaning of the new school term. "The earth in its annual revolution," he wrote, prompts us to consider again "what has been done during the year that has past and what can be done during the year to come in the school in our neighborhood to forward the great enterprise of educating the human race." No task was more important than "to devise means to forward the education of our children who are soon to succeed us in active life and be our representatives for ages to come" (quoted in Turner, 1940, pp. 18, 91). To carry out that mission, however, required more than rhetoric. The school board also needed to levy local school taxes, to fix a leaky roof, to hire a teacher each term, and to make sure that the citizens cut firewood small enough to fit into the school's stove. Two years later, Atwater himself taught the school for 43 days at a salary of $14 per month.

In Mantua Village, this mixture of the mundane and the eternal, the local and the cosmopolitan, captured the work of rural school trustees as the common school movement spread across the nation. They were expected not only to see to the everyday details of running the local school district but also to mobilize collective choices, to help neighbors negotiate a sense of the common good. Consensus on education was often tenuous and temporary, for every community had its factions, but without some agreement on purpose as well as practical matters such as taxes and firewood, schooling would have faltered. The invisible hand of ideology was a far more powerful force in shaping the common schools than the visible arm of state governments.

Districts like the one in Mantua Village, with its one-room school, had a long political lineage and a strong hold on American society. Thomas Jefferson and starchy New Englanders might have agreed on little else, but on the virtues of the town-meeting form of democracy they had a meeting of minds. Jefferson tried to persuade his fellow Virginians to divide up the state's counties into wards (or groupings of about a hundred families) that would function like Yankee school districts. Each ward would have its own school and elected official to look after its welfare. Jefferson believed that such face-to-face small political units were seedbeds of citizenship, small civil societies where adults as well as children might learn how to exercise their republican duties and preserve their rights and liberties (Sheldon, 1991).

Jefferson never managed to persuade Virginians to create these ward schools, but local control, carried by migrants from the Northeast, took root rapidly in the new states carved out of the public domain in what is now the Midwest. And the one-room school district persisted: As late as 1918 there were still more than 90,000 one-teacher schools in the Midwest, and in the nation as a whole almost half of schoolchildren attended such schools. In the school district meetings, historian Wayne E. Fuller (1994) observes:

> both native and foreign-born Americans learned to participate in making decisions and took their first lessons in politics. Sides were taken and debated; arguments were won and lost. Elections, often hotly contested, removed some from office and elevated others to places of responsibility on the school board. (p. 1)

Through such practices, "the mechanisms of democracy became almost second nature to them" (Fuller, 1994, p. 4).

One reason Americans chose *locally controlled* public schools is simply that the population was very scattered and rural. Other nations, however, have produced *centrally controlled* rural schools. The choice depended on the political cultures of the nations. In the United States, a powerful incentive for local control was the deep American distrust toward distant governments, whether that of King George III or the federal government in Washington. In the 19th century, citizens also tended to regard state governments as distant and prone to mischief. When they wrote and rewrote their state constitutions, Americans did their best, over and over again, to limit the powers of state governments.

Given distrust of distant governments, the best way to govern schools was to elect local school trustees to run local districts. Then communities could retain collective decisions about schooling—who would teach, how much schools would cost, and what kind of instruction to offer. If district voters disagreed with school trustees, they could elect others. Citizens came to think it was their right to settle questions locally since they paid most of the bills and knew local circumstances.

A powerful incentive for scattering common schools across the land was a pervasive common school ideology that taught that all citizens should receive sound moral and civic training in a *public* institution responsive not only to parents but to the entire community. The education of all was a common good, and shaping and supporting this common good was a task for local people.

But there was a puzzle about this American system: Even though the control of public schools was highly decentralized, the schools themselves were surprisingly alike in message and form. A strong common ideology, more than state regulation, produced this Victorian-era standardization (Tyack, 1993). In Europe, wrote a Swedish observer in 1853, ministers of education gave their fiats in "Egyptian darkness," but in the United States local schools depended on "the power of persuasion and on the activity of the people itself, when it shall have been raised to consciousness" (Siljestrom, 1853, pp. 11, 39).

The term *school trustee* is revealing: Reformers argued that these elected representatives held in trust not only the education of all the children of their community but also the future of the whole society. School trustees, wrote Horace Mann (1891), were responsible for the duties "of improving the young, of advancing the welfare of the state and of the race" (p. 245). Mann argued that school committeemen should be aristocrats of character, exemplars of the values they sought to inculcate in the children. They "are more worthy than any other class of men, to be considered as the pilots, who are directing the course of the bark that contains all the precious interests of mankind, and steering it either for its rescue or its ruin" (p. 246). Mann wanted more state regulation of schools, but he recognized that even in the urban commonwealth of Massachusetts, local control was a firmly established tradition.

In 19th-century cities, as in the countryside, school board members were expected to be, in Mann's idealized version, "the administrators of the system; and in proportion to the fidelity and intelligence exercised by them, the system will flourish or decline" (pp. 245–246). In some communities, of course, school trustees became better known for graft and patronage than for faithful service. Even in cities that employed superintendents, busy school board members were expected to attend to administration—selecting textbooks, approving the curriculum, contracting for schoolhouses and equipment, hiring teachers, mediating community conflicts over schooling—and to create enough subcommittees to accomplish the work (Reller, 1935). One reason most urban school boards were large was that it took many people to supervise the operation of large systems. Indeed, when reformers in New York City proposed abolition of ward boards and a reduction in the size of the central board, teachers and community residents protested that so few trustees could not possibly handle all the work or adequately represent all the ethnic groups in the city. On cold days, asked one teacher, if there were no ward trustees, who would check to see if there was enough coal to keep the children warm (Tyack, 1974)?

At first, patterns of governance of urban schools resembled those in the countryside and small towns. In Boston in the 1850s, for example, there were 190 committeemen who supervised that many small primary schools scattered across the city. As cities expanded, they added wards, each of which might have its own local school committee to oversee the operation of local schools. Since ethnic groups clustered in different quarters of the city, often these elected ward school committees represented different immigrant groups (Schultz, 1973). Central and ward school boards—and sometimes other agencies of government—fought over the perquisites and duties of office; the pattern of politics differed from city to city. In 1904 in Philadelphia, there were 504 members of ward boards and 42 on the central board—a total of 546 trustees elected to represent the public interest and to oversee the administration of the schools (Shaw, 1904). Elites considered such widespread participation by lay trustees not a virtue but a defect to be remedied. It led, they thought, to corruption and lay meddling in what should have been a professional domain. The machine politicians and the educators of immigrant stock were foxes in the educational chicken coop. It was time to take the schools out of politics and turn them over to experts. The strategies for doing this varied between countryside and metropolis.

THE COUNTRYSIDE: CONSOLIDATION OF RURAL SCHOOL DISTRICTS

By the early 20th century, professional leaders in education came to agree that there were entirely too many school districts. They had a name for the defect: "the rural school problem." Educational leaders of the first half of the 20th century would have been astonished to find that school reformers today are turning to country schools as models of effective schooling. For the most part, the administrative progressives regarded small rural districts as the most problem-ridden sector of public education. A major cause of retrograde country schools was local control by laymen, "democracy gone to seed," as Cubberley (1915) said (p. 95). The problem was even worse when Petar Petarovitch and other immigrants served on the school committees.

Their answer was to eliminate small districts through consolidation, which would restrict local control and enhance professional autonomy. The consolidation of tiny school districts radically reduced the number of rural school districts and put school boards at a greater distance from local neighborhoods. Although the total population mushroomed from 1930 to 1991, the number of districts dropped from about 130,000 to 15,378. In 1930, there were about 150,000 one-teacher schools; in 1950, 60,000; and in 1991, fewer than 1,000.

The activists who sought to consolidate and standardize rural education found many faults in tiny districts and one-room schools. The local school board trustees, they thought, were apt to be provincial if not ignorant, parsimonious if not outright stingy, and incompetent in professional matters. Unfortunately, trustees gave local patrons what they wanted: schools that were cheap, that reflected local notions of morality and useful learning, and that gave employment to teachers who fit in well with the community. Rural teachers tended to be young, poorly trained, and grossly underpaid (the most capable instructors often migrated to large districts). Many schoolhouses were dilapidated, were cold in winter and hot in summer, and possessed only the most rudimentary teaching aids (sometimes even lacking textbooks). The curriculum was formal and narrow, said advocates of consolidation, and teaching by rote was common. Schooling prepared students neither to prosper as farmers nor to adapt to jobs in cities. Schooling should, but didn't, liberate children from the provincialism of their parents (Cubberley, 1914).

People in rural communities dissented from such an indictment and fought consolidation in pitched battles from Maine to Oregon. The critics often took the worst schools as the average. In much of America, particularly the rural schools of the Midwest and West, one-teacher schools were reasonably well supported and effective, producing citizens who were more literate than graduates of urban systems. As Fuller (1982) shows, such school districts often gave citizens skills and practice in face-to-face democratic decision making.

Not all rural families enjoyed the advantage most cherished by most small school districts—the tradition of local control. African Americans, Native Americans, and Mexican Americans did not have the kind of local control of public schools reserved for rural White Americans. Black schools in the South were subject to White county boards and superintendents. The Indian Bureau in far-away Washington, D.C., set the curriculum and managed the budgets of rural schools for Native Americans. When itinerant Mexican field workers' children attended rural schools—which was not often—they found that Anglo teachers and children often stereotyped them and denigrated their culture. In the era of World War I, even rural Whites often faced draconian state-decreed methods of assimilation to "American" ways if they were immigrants. O. L. Rolvaag described how one Norwegian boy felt about being an outsider in a one-room school:

> Directly in front of him hung the blackboard; at the top of it was written in a beautiful hand, "This is an American school; in work and play alike we speak English only." He read the commandment twice; a feeling of shame came over him and he slunk even lower in his seat. (quoted in Gulliford, 1986, p. 96)

At their best, however, and perhaps even at their average, rural schools were not quite the "problem" that the reformers complained about. Many themes of present-day reform were foreshadowed in country school districts: the virtues of smallness, the view of the school as a community and the community as a school, responsiveness of schooling to the values and commitments of local citizens, and a lack of bureaucratic buffers between parents and teachers. All of these give meaning to "local control," a concept that has resonance for both conservatives and liberals today. Most important, perhaps, though largely unselfconscious, were the lessons taught about political participation. In cities and suburbs, present-day advocates of democracy often try to reproduce contexts that occurred spontaneously in rural communities when *democracy* and *local control* seemed synonymous terms.

And inside the classroom, many notions that seem new and progressive today were standard practice in America's country schools in the past: older children teaching younger ones, nongraded classrooms, flexible scheduling, and instruction that was personalized because the teacher knew the pupils as individuals. Obviously, not all one-teacher small schools had these virtues, but country schools had a potential that their critics ignored and a vitality that continues to attract those who favor decentralization today (Fuller, 1994; Gulliford, 1986).

But the people who won the contest over consolidation of rural schools were the educators who lobbied for state laws to combine country schools and eliminate little districts. They sought to standardize curriculum on an urban model, to provide greater state financing, and to upgrade and supervise rural teachers. As the American population became more urban, so did the character of education, even in the hinterland. This constituted progress to the reformers, who wanted to professionalize what they regarded as an unequal and retarded sector of the educational system. The decimation of districts was their crowning achievement.

"TAKING THE SCHOOLS OUT OF POLITICS" AND SYSTEMIC REFORM IN URBAN DISTRICTS

The administrative reformers of the 20th century had a clear-cut plan for transforming public education. They proclaimed the traditional forms of democratic local control of schools a failure, especially in cities heavily populated with immigrants. There was too much lay meddling with the proper business of professionals, too much opportunity for patronage and corruption, too little scope for experts to make decisions. The messiness of "politics" and adaptation to ethnic constituencies produced favoritism and inefficiency. The older concepts and forms of democracy had failed.

So first they wanted to "take schools out of politics" in the cities. Then— supported by allies in business, the professions, and foundations—they used urban districts as the sites for systemic reforms. Reformed urban schools were to be the template for systemwide transformation of public education everywhere. Here, as in consolidating rural districts, policy elites were remarkably successful (if "successful" means accomplishing what they set out to do) (Tyack & Cuban, 1995).

Today, when critics call large city schools ineffective, chaotic, and pathological, it is easy to forget that in the Progressive era at the turn of the 20th century leaders chose urban education as their laboratory for creating a one best system of public schooling. These districts were Meccas for teachers and offered promising career paths for ambitious administrators.

Administrative reformers and their allies said that the first job of reform was to clear away the political underbrush of patronage and graft and to get rid of overactive laypeople on boards who were micromanaging the system. The way to do this was to abolish the ward committees, cut the size of the large central boards, elect trustees at large rather than by district, and find a way to attract "the better citizens" to the board.

Even more important was to install a new ideal and structure of governance, an apolitical corporate model in which the board acted like the trustees of a bank and the superintendent had the authority of a business CEO. The whole notion of representative lay democracy was wrong-headed in urban public education, reformers thought. Columbia president Nicholas Murray Butler told Chicago businessmen that he should "as soon think of the democratization of the treatment of appendicitis" as to speak of "the democratization of schools" (quoted in Chicago Merchants' Club, 1906, p. 40). Schools should be run like businesses. The small board should select a good manager and delegate the running of the district to him (the reformers assumed that the superintendent should be a man). "There is but one best way" of running schools, said a president of a school board, "and this centralized and specialized system should be adopted everywhere" (Ellis, 1900, p. 633). The public deserved to have its schools managed well—that was the meaning of democracy.

Once that model was in place in cities, the policy elites thought, professionals could have a free hand in aligning the elements of systemic reform, city by city. Using "scientific" methods of curriculum building, experts would determine what students should know and be able to do as adults, backward mapping from adult tasks and duties to the program of studies needed to prepare the young for "life." These experts assumed that students differed in abilities and in the future destinies for which schooling should equip them; hence, curricula should be differentiated. They believed that teachers should be trained in city normal schools or inservice programs aligned to that district's course of study. And, finally, they developed complex systems of tests to appraise how well students had mastered the subjects they studied. Thus, within city school systems they sought to align and institutionalize aims, standards, curricular frameworks, teacher education, and testing (Cubberley, 1916; Strayer, 1930).

The advocates of the corporate model of school governance wanted to change not only how schools should be run but also who should run them. They did not abandon the moral and personal qualities Horace Mann prescribed for the ideal school trustee but added further prescriptions. They wanted board members to be "successful" men (not women), preferably business and professional leaders, well educated, and prosperous. Such trustees, said the U.S. Commissioner of Education, "have no personal ends to serve and no special cause to plead" (Harris, 1892, p. 168). They would not control schooling directly—that was unprofessional—but rather indirectly through superintendents trained in "scientific management." They would know how to delegate the management of schooling to experts who would be best able to understand and "really represent the interests of the children" (Chancellor, 1915, p. 12).

All this, of course, was not "taking the schools out of politics" but instead substituting one kind of political control for another and restricting the kinds of people thought to be fit trustees. As school board members came to be drawn more and more from the upper strata of their communities and as they turned over more decision making to experts, the "reforms" restricted the kinds of choices citizens had exercised under an older, more localized and pluralistic system of political control.

Even among superintendents, who were the group that presumably stood to gain most from the new "corporate" system of district governance, a few had their doubts about its wisdom. The school chief of Omaha, Nebraska, argued that

> we must remember that this is a representative government—a government by all the people, not by those we think are the best people; and we cannot always have members all of a kind who move in the highest circles of society. . . . I am not sure but that the residents of "Hell's Half Acre" are sometimes entitled to representation. (Pearse, 1903, p. 162)

He further argued that

> all citizens should be directly interested in the schools, and one of the best ways to have them interested is for them to have some voice in the selection of the men who manage the schools. The educative influence in the community of a general election of school-board members, in which general school policies are discussed, is good. (Pearse, 1903, p. 162)

As the corporate model of school governance took hold in cities during the Progressive era, city superintendents more and more talked about business efficiency and science as guides to policy. A number of universities had created schools and departments of education and were turning out specialists in a variety of fields. Curriculum designers specified what different students would need to know and do as adults; educational psychologists created "intelligence" tests to sort "slow," "normal," and "gifted" pupils into tracks; and experts taught "scientific management" to superintendents. On school boards and in their associations, business and professional elites gave political and organizational support to this program of centralized systemic reform in urban districts (Tyack & Hansot, 1982).

Whereas 19th-century school administrators had worked to create *uniform* city systems, the administrative progressives saw sameness as a defect and *diversification* as a virtue. They were proud when no two high school students took exactly the same courses. Science, they thought, showed that children had different mental capacities and destinies in life. Thus, the most efficient educational system provided different paths for them. Lewis Terman (1919), a psychologist in the vanguard of applying IQ tests to schools, declared that "educational reform may as well abandon, once and for all, all effort to bring all children up to grade" (p. 73). A good school system was one that tailored the nature and pace of instruction to individual differences and prepared students for their different lives as adults—at work, in the family, as citizens, and at leisure. Curricular reform meant differentiation. In one respect, however, the administrative progressives insisted on the school producing uniform products: They were ardent Americanizers who believed that education should ultimately erase ethnic differences in the interest of producing a common language and civic culture.

In their top-down mode of systemic reform in urban districts, the administrative progressives tried to substitute public relations for the sort of active lay involvement that had characterized much decision making in the 19th century. Acutely conscious about being ahead of the reform curve, they used city systems as experimental stations of innovation in curriculum and instruction. They emulated one another and shared success stories at meetings of the NEA. Professors moved their protégés into city superintendencies across the United States, gaining local allies committed to the new forms of systemic reform. Foundations and the U.S. Office of Education sponsored urban school surveys to assess how well cities were implementing the new model of schooling. Test companies and textbook manufacturers sold their goods to districts nationwide. While individual city districts were the sites of systemic reforms, the culture of reform was competitive, cosmopolitan, and national (Tyack & Hansot, 1982).

At the close of the first half of the 20th century, the administrative progressives looked back with pride on their achievements. They had mitigated the "problem" of lay control of urban schools by contracting the roles of central school boards and by abolishing ward boards. Thus buffered, the experts were able to diversify programs of study so that there was a niche for every child. They looked on city districts as the flagships of their educational fleet. Little did they suspect that in the next half-century most observers would consider urban schools to be the sector of public education most in need of reform.

REFLECTIONS ON LOCAL DISTRICTS AND REFORM TODAY

Throughout the 20th century, policy elites in education were often ambivalent or hostile toward the basic building block of the American system of public education—the local district governed by an elected school board. Reformers successfully pruned this form of representative government.

They eliminated about 90% of school districts through consolidation. From time to time they even proposed the complete abolition of local districts. They destroyed local ward boards in cities and sought to model urban school governance on a corporate model borrowed from business. Within that corporate model, policy elites largely set the agenda of reforms. State and federal agencies policed local compliance with mandates and regulations. Although recent reformers have advocated decentralization of control, most of the long-term trends have moved toward greater centralization, albeit in a somewhat fragmented form (Meyer, 1980).

After a century of attacks on local control, the remaining American school districts—14,883 of them in 1997—are still hardly monolithic (U.S. Department of Education, 1997). The smallest one-third of districts contain about 3% of the total number of students. Half of all districts have fewer than 1,000 students. But the 5% constituting the largest districts enroll almost half of all students in K–12. Local districts vary enormously in resources, in their levels of conflict or consensus, and in their mix of classes and ethnic and racial groups. They also differ in professional sophistication. Some favored school districts have at least as much educational expertise as do most state departments of education, while others are so far behind the curve of innovation that they do not even realize that there is a curve. No one program of reform could possibly fit them all. In these reflections, I'd like to focus on small and medium-sized districts, which are often ignored in discussions of school governance.

Despite decades of criticism and constriction of local control, the public still trusts local officials more than state and federal governments. Today, increasing numbers of leaders, both progressive and conservative, are insisting that public education be deregulated and that local districts recapture more power to make decisions about schooling in their communities. Although districts and their school boards are flawed instruments of democracy, if they disappeared, we would probably reinvent something similar. Local control offers a chance to make collective decisions about an important matter: the education of the next generation (Martin, 1987).

Although local control is more popular than state or federal policy making, local school districts are not—and should not be—free-standing and totally autonomous agencies. They are the creatures of the states and serve broad national purposes, now as in Mann's time. The history of local control should not be romanticized. Many districts have had a sorry record in securing racial and gender justice, in serving economic classes equitably, and in guaranteeing religious freedom. Federal and state action has been necessary to guarantee civil rights and liberties in education. In addition, only federal and state governments can remedy the "savage inequalities" in financial resources between districts (Kozol, 1991). Whether control should be centralized or localized depends on the issue at hand. What are some of the functions appropriate for local governance in education?

Three jobs—everyday managerial competence, mediation between reformers and the public, and negotiation of the common good—are particularly important, it seems to me, for district leaders intent on preserving what is valuable and fixing what is not in their local schools. What counts in school reform, finally, is what happens in classrooms, and this depends heavily on what happens in school districts. One could say that all educational reform is local (in the sense in which Tip O'Neill said "all politics is local").

One function—everyday competence in running schools—is often dismissed as "mere management" (rather than leadership). Yet ask teachers and parents whether these matters are important: bus schedules that deliver children safely and efficiently, plumbing that works, adequate photocopy machines, roofs that don't leak, modern textbooks, playing fields that are level and mowed, and opportunities for teachers to reconsider what and how they teach. If classroom instruction is to proceed smoothly, someone has to see to such matters, and this is an important part of the business of school districts and their trustees and administrators.

Competence in performing ordinary tasks is not trivial but necessary in carrying out ambitious policy—even if the administration is lambasted as a "bureaucracy." Founders of public charter schools are discovering that the practical demands of running a school require careful attention—small businesses and small schools have a high mortality rate—and some charter schools have asked local school district administrators to handle complex tasks such as payrolls and health plans.

A second job that seems vital in local districts is mediation between innovators and the lay public. For instructional reforms to succeed in practice, local citizens and teachers need to understand and support the innovations. The public's notion of what constitutes a "real school" exerts a cultural brake on reforms that exceed the speed limit of pedagogical innovations. School districts need to be open to new currents of educational thought and promising practices. They can learn from expert outsiders. But districts, with their elected boards and professional staffs, also need to balance the cosmopolitan and the local, the traditional and the new, by relating educational programs to the goals and experience of local communities (Metz, 1990; Tyack & Cuban, 1995). Trustees might conclude that the common sense of the community dictates doing "nothing innovative for a while," writes a former editor of the *School Board Journal*,

> whatever the blandishments of reformers: After you go through a few cycles
> of tearing down walls for open classrooms and then putting them up again

> . . . or throwing out the old math for the new math and then pitching the new math for some version of the old math, you begin to recognize the virtues of being stodgy. (Martin, 1987, p. 29)

This may result in fewer reforms but a longer and happier life for those innovations that the community does decide it needs.

Where it is successful, such mediation and deliberation about improving local schools can produce greater coherence in goals, healthier morale among professionals, and more trust between communities and their schools. Lay and professional leaders in school districts can do much to enhance coherence, morale, and trust—or the opposite—as Milbrey Wallin McLaughlin (1992) found in her analysis of contexts for teaching. Teachers can feel infantilized or respected, collegial or alienated, depending on the dominant climate of values sustained at the district level (see also Purkey & Smith, 1985).

One reason the general public trusts local educational leaders more than distant authorities is that school boards and professional leaders are expected to be responsive to the people who elect them or hire them—a person at the end of a telephone instead of an electronic shuffle, a board member who has breakfast with a group of retired people in the local coffee shop. "The reality," says a seasoned observer of school trustees, "is that hearing complaints and comments from the public is not a sideline for boards but lies at the heart of why boards exist in the first place" (Martin, 1987, p. 29). If they are skilled and patient, local trustees can be useful ombudspersons for the public schools, even though such activity has often been condemned as lay meddling in professional business.

A third function of leaders in the local district is related to the other two. The most important job of leaders at the local level is to help communities generate a sense of the common good as represented in the education of children. Deeply embedded in the history of American democracy, but often forgotten of late, this conviction holds that all citizens, not just parents, have a stake in the civic education of the next generation of students. As Darwin Atwater knew, being a trustee requires thinking about the welfare of the schools over the long term, preserving the best of tradition, responding intelligently to issues in the present, and bearing the future—even the distant future—in mind in making decisions. Jefferson argued that there was no better school of citizenship for both adults and the young than deliberating about common needs and values in a face-to-face community; for him the ideal school governance was a town meeting (Sheldon, 1991).

Deliberating about the common good is perhaps best done at the district level, where people have to live with the consequences of their advocacy and actions. One essential kind of democracy in education is the ability to vote for public representatives who can, in the words of Jacqueline Pilcher Danzberger, "filter, interpret, and translate the education goals" of local communities into educational programs for their constituents (1987, p. 58). These are collective choices, not simply individual consumer choices. National discourse about the purposes of education has all too often been narrowed to a distorted claim that good schools exist to assure success in international competition or individual advancement, and the measure of success has too often been reduced to higher test scores. The democratic purposes of education need new advocacy at every level, but particularly in school districts.

Talking of the public good may seem hopelessly naive in a time when discourse about individual and international competition dominates policy talk about education, when confidence in public institutions sags, and when people seem careless if not niggardly about what they hold in common. The public good is not some bland consensus that disguises differences or obscures inequalities. It is not achieved by delegating decisions to experts who presumably know what is good for the society. It is an ever-changing attempt to chart goals through debate, negotiation, compromise, and trials of ideas in action. Through feedback, local citizens can observe concrete results and modify their notion of the common good in practice. This process of negotiating the common good reflects the democratic values the society claims to honor and moves toward a community of commitment.

CHAPTER 2

How Districts Relate to States, Schools, and Communities: A Review of Emerging Literature

JULIE A. MARSH

Until recently, education reform movements have paid little attention to school districts. State and federal policies have concentrated on schools as central units of change, rendering local districts virtual nonactors in the educational improvement process (Elmore, 1993, 1997; Elmore & Burney, 1999; Fullan, 2000; Massell & Goertz, 1999; Spillane, 1996). The focus on state-level education standards, curriculum frameworks, assessment, and accountability systems, as well as state and federal efforts to restructure schools, increase site-based decision making, serve specific populations through categorical programs, and promote parental choice, exemplify this education policy trend.

To some reformers, districts are the problem. Critics claim that districts play no significant role, are inconsistent with sound policy, and are inefficient bureaucratic institutions (Chubb & Moe, 1990a; Elmore, 1993, citing Finn, 1991). To others, districts have become overly politicized and unresponsive to public, teacher, and student needs (Hill, 1999) or are viewed as conduits through which policies and funding reach more important school-level actors. Finally, some reformers have invented new organizational forms and networks (e.g., New American Schools Development Corporation) that bypass districts to target resources and support to schools.

Despite this policy trend, studies are now documenting roles that districts play in enhancing teaching and learning. While formerly there was little evidence that districts played a constructive role in instructional improvement (Elmore, 1993), a growing body of research is building evidence that districts can be important agents of instructional change.

School Districts and Instructional Renewal. Copyright © 2002 by Teachers College, Columbia University. All rights reserved. ISBN 0-8077-4266-X (pbk), ISBN 0-8077-4267-8 (cloth). Prior to photocopying items for classroom use, please contact the Copyright Clearance Center, Customer Service, 222 Rosewood Dr., Danvers, MA 01923, USA, tel. (508) 750-8400.

Overall, this literature follows two lines of inquiry, exploring district–state relations (e.g., how districts respond to state policy) and district relations with schools and teachers (e.g., how district strategies for systemwide improvement, in context, affect schools and teachers). Methodologically, these studies vary widely in theoretical grounding, data collection, research procedures, and apparent quality. (See Marsh, 2000, for details regarding these studies' research questions, samples, and methodologies.)

This chapter examines both the state–district and district–school literatures, focusing on research from the past 15 years that treats districts as primary units of analysis. The review explores roles districts play in supporting improvements in teaching and learning, and factors that enable districts to do so. This chapter concludes with unanswered questions and suggestions for future research on districts.

FINDINGS ON STATE–DISTRICT RELATIONS

Several studies demonstrate a basic conception of school districts as implementers of state policy, with implementation often varying by type of state policy and by magnitude (Firestone, 1989b; Marsh & McCabe, 1998; Swan, 1998). Based on a typology of policy "instruments" (McDonnell & Elmore, 1987), a survey of 24 districts found a preference for implementing *mandates* (e.g., textbook approval systems, school report cards), *inducements* (e.g., alternative schools, pay for performance), and *capacity-building* policies (e.g., local-option sales tax, expanding technology for instruction) (Swan, 1998). Districts had partially or completely implemented all five mandates and three of the four inducements listed on this survey. Further, *systems-changing* policy actions were the least likely to be implemented.

Districts often "actively used" state reforms, such as a pilot career-ladder program, a program for merit schools, and curriculum policy (Firestone, 1989b). The "magnitude" of district use also varied widely. For example, 9 of the 24 districts in this analysis anticipated or exceeded minimum requirements of one or more state reforms. Other research indicates that often when districts report implementing a new state reform, many of the reform's components existed locally before the reform's initiation (Marsh & McCabe, 1998).

Research on district responses to state assessment policy distinguished three main approaches: *fragmented* (little leadership for change, little interest in the state test), *communicating* (efforts made to coordinate instruction and support higher-order thinking, but still little interest in the state test), and *coordinated* (deliberate effort to raise test scores, district-run instructional activities, formal use of data) (Firestone & Fairman, 1998).

Responses to state policy vary not only across districts (Spillane, 1996, 1998a; Spillane, Thompson, Lubienski, Jita, & Reimann, 1995) but also within them (Spillane, 1998b). Two Michigan districts highlight contrasting responses, with one largely ignoring state reading reforms and the other substantially revising its policies to align with them (Spillane, 1996, 1998a). Within these districts, responses varied as well, at both school and district levels. For example, in the less responsive district, some policies that contradicted state policy (e.g., traditional curriculum guide, standardized tests focused on discrete decoding and comprehension skills) were left unchanged, while others were revised to align with state policy (e.g., a few workshops, Chapter I curriculum revision).

Districts can be more than simply recipients or implementers of state policy—as in nine Michigan districts that generally focused on topic coverage at the expense of encouraging fundamental changes in teachers' ideas about teaching and subject matter envisioned by state and national math and science reforms (Spillane et al., 1995). In two other districts, administrators repeatedly and proactively ignored or weeded out certain state policies or ideas and replaced them with their own (Spillane, 1996, 1998a).

District leaders not only intentionally ignore or knowingly rework state policy, but also may deviate from state policy intent by interpreting and misconstruing policy messages or content. For example, local policies and programs in six of the nine Michigan districts failed to reflect core themes of state/national math and science reforms (Spillane & Thompson, 1997). In summary, district policy making can (1) undermine state policy makers' efforts to streamline instructional guidance (e.g., by shaping practitioners' opportunities to learn about instruction and state policy); (2) influence state policy makers' efforts to transmit messages for instructional change to practitioners; and (3) influence state efforts to increase the coherence of messages (Spillane, 1996).

Other studies confirm a pattern of districts adapting state policy and actively constructing their own policy environments. One suburban district defied and bent some state policies (e.g., Title I, decentralization) perceived as misguided and embraced and adapted others (e.g., magnet schools) when these reinforced existing goals and ongoing efforts (Kirp & Driver, 1995). Parallel research documents considerable adaptation to state accountability systems (Goertz, Massell, & Chun, 1998). Some districts exceeded state policy expectations—raising standards higher, creating more performance incentives, and expanding testing. Many districts, particularly from "strong" accountability states, "proactively" identified schools that risked not meeting state criteria and devised capacity-building systems for them, such as differential governance arrangements granting schools autonomy contingent on their performance.

Similarly, districts in one California county created their own policies in response to shifting state curriculum and assessment policies (Chrispeels, 1997). Even after the demise of the state's assessment system, many districts continued to implement alternative assessments in the spirit of the failed state policy because such approaches to assessment "made sense to local educators" (Chrispeels, 1997, p. 470).

These studies corroborate earlier findings that state policy often spurs additional district-level policy making (Fuhrman & Elmore, 1990). Rejecting the notion of state–district relations as zero-sum games in which increased state policy making diminishes local control, this research in 24 districts in six states indicates that increased state policy can enhance both state and local control. Ambiguity and contradictions in state policy, along with little state capacity to enforce policies, created opportunities for district discretion and enhanced local activism. For example, districts enacted policies in anticipation of state action, wove together multiple state policies to meet needs, and used state policies to catalyze local improvement efforts. Ten of these districts had strong forms of curriculum centralization in progress, in which administrators aligned and standardized curriculum frameworks, course syllabi, assessments, textbooks, and sometimes teacher evaluation instruments. Districts are portrayed—as in other research in this line of inquiry—as change agents with local actors who are

> very sophisticated players, adept at anticipating new policy initiatives and using them to their advantage. Local leaders know how to use state and federal mandates as leverage to accomplish what they might wish to anyway— as opportunities and as rationales for persuading reluctant educators or citizens. They also know when and how to ignore or circumvent regulations that trouble them, when the state will fail to notice or "blink" in not noticing. (Fuhrman & Elmore, 1990, p. 93)

Throughout these studies, several factors account for district responses to state policies, including capacity, size, leadership, organization and governance, political climate, and nature of state policy. These factors help explain why certain districts adopted policies while others ignored them or why some districts implemented policies with fidelity to state policy intentions and others failed to.

Capacity

As various studies attest, a district's capacity influences its response to state policy (McLaughlin, 1987). An examination of why some districts made more progress at realizing the state's vision for more challenging math and science instruction while others made significantly less showed that much of this variation results from differences in districts' capacity to *learn* core reform ideas, *do* what the policy asks, and share reform ideas with others (Spillane & Thompson, 1997).

Three interacting dimensions of district capacity—human, social, and physical capital—emerge from research. As this research demonstrates, these greatly influence districts' ability to interpret, implement, and sustain state policies and programs.

Human Capital. Human capital includes personal commitment, a disposition to learn about instruction and view learning as ongoing, and substantive knowledge about reform ideas (Spillane & Thompson, 1997). Another key dimension of this form of capacity is "the extent to which the [district] used it to move from a few knowledgeable individuals to a knowledgeable collective"—thereby developing a cadre of educators with the skills and knowledge to lead reform (Spillane & Thompson, 1997, p. 193).

For example, districts' active use of state policy depended on the will of district administrators, board members, and school principals, as well as their capacity to mobilize diverse personnel (e.g., technical specialists, members of the dominant coalition, interest-group representatives) and perform technical functions (e.g., selling a vision of change, monitoring reform, and handling disturbances) (Firestone, 1989b).

Local capacity building through professional development for teachers and administrators builds human capital in another way; for example, encouraging districts to sustain state curriculum and assessment initiatives (Chrispeels, 1997). Districts that moved farthest in experimenting with and implementing alternative assessments and continuing this activism after the demise of the state test demonstrated the will and capacity to continue.

Social Capital. Social capital resides within relationships among individuals that result from norms encouraging trust, collaboration, and a sense of obligation (Spillane & Thompson, 1997). For example, linkages to knowledge sources outside the district (e.g., through networks) enabled some districts to gain substantive knowledge about state reforms. Additionally, districts with a history of collaboration and established norms of trust were better able to discuss instructional reform and work together to achieve it (Spillane & Thompson, 1997).

Similarly, district administrators' encouragement and recognition of educators, as well as their inclusion in decision making, may also build social capital (Firestone, 1989b). In this study, teachers and principals were more supportive of a policy if they participated substantively in its development or design. Accordingly, districts enabling educators to influence issues important to them enhance the potential buy-in and trust among the key actors necessary for change.

Physical Capital. Physical capital includes the financial resources allocated to staffing, time, and materials (Spillane & Thompson, 1997). For example, adequate time enabled educators to understand substantive ideas. The way in which time was allocated and used was equally important (i.e., it needed to be consistent and steady over the long run). Curricular materials also became an important opportunity for teachers to learn about the math and science reforms (Spillane & Thompson, 1997). In other research, limited resources—presumably financial but also possibly human capital—prevented districts from implementing various types of state policies (Swan, 1998). Given resource limitations, districts were able to implement only a couple of key policy actions that were mandated.

District Size

Closely related to capacity, a district's size can affect its responses to state policy. A study of five school districts in Maine and Maryland found that differences in districts' institutional configurations, including their size, contributed to how they approached teachers' instructional improvement and response to state tests (Firestone & Fairman, 1998). Six times smaller than their Maryland counterparts, Maine districts lacked staff capacity to support teachers (e.g., two of the three Maine districts had no systemwide inservice days). Maryland's size also influenced its "network capital," enabling it to bring in outside experts and organize many more activities for teachers. The study concluded:

> Larger districts appear to have more human and social capital to respond to state testing mandates. Curriculum coordinators have access to knowledge outside the district and can make it available to teachers while promoting sharing of locally developed solutions to the problem created by the state test. Moreover, the larger districts are more insulated from local concerns—which rarely focus on test results unless scores are embarrassingly low. (Firestone & Fairman, 1998, p. 42)

District responses to federal policy also demonstrate size effects (Hannaway & Kimball, 1997), with smaller districts reporting less understanding of, and progress implementing, standard-based reform legislation. This size "disadvantage" may reflect the districts' lack of connections to outside sources of information and technical assistance.

Leadership

District leadership—including leaders' knowledge, skills, exercise of influence, and understanding of reform content—also influences the implementation of state policy. One study concluded that "the beliefs, skills, and energy of people in specific positions made a difference" in district responses to state assessment policy (Firestone & Fairman, 1998, p. 36). Strong leadership from the superintendent and curriculum coordinator communicated explicit support for instruction and interest in the state testing program, as contrasted with districts with lower levels of support for state policy. In another study, stable leadership—from three superintendents over a quarter of a century—accounted for the consistency of policy in one suburban district (Kirp & Driver, 1995).

Policy makers' understanding of state policy and reforms also appears to shape their responses to it. Local policy makers construct varying ideas of instructional reforms (e.g., in reading instruction, constructing meaning in literature) and promote these ideas when implementing the state's reforms (Spillane, 1998a). How leaders understand the reform affects the degree and focus of support for realizing reforms. Leaders' understandings were shaped by various things: their sources of information (e.g., conferences, state test), local context (e.g., attitudes about state government), and personal beliefs and experiences (e.g., in reading). Here, ties to state and national professional associations, as well as to the back-to-basics or Effective Schools movement, often mediated the ways in which administrators viewed state policy (Spillane, 1998b). (See Spillane, 2000a, 2000b, for a similar cognitive analysis of district policy and practice.)

Organization and Governance

Organizational and governance structures also affect district responses to state policy. Horizontal and vertical segmentation within districts can alter the way districts enact state policy (Spillane, 1998b, building on Cohen & Spillane, 1993; Weick, 1976). For example, because specialized subunits within districts often work "in parallel not partnership," some subunits can make state policy a priority while others ignore it (Spillane, 1998b). In another study, differences in governance structure helped account for variation in district responses to state testing: Structures fostering tighter linkages to the community (e.g., more elected officials for smaller communities) tended to deflect attention from state tests (Firestone & Fairman, 1998).

Political Culture and Reform History

Additionally, contextual factors such as the history of reform activity and political climate appear to influence how state policies are received, interpreted, and enacted locally. Differences in political culture between states can account for organizational differences among districts and their responses to state policy. Given Maryland's sophistication in dealing with the public and its history of policy activity—adopting two state tests, high school graduation requirements, and other curricular guidelines—educators in this state were more likely than educators in Maine to "take the state seriously if it said that high test scores were important" (Firestone & Fairman, 1998, p. 32).

Other research identifies local contextual factors that can be influential, such as the fit between state policies and local values and initiatives. For example, a suburban district with a strong commitment to racial equity was quick to participate in the state desegregation program because it reinforced existing local goals and efforts (Kirp & Driver, 1995). The same was true for the district's adoption of state curricular guidelines. Conversely, districts in which resentment toward state "meddling" in local affairs is high may pay little attention to state policy (Spillane, 1996).

Nature of State Policy

Finally, characteristics of state policy itself can influence a district's response to it. For example, distinct patterns of district responses to state policy manifest in states with "strong" versus "weak" accountability systems—defined by prescriptiveness, rigor of measures used, alignment of the system with other federal and state policies, and stability of the system uncovered (Goertz et al., 1998). In strong-accountability states, districts exceeded state policy expectations in establishing accountability systems, whereas in weak-accountability states, districts varied considerably in alignment with state systems.

Similarly, state policies can affect district approaches to instructional reform by creating "stakes that affected local will to comply and in their efforts to build local capacity" (Firestone & Fairman, 1998, p. 32). For example, formal sanctions such as reconstitution were more effective in prompting districts to pay attention to state testing policy than the threat of embarrassment from public comparisons.

FINDINGS ON SCHOOL–DISTRICT RELATIONS

This second body of literature examines district interaction with schools to improve teaching and learning. Like the literature just described, these studies characterize districts as proactive change agents. A study of 22 districts concluded that districts "do continue to play a large role in the life of public schools" and should not be treated "as ancillary to the change process" (Massell & Goertz, 1999, p. 1).

New York's Community School District #2 offers "an 'existence proof' that it is possible for local districts to be agents of serious instructional improvement" (Elmore & Burney, 1999, p. 264). On the theory that "changes in instruction occur only when teachers receive more or less continuous oversight and support focused on the practical details of what it means to teach effectively" (p. 272), the district used professional development as a management strategy. Through extensive professional development opportunities and a strong culture of shared values around instructional improvement, District #2 altered instructional practice, dramatically improving test scores among its diverse student population over time (Chapter 4, this book).

Other studies link district practices to student performance and suggest factors that make districts "instructionally effective," achieving high levels of student performance across subjects, growth over time, and consistency across subpopulations (Murphy & Hallinger, 1986, 1988). These studies presume a more top-down conception of districts, in which superintendents take primary responsibility for directing and enforcing change. (The generalizability of these studies, however, is limited by reliance on self-reported data from superintendents and changes in educational context since the time of research.)

Several studies also examined the specific ways in which districts influenced local schools and practitioners. For example, districts engaged in restructuring created new roles for teachers and administrators (David, 1990). Similarly, the district's level of professional community affected teachers' commitment to the profession and their sense of pride as teachers (McLaughlin, 1992; McLaughlin & Talbert, 1993). Moreover, teachers' perceptions of district settings often dampened or enhanced aspects of their school or department culture. For example, a strong district community increased the professional motivation of teachers in a weak department (McLaughlin, 1992; McLaughlin & Talbert, 1993).

District organization and culture can affect teacher attitudes and commitment, as suggested by research on low-income and rural districts in Tennessee (Rosenholtz, 1989). For example, "moving" districts—those providing a clear focus on and coherence to instruction, informing educators of current thinking on best practices, and encouraging educators to take risks and grow professionally—tended to have more "moving" schools with high levels of teacher commitment. On the other hand, "stuck" districts—those with fragmented instructional goals, policies, and practices—resulted in schools and teachers with little sense of progress or commitment.

Finally, research on rural districts volunteering to participate in a particular state reform suggests that district organization affects schools and teachers (Goldring & Hallinger, 1992). Teachers in *decentralized* and *centralized* district contexts reported more positive internal organizational processes (e.g., high amounts of instructional leadership, good teacher rapport, high sense of peer commitment, clear school missions, high sense of teacher competency) than *fragmented* districts.

As with state–district relations, a similar set of forces and conditions explain why districts were more or less able to enact educational improvements—including capacity, balance between district authority and school autonomy, and leadership. Unlike the state–district literature, the findings in these studies are more mixed or conflicting.

Capacity

As in studies of state–district relations, this body of literature repeatedly found that the kinds and levels of human, social, and physical capital contributed to districts' ability to enact change.

Human Capital. Several studies revealed the importance of practitioner *knowledge* and *skills*. "Pioneering" districts cultivated new teacher roles by providing access to professional development that enhanced knowledge and skills (David, 1990). Similarly, one of the five "major capacity-building strategies" identified in another study included districts' ability to build teacher knowledge and skills (Massell & Goertz, 1999). Districts embracing this strategy developed "learning communities" by offering teachers traditional and nontraditional professional training (e.g., workshops, on-site teacher leaders and staff developers) and encouraging teachers to become "consumers of professional literature" (p. 3).

The research on rural Tennessee districts, noted earlier, empirically linked principal and teacher learning opportunities to teacher commitment—with "moving" districts providing extensive district inservice on topics matching principal and teacher needs, while "stuck" districts failed to take responsibility for expanding learning opportunities (Rosenholtz, 1989). Similarly, the key to District #2's success was the way in which professional development permeated the work of the district—including not only discrete workshops and a professional development laboratory, but also institutionalized practices such as intervisitations and internal and external consulting (Elmore & Burney, 1997a, 1999).

Social Capital. The district's *normative culture* may also play an important role in enabling reform (Elmore & Burney, 1999; McLaughlin, 1992). As one study concluded, "The relationships between teacher and district that are powerful influences on teachers and teaching have little to do with hierarchical structure and controls and everything to do with the norms, expectations, and values that shape the district professional community" (McLaughlin, 1992, p. 35).

Professional development can convey critical norms that build a sense of district professional community, influencing teacher commitment and pride, as noted earlier, and contributing greatly to success, as in District #2 (Elmore & Burney, 1999). The ability to foster a culture and collective identity is crucial to successful large-scale reform efforts (Fullan, 2000). This emphasis on norms and culture was absent from earlier research on effective districts, which focused on technical and physical dimensions of capacity (Murphy & Hallinger, 1986, 1988).

Practitioner involvement and collaboration may serve to build a different kind of social capital within districts. One study concluded that school staff needed authority and autonomy to create new roles and environments appropriate to their needs (David, 1990). In another study, when teachers engaged actively in constructing their school reality, school goals became mutually shared and risk taking more prevalent (Rosenholtz, 1989). On the other hand, in settings in which teachers and principals felt professionally isolated and were uninvolved in goal setting, they experienced uncertainty, self-defensive posturing, and resistance to change. The study concluded that "to assure that schools will be healthy educative places, teachers must share responsibility for their professional destiny by engaging in decisions through which that destiny is forged" (p. 203).

Earlier research, however, did not support this notion of joint goal setting and decision making (Murphy & Hallinger, 1986, 1988). In these studies, "instructionally effective" superintendents did not involve teachers or the community in goal setting, instead controlling the goal development, establishing districtwide instructional and curricular foci, and selecting professional development activities themselves.

Social capital residing in internal and external "relationships" can contribute to districts' capacity to support local reform. These relationships can help promote communication and align goals and actions of various constituencies (Florian, Hange, & Copeland, 2000). This 16-district survey of administrators showed that standards-based reform across schools was enabled in most instances by relationships with external organizations and agencies, teams of staff or administrators, parents, and community. Relationships with school board members, other districts, teacher unions, and local businesses were also identified as important in some districts.

Physical Capital. Several dimensions of physical capital appear to affect district–school relations. By increasing the time available for professional development—including the provision of planning time, release time, and paid time in the summers, as well as running meetings efficiently to save time—"pioneering" districts cultivated new roles among educators (David, 1990). Elsewhere, by phasing in the introduction of instructional change gradually over many years, while maintaining a consistent focus, the district provided adequate time for change to occur in successive parts of the system, instead of forcing change simultaneously all at once (Elmore & Burney, 1997a, 1999).

Investment in high-quality materials, another aspect of physical capital, is also important to successful large-scale change efforts at the school, district, and national levels (Fullan, 2000). However, the presence of materials alone is not sufficient to enact change and can easily be used superficially.

Balance Between Central Authority and School Autonomy

Districts' success in enacting school-level improvement often hinges on a delicate balance between centralized and decentralized control. In some districts, school empowerment is a key strategy to supporting instructional reform, while other districts display a "mosaic of loose and tight control" (Massell & Goertz, 1999, p. 13). Despite efforts to maintain district-level direction and consistency, "instructionally effective" district leaders indicated that they allowed principals and schools a degree of flexibility, suggesting a dynamic tension between district control and school autonomy (Murphy & Hallinger, 1986, 1988). "Pioneering" districts delegated to schools functions most directly related to teaching and learning, while retaining control of districtwide functions such as transportation, food services, and maintaining lines of communication (David, 1990). Finally, setting clear expectations and then decentralizing responsibility enabled District #2 to "walk a fine line" between central authority and school autonomy (Elmore & Burney, 1999).

Mixing centralized and decentralized control, however, can hinder district efforts to enact school improvement (Goldring & Hallinger, 1992). In districts characterized by "fragmented centralization" (displaying centralized control on some indicators and autonomy on others), teachers reported less positive internal organizational processes than teachers in either centralized or decentralized settings. Perhaps these districts conveyed mixed or confused messages: "The important issue may be one of signal-ing to schools, not one of control" (Goldring & Hallinger, 1992, p. 17).

Leadership

District leaders' knowledge, understanding, skills, and exercise of influ-ence also emerge as important in the process of enacting change. The su-perintendents in "moving" districts were more experienced and availed themselves of ongoing learning opportunities, thereby "typifying organi-zational norms through their action" (Rosenholtz, 1989, p. 182). District leadership styles can also signal "the presence (or absence) of a vital, co-hesive professional community" (McLaughlin, 1992, p. 34). For example, by invoking "coercive authority" to implement district policies, one dis-trict perpetuated a feeling of paternalism among teachers and a divisive sense of "us/them" that lead to fragmentation of work culture.

District leadership was also an essential ingredient of effective districts identified in earlier research (Murphy & Hallinger, 1986, 1988). However, the conception of leadership in these studies focused on active involvement in and control over goal setting, supervising and evaluating staff, select-ing professional development activities, and monitoring school activities. Unlike other studies (McLaughlin, 1992: Rosenholtz, 1989), this research did not emphasize the normative aspects of leadership.

District administrators' knowledge about and understanding of re-forms also appear to affect how districts enact school-level policies (Price, Ball, & Luks, 1995; Spillane, 1998a, 1998b). One district's allocation of mini-mal resources to math reforms, for example, reflected curriculum admin-istrators' limited understanding of and commitments to these reforms (Price et al., 1995).

SUMMARY AND IMPLICATIONS FOR FUTURE RESEARCH

The preceding review provides evidence that districts can play a poten-tially critical role in improving teaching and learning. Studies on district–state and district–school relations demonstrate that districts were more than passive recipients of policy. Instead, they often ignored, adapted, and in-terpreted higher-level policies, as well as developing their own policies and programs to support school change and guide instructional practice. This research highlights variation in districts' implementation of state policies, as well intentional and unintentional efforts to alter state policy to fit local contexts. Studies of district–school relations also found that districts act-ing strategically could create new roles for teachers; alter teaching practice; improve student achievement; and enhance teachers' pride, sense of competency, and commitment to the profession.

Additionally, this research offers insights into forces and conditions that facilitate or constrain district improvement efforts, three in particular. First, districts that mobilize human, social, and physical capital appear more able to enact and sustain state and local reform goals and policies. These forms of capital represent capacity beyond fiscal and staff resources, including normative aspects of district culture and values, as well as the relationships, networks, and trust among individuals.

Second, an important source of the district's capacity resides in district administrators' knowledge, understanding, and informational resources. District staff's knowledge of reform greatly influences how resources are allocated, how policies are interpreted and implemented, and the level (or lack) of support given to reform ideas, policies, and programs. Efforts to increase the information accessible to local policy makers and administrators play an important role in building districts' capacity to undertake instructional change.

Third, both the exercise and stability of district leadership over time appear to affect how instructional reform plays out across a system. Beyond the personal attributes of top administrators (e.g., competence, beliefs), district leadership includes the ability to build a cohesive professional community and normative culture.

This growing body of evidence on districts' relationships with states, schools, and teachers sheds little light on district–community relations. Focusing on the formal policy system that treats "district" as central office, most of the research reviewed views community as a *context* rather than an *actor* in reform efforts (David, 1990; Kirp & Driver, 1995; Spillane, 1998b). More often than not, the literature portrays the community as a barrier, not a resource (Firestone, 1989b; Firestone & Fairman, 1998; Murphy & Hallinger, 1986, 1988).

Despite what we have learned over the past 15 years, many questions remain about districts and their role in educational improvement. Several lines of inquiry would enhance our knowledge base on this topic. First, theoretical work and methodological improvements are needed. Much of the current literature is atheoretical. Spillane's (1998a, 1998b, 2000a, 2000c) cognitive framework offers one example of a useful, fully developed theoretical base, as does research applying Wenger's (1998) communities of practice framework to school districts (see Wechsler, 2001). More longitudinal studies and less reliance on self-reported information from district administrators would improve the knowledge base as well. Research capturing the bottom-up perspectives of school-level educators could further strengthen understanding of district practice and its consequences (e.g., Firestone & Fairman, 1998; Rosenholtz, 1989; Spillane, 1996).

Armed with better frameworks and designs, scholars are ready to develop more nuanced understandings of how districts manage their policy environments to enact instructional change. The extensive research on District #2 illustrates a kind of deep examination of the district structures, strategies, and impacts that are needed in other settings and with other facets of the story of the school district in instructional renewal (e.g., the tools district leaders employ to create shared norms and build opportunities for continuous learning by school and district staff). Building on Spillane and Thompson's (1997) work, further study of relations and interactions among the various resources of human, social, and physical capital would help illuminate how districts develop capacity for instructional improvement, as would more work on how districts mobilize and activate these resources (see Chapter 5, this volume). Some research currently being conducted by the Center for the Study of Teaching and Policy (CTP), by the Learning Research & Development Center, and by Spillane and colleagues is addressing some of these critical questions.

Work on "nonsystems actors" (Cohen, 1995) raises important questions about district–community relations, suggesting yet another line for further inquiry. In this view, much activity within districts occurs in a fragmented organization that in some respects is a "nonsystem" of schools governed and influenced by countless government agencies and private organizations. In this context, social resources supporting teaching are critical to the progress of systemic reform. By expanding the definition of instruction to include resources outside schools that influence students' motivation and preparation for engaging in school, parents, citizens, businesses, professional development groups, and other organizations become potentially critical actors in the process of districtwide instructional improvement.

Combined with existing research that construes the community as a barrier to district reform, these ideas provoke several important questions. For example, to what extent and in what ways is community a resource to districts as they try to enact educational improvement? How much does community involvement and collaboration affect a district's human, social, and physical capital? Are internal focus and insulation from the community helpful to districts (as suggested by Firestone, 1989b; Firestone & Fairman, 1998; Murphy & Hallinger, 1988)? Conversely, if community is a critical instructional resource, then how do districts engage citizens and organizations to enhance the social resources of its students and teachers?

Finally, unanswered questions concern the degree to which school districts affect the implementation of state policies and the enactment of school-level instructional changes. While we now know that districts are key actors in educational improvement efforts, *how* significant are their contributions relative to other actors? In other words, do districts matter as much as states? As schools? Research that considers the joint and relative contributions of states, districts, and schools can do much to shed light on these questions.

NOTE

The author gratefully acknowledges James Spillane for his thoughtful comments on an earlier draft of this chapter.

PART II

Provocative Possibilities, Emerging Questions: The District as Catalyst and Critical Support for Instructional Renewal

A close examination of particular cases, studied individually or comparatively, reveals how districts can move beyond the enduring perceptions of the district as an obstacle to reform. Accounts of these cases detail how policy makers and leaders can fashion strategies that give the district a more vital role in instructional renewal.

The case accounts we have included—by Goertz and Massell, Stein and D'Amico, Hightower, Snyder, and Burch—illuminate different aspects of the district's role in instructional renewal in a variety of settings, from among the smallest districts in the nation to the largest. In particular, the chapters explore the districts' efforts to build instructional capacity, guide professional learning, engage in simultaneous systemic change at the school and district levels, and establish a system of supports for a strong and effective teaching force. The chapters also keep in view dynamic conditions that have the potential to alter the district's place or presence in instructional renewal, including turnover of district leaders, resistances of many kinds, the policy "flux" that characterizes many urban districts, and the fragility of coalitions that support the district's activity in instructional renewal.

CHAPTER 3

District Strategies for Building Instructional Capacity

DIANE MASSELL AND MARGARET E. GOERTZ

This chapter explores the promises and challenges of district-level strategies to build capacity for instructional improvement. We highlight three strategies that were most common among the districts we studied: (1) increasing professional knowledge and skill, (2) strengthening and aligning instructional guidance, and (3) using data to guide instructional improvement efforts. Although these strategies are prevalent in most districts (all districts support some kind of professional development, for example), the districts that we discuss deployed them in innovative and focused ways to improve instruction in schools and classrooms. We analyze how districts enacted each of these strategies, examining in greater detail practices in eight districts that illustrate important differences in approaches (see Table 3.1 for district demographics). In this more focused look, we discuss how a small group of teachers and/or administrators viewed their district's capacity-building activities and the implementation issues that arose.

Data for this chapter come from a 3-year study of standards-based reform in 23 school districts across eight states—California, Colorado, Florida, Kentucky, Maryland, Michigan, Minnesota, and Texas. Identified only by pseudonyms in this chapter, these districts were selected for their improvement and standards-based reform initiatives. We conducted site visits in 1998 and 1999; in each district, we interviewed central office staff responsible for accountability and assessment, curriculum and instruction, professional development, low-performing schools, and federal programs. We also interviewed principals and school improvement committee chairs in a sample of 57 elementary schools in all states but Minnesota, and we observed and interviewed teachers in 33 of these schools. The findings reported here draw

School Districts and Instructional Renewal. Copyright © 2002 by Teachers College, Columbia University. All rights reserved. ISBN 0-8077-4266-X (pbk), ISBN 0-8077-4267-8 (cloth). Prior to photocopying items for classroom use, please contact the Copyright Clearance Center, Customer Service, 222 Rosewood Dr., Danvers, MA 01923, USA, tel. (508) 750-8400.

Table 3.1. Demographic Data on Eight Focal Districts

District Pseudonym	State Code	Rural, Urban, Suburban	Size [a]	Student Demographics	
				Concentration of Students of Color [b]	Students Who Qualify for Free or Reduced-Price Lunches (%)
Farmington	05	Rural	Small	Low	42
Wilder	04	Rural	Small	Low	40
Barton	05	Urban	Very large	High	67
Livingston	01	Urban	Very large	High	64
Hazelcrest	05	Suburban	Large	Low	17
Midview	06	Rural	Small	Low	30
Alpine	02	Suburban	Medium	Medium	23
Sandalwood	08	Urban	Very large	High	91

[a] "Small" is fewer than 10,000 students; "Medium" is 10,000 to 30,000; "Large" is 30,001 to 75,000; and "Very large" is more than 75,000.
[b] "Low" is a concentration of 25% or less; "Medium" is a concentration of 26% to 74%, and "High" is a concentration of 75% or greater.

heavily on the district-level interviews across the study sites and on administrator and teacher interviews in a subset of our study schools.

We do not intend to evaluate the impact or effectiveness of the strategies. These strategies were not mutually exclusive; within a district, they could and did overlap in ways that often reinforced each other. Rather, we hope to convey the organizing principles that, in the words of Elmore and Burney, "give the overall strategy its meaning" (1997a, p. 7).

STRATEGIES TO INCREASE PROFESSIONAL KNOWLEDGE AND SKILL

Providing support for teachers' professional development is a regular, institutionalized district practice. Nevertheless, the *way* districts seek to improve teachers' knowledge and skills varies markedly from place to place. Differences arise in the formats and content of professional development. For example, one California district in our sample offered extensive workshops, while a Colorado and a Maryland district provided almost none. Some districts focused heavily on providing generic pedagogical strategies, while others centered their professional development more strongly around school subjects. Districts used a mix of professional development formats, sometimes only a few and sometimes many. The type and number of activities depended primarily on the size and relative abundance of resources inside and outside the district. In addition to these variations in form and function, there were important, if difficult to measure, differences in the degree to which professional learning was at the heart of the district's "theory of action," that is, the set of beliefs about what can cause the behavior of people and organizations to change (Argyris & Schön, 1974). While the leadership in nearly all our districts expressed the belief that increasing teachers' knowledge and skills was an important part of any change process, only a few demonstrated a deep commitment to professional learning as the linchpin of sustained improvement. These district leaders devoted not only resources but also creative energy to the task, finding and building opportunities for growth into many different kinds of activities.

Although these differences were strong, there also were discernible common trends across districts. The most striking was the growing interest in nontraditional forms of professional training and support. While menu-driven workshops were still prevalent in our sample, district staffs increasingly believed this format had limited benefits. One of our Minnesota districts funded an external evaluation of its professional development workshops and found that teachers often chose not to participate despite receiving inservice credit and clock hours with financial benefits. A Kentucky respondent acknowledged that despite heavy financial investment in Different Ways of Knowing (DWOK) training, teachers did not use these techniques because the professional development they received occurred "too often with no follow-up to see if it was effectively implemented, if it had an impact on the classroom." Indeed, the literature on professional development strongly critiques the traditional "one-shot" workshop, finding that such brief exposure to new ideas often has only a marginal effect (Cohen & Hill, 1998; Little, 1993b; National Commission on Teaching and America's Future, 1996).

Consequently, districts experimented with nontraditional forms of professional development. Most frequently, they deployed district staff in schools for continuous professional development tailored to individual needs, identified teacher leaders to receive special training and then deliver it to their colleagues, and engaged teachers in policy development, such as creating assessments or standards. In addition, many tried to fix the ailing traditional workshop concept by expanding these events to multiple days or weeks and, in one case, years. Districts also provided some kind of follow-up throughout the academic calendar year.

Two pairs of district cases illustrate different approaches to the perceived professional development problem. Farmington and Wilder almost completely abandoned workshops in favor of school-based and other formats. By contrast, Livingston and Barton retained workshops as a central component of their professional development opportunities—but did so in very different ways. Livingston was also notable for the rich array of learning opportunities it provided.

Farmington and Wilder: Examples of School-Based Professional Development

Farmington. Farmington, a small and poor rural district, deployed its resources for professional development in three primary ways. First, the district central office designated a teacher specialist to reside at each of its elementary and middle schools to individualize support. This was part of a larger management strategy of trimming back the central office and reassigning staff to work more closely in the schools. According to one district respondent, "Teacher specialists are the most effective thing we've done because they are the point of contact, and they individualize their help to meet the needs of specific teachers." These specialists received common district training, often on subjects related to the kind of teaching and student preparation implicit in the state's testing program. But, because they were school-site staff, the aim of the program was to have them work regularly with teachers and schools in ways that were best suited to the needs of the teachers and schools, although the district sometimes required them to provide workshops on specific subjects of interest districtwide. These specialists coached teachers one-on-one, offered schoolwide workshops, and carried out other tasks at the behest of the principal. Additionally, in keeping with the idea of bottom-up change, Farmington also devolved its mandated professional development days to schools to use as the schools saw fit. Finally, since it is in an isolated, rural area, Farmington focused on expanding the supply of professional development opportunities for teachers by creating a separate, for-profit professional development center.

Wilder. The professional development strategy of Farmington was similar in many respects to that of Wilder, a small, poor rural district in another state. Like Farmington, this district also offered little districtwide professional development, although in this case it was because the state mandated decentralization of curricular and professional development decisions and resources to schools. The central office and schools collaborated to jointly fund a program of school-based resource teachers at the elementary level, having found that without follow-up support, subject-matter initiatives and new programs were not having an impact. Resource teachers modeled lessons, mentored teachers who had questions and concerns about how to implement specific instructional programs and approaches, and directed teachers to more information on good instructional practice. The district used federal and private foundation grants to help pay for the resource teachers and to respond to other school-identified needs, such as technology training.

Barton and Livingston: Examples of District-Retained Professional Development Workshops

Barton. Barton, a very large, impoverished urban district, deployed its professional development strategy through a set of extended district workshops in reading/language arts and mathematics. In previous years, Barton schools had been given considerable leeway choosing curriculum materials and programs as well as in allocating time and resources for staff training. But poor student achievement, coupled with concerns about the way schools were using professional development resources, stimulated significant recentralization. The district adopted and mandated common reading/English-language arts (ELA) and mathematics materials, and it tied summer workshops to the new textbook curricula. Previously, Barton's training had been more generic because the district had no common, districtwide curriculum material. The district also made its workshops extended affairs. It offered 5-day summer institutes for the reading/ELA material, and it planned to offer 10 days for mathematics with follow-up support to be provided by the textbook publishers during the schoolyear. Barton offered financial incentives to teachers to attend, and about half of the teachers participated that first summer.

Barton also placed retired educators in many schools to support new teachers and hired content-area specialists to rotate among schools and provide support for certain district instructional initiatives. At the time of our visits, however, this support was not the district's major professional development initiative, and our study schools were using the retired teachers for a variety of purposes that ranged from performing administrative tasks to teaching small groups of students.

Livingston. Like Barton, Livingston is a very large, high-poverty urban district, and central office leaders used district workshops as a primary strategy for teachers' professional development. However, Livingston developed a different approach. First, all teachers entering the district were required to participate in an extensive series of courses and workshops in literacy and mathematics over a 2-year period. Basic literacy training the first year involved 30 hours of coursework plus professional reading. Unlike Barton, classes were not tied to a particular curriculum package or textbook (schools in the district selected and used different materials) but rather were oriented toward instruction in the content areas. In mathematics, for example, the staff focused on the development of learning and instructional strategies; the use of logic and language; available resources; lesson design; and the use of technology for algebra, geometry, probability, and other mathematics areas. After the first 2 years of basic training, teachers were offered courses that built on this common foundation. Training for parents and volunteer tutors was based on the same pedagogical approaches used in the teachers' courses, in an effort to ensure that students received a consistent instructional message.

Livingston's approach to professional development differed in other ways as well. District leadership and administrators in the schools we visited embraced the notion of creating learning communities and instituted other professional development strategies to try to make learning a regular part of teachers' and administrators' lives. For example, two of the districts' three area superintendents required their principals to conduct action research and collect data. The principals met to discuss their research with their area superintendent and peers, and they were encouraged to imitate this learning strategy with their teaching staff. The district supported teachers' participation in study groups and strongly encouraged teachers to become consumers of professional literature. For example, Livingston offered a book on guided reading to any K–3 teacher who requested one. Teachers were also engaged in developing district standards, benchmarks, curriculum, new materials, assessments, and other initiatives. Like others mentioned here, this district had a modest school-based strategy. They deployed a few district coaches to schools to support individual teachers or provide professional development for entire school staffs in literacy or math. The district was also in the process of developing teaching standards and examining the range of its professional development activities to try to build a more coherent conceptual foundation for its work in this area.

Implementation Issues: School-Level Responses to Districts' Professional Learning Strategies

Our conversations with small groups of teachers in each district suggested several things about professional development strategies that ran counter to our expectations. First, teachers we interviewed in Barton and Livingston greatly appreciated the workshop initiatives sponsored by their districts.

Far from the usual image of the district workshop as a meaningless, frustrating event, these professional development opportunities were fulfilling teachers' own perceived needs. After years of trying—on their own—to improve student learning in reading and mathematics, many of the Barton teachers seemed to welcome a stronger district role in directing these practices through central textbook adoptions with extended professional development geared to these materials. District administrators themselves talked about the difficulty of providing useful professional development without a common set of curriculum materials in use across the schools. Livingston's approach, by contrast, was not specific to any curriculum materials, although it was oriented to the teaching of particular school subjects. It was still perceived by the teachers we interviewed as highly useful, in part because it was very intense, extended over a period of years, and fostered shared teaching strategies.

Teachers were less likely than administrators in Wilder and Farmington to point to school-based resource teachers or specialists as useful professional support. When we asked them about the most effective or important support they received, only about one-fifth of the classroom teachers we spoke to in Wilder mentioned resource teachers. One explanation for this finding may be that the resource teachers, who were shared across schools, primarily supported new teachers or teachers in state-tested grades, and we interviewed a broader mix. However, although the teachers in Farmington often described their teacher specialists as helpful, a survey sponsored by the district during the second year of our study found teachers willing to eliminate these roles and have these staff return to the classroom to teach. One district respondent speculated that this attitude arose from the fiscal crises in the district and the feeling that specialists should return to the classroom to "pull their weight." In fact, the district ultimately decided to return specialists to the classroom part time to serve gifted-and-talented students.

Livingston's strategy of creating school-based learning communities appeared to have fostered (or at least supported) a climate for professional learning in the schools that was school-based and job-embedded. Teachers' conversations with us about their professional development experiences stood in sharp contrast to those in Farmington, Wilder, and Barton. Norms of professional learning seemed quite high, which was certainly an artifact of the leadership within the schools. For instance, although one school had been considered a "lighthouse" in the district for many years, there also were strong imprints of the district's recent approach to fostering these norms. Their teachers much more frequently discussed the importance of colleagues, study groups, professional reading, and visiting classrooms to observe (part of the support system for new teachers), as well as attending district-financed outside conferences in language arts or mathematics. For example, one teacher said, "Everything we [partners on a team] do together is so powerful because we play ideas off each other, we talk them through, and we read books together to support what we're studying. That has been so powerful!" This and other comments suggested a kind of self-motivation for learning that was more frequently expressed by staff in these schools than in the schools we visited in Farmington, Barton, or Wilder.

STRATEGIES TO STRENGTHEN AND ALIGN INSTRUCTIONAL GUIDANCE

Some district leaders in our study believed that strengthening and aligning curriculum and instruction was a central lever for improvement. Again, as with professional development, the focus on curriculum and its alignment with testing, instruction, and other tools are certainly not uncommon. Nearly all of our study districts voiced concern about aligning their curriculum and instruction, both vertically to state standards and assessments and horizontally to other elements of district and school policies and programs.[1]

But the districts varied substantially in how they tried to improve curriculum and instruction as well as achieve alignment. One difference was the degree to which districts sought to build alignment through changing curriculum, instruction, or both. A Michigan district, for example, had a highly centralized mastery learning curriculum that identified very specific grade-level objectives in core subjects, had a single textbook series, and required teachers to teach to mastery in the order given in district documents. One of our Texas districts guided its elementary language arts program primarily by aligning professional development to a set of principles and standards; it did not adopt textbooks. Districts also made strategic choices about whether and where to centralize curriculum and instruction. Central control often varied by subject matter, with stronger district direction typically occurring in mathematics. However, during our time in the districts, some began to assert more guidance over formerly decentralized language arts curriculum and instruction in response to lagging student test scores and teachers' confusion about how to achieve balance between whole-language and more traditional phonics approaches.

Hazelcrest and Midview provide examples of school districts that used centralized curriculum reform aligned to state standards as their overarching capacity-building strategy. These districts tell interesting stories about how the specificity of guidance for curriculum and instruction can differ and illustrate different strategies for generating teacher understanding.

Hazelcrest: An Example of Centrally Managed Curriculum Development

Hazelcrest is a large and growing suburban district that, in response to low scores in the first year of the state test, launched a 5-year plan to align its curriculum to meet state expectations. Hazelcrest teachers helped develop lengthy and highly specified curriculum guides with standards, frameworks, and scope and sequence documents. The guides contained a hierarchy of outcomes that ran from state to district to grade level to unit outcomes. They included resource guides for each grade level, planning guides for each unit outcome, and lesson indicators or "essential learnings." The language arts guide, for example, suggested how teachers might allocate their time and contained a sample year-long planning matrix of how to cover all the outcomes. It contained periodic running records and mid-year assessments in which students had to respond to a reading activity and writing prompt. The district was also developing assessments in language arts and mathematics to track individual student progress against district outcomes and had adopted a recommended textbook in mathematics.

Curriculum revision was accompanied by professional development linked to the emerging curricular changes. Teachers were trained by grade level in one subject for 2 years, before turning to a second subject area. Staff development, which was strongly controlled by the central office, focused on use of the guide, the philosophy behind the new approach to instruction, the scope and sequence guide, instructional practices, and expected student outcomes. The district trained principals and teachers in what appropriate instruction would look like—for example, instruction that matched the models in the curriculum guide—and used a system of "look-fors," instructional elements for teachers and administrators to use to monitor teachers' implementation of new instructional approaches. Similarly, the district assigned six teacher specialists to five to seven schools each to assist teachers in changing practice. In addition to providing professional development, they planned with the principal to address the instructional needs of teachers in the school. Hazelcrest tried to insure that all its professional development was based on Dimensions of Learning (DOL). DOL was a state-endorsed program providing instructional strategies organized around five categories, or dimensions, of student thinking. One respondent noted, "We've been reluctant to bring people in to do whole-scale professional development . . . when their model was not exactly aligned with ours. We haven't wanted to give teachers mixed messages."

Midview: An Example of Teacher-Initiated Curriculum Development

The Midview School District is a small, rural community located in another state. Like Hazelcrest, it also mandated the use of specific curriculum—the Reading/Writing Workshop in English/language arts (ELA) and the Everyday Mathematics program in mathematics. However, in contrast to Hazelcrest's centrally managed curriculum development, a small group of teachers had introduced Midview to the workshop approach to ELA in the early 1990s. They had learned about the program from a local college professor and through their own reading. As interest in the workshop method grew among the faculty, the district became a demonstration site for a Goals 2000–funded revision of the state's ELA standards and curriculum framework. Our project co-directors (and Midview site visitors) found that participation in the state standards revision process both broadened (to include more teachers) and deepened discussions about what students should be learning and how teachers would help students (Wilson & Floden, 2001). The district subsequently endorsed the Reading/Writing Workshop in its regular ELA curriculum adoption.

Like Hazelcrest, Midview implemented the new program gradually, with a heavy investment in professional development and materials. Implementation was developmental, however, rather than sequential by grade level. As one teacher described the process, teachers first removed workbooks and supplemented the basal stories with reading, writing, and art projects; then, over time, they replaced textbooks with their own trade books. After most teachers had adopted the workshop strategies, the district pushed teachers to expand their mastery of the workshop approach, use of portfolios, and commitment to whole-language strategies. While the community expressed reservations about the district's movement away from phonics instruction and familiar spelling lists, the new superintendent strongly supported the workshop approach. In addition to paying teachers to attend summer programs, the district offered regular refresher courses on the workshop method. Principals also were required to take courses on the Reading/Writing Workshop.

In contrast to the ELA curriculum, where the impetus and support for change came from the teachers, the new mathematics curriculum was developed by a district committee as part of its regular curriculum review cycle. Midview allowed teachers to become more familiar with the new mathematics curriculum before requiring full-scale adoption of the program and more fundamental changes in instruction. But while participation in the ELA demonstration program had served as a natural teacher network for development and implementation of this subject, mathematics lacked such support. Summer institutes and optional training offered by the district generated little interest among the teachers.

Implementation Issues: School-Level Responses to Districts' Instructional Guidance Strategies

In both Hazelcrest and Midview, district-driven curriculum and instruction were a major, although not exclusive, influence on what and how teachers taught. Teachers across the three study schools in Hazelcrest reported that their district curriculum guides gave them outcomes and some scope and sequence (e.g., genres to read at each grade level), but teachers had flexibility in how to achieve the outcomes. As one teacher noted:

> I used to look at a unit of study and decide how to teach it. Now I look at the outcomes required by the [district], the final assessment, the scoring tool to see what it is they are looking for, and I use those as guides to my instructional planning.

While the guides included unit plans, teachers designed ELA activities around trade books chosen by their grade groups or schools. Similarly, Midview teachers spoke about a language arts program built around trade books they had selected, the writing process, and student writing. Teachers in both districts, however, modified district curriculum as necessary to meet state assessment demands—reorganizing the order of topics, focusing writing instruction on categories used in state scoring rubrics, and sometimes dropping content not covered on the test.

Three factors facilitated the implementation of a common curriculum in each district. First, with the exception of mathematics in Midview, both districts expended considerable resources on training teachers on the underlying principles, pedagogical techniques, and content of the new curricula and provided ongoing support through follow-up training, school specialists, and/or teacher group time to discuss implementation of curriculum.

Second, the districts phased in new curriculum by grade level (Hazelcrest), subject area (both districts), or developmental level (ELA in Midview). Phase-in gave teachers needed time to become familiar with new approaches to teaching, participate in professional development, and try out new techniques in the classroom. It also gave them time to develop supplemental materials and activities to address state and local standards. Yet, even with a phased implementation, the addition of the second curriculum placed considerable stress on teachers in both districts. One teacher in Hazelcrest commented, "Sometimes I feel like we have 300 days of curriculum for 180 days [of school]." A district respondent in Midview felt that teachers' lack of interest in summer mathematics institutes was due in part to teacher burnout, to the fact that teachers "had so many things coming at them from so many directions that they just . . . had to have a summer."

Third, most of the training and ongoing support was provided by local educators, such as curriculum specialists, a cadre of teachers such as the ELA network in Midview, or faculty at nearby colleges. When teachers in Midview were expected to implement their new mathematics curriculum aided primarily by summer institutes, their principals, and telephone calls to their textbook representative, they called for additional follow-up training to address loopholes and unanticipated problems.

STRATEGIES TO USE DATA TO GUIDE INSTRUCTIONAL IMPROVEMENT

District staff increasingly viewed the use of data in instructional and other practice-related decisions as a way to more effectively drive change (Massell, 2001). This view stands in contrast to previous attitudes, when data were often considered part of tedious reporting mandates rather than engines for improving practices and student learning (see, e.g., David, 1978). By contrast, the majority of administrators in our study districts and schools actively promoted and supported data and research, and veteran educators believed their own attitudes about data were changing. For example, one Texas principal said:

> I can remember being in the classroom as a teacher and not ever looking at TAAS [Texas Assessment of Academic Skills] . . . or whatever data. And nobody talked about it. . . . I think the good thing about all the publicity with TAAS is that it has made us take a good look at [those] data. What does it say, what does it mean, what do we need to do differently, better, more of? . . . And those results have to guide what we do so that we can continue to improve.

Predictably, district and school educators used data to align curriculum and instruction with tested outcomes. But they also used the data in some uncommon ways—for example, to identify and network with schools or districts that had similar demographics but better student performance, a move to alter stubborn beliefs that students' family circumstances immutably determine how well students achieve. A Kentucky district paired its more successful principals with those in low-performing schools to model different administrative strategies. A few districts and schools in our sample also began to use student achievement data to identify professional development opportunities, in contrast to the typical needs or satisfaction surveys districts use to decide which opportunities to offer or which are successful (Guskey, 2000). A Florida district, for example, examined and compared test scores over time, identified needs for schools, and helped principals set up training programs.

To encourage their schools and teachers to use data, districts paid particular attention to interpreting the information for schools or developing schools' understanding of data. Their strategies differed according to who received the training—staff inside or outside the schools. Most districts hired or trained experts to provide interpretation. Assessment staff from a Florida district held more than 100 meetings with individual schools to explain test results. By contrast, some districts taught staff within the schools to do their own analyses of data generated by the state, district, or others, although they usually provided the training to a select group, such as principals, school improvement team members, or a designated teacher or noninstructional staff member. Finally, a few districts and schools in our study encouraged teachers and administrators to produce data themselves, in part to improve their understanding of data for instruction but also for other purposes, such as to create information more relevant to their particular curriculum.

In addition to training, many districts generated their own data on student achievement to supplement the information collected by the state. Some districts wanted these data to measure continuous progress toward district and/or state standards, provide instructional feedback to teachers, offer student-level information for parents and teachers, reinforce constructivist teaching through performance assessments, and/or evaluate programs. They asked for more data particularly when their states tested only a few benchmark grades or a small number of subjects, or when the test used a matrix sample that lacked reliable information about individual student performance.

Finally, districts and schools created new incentives to encourage schools and teachers to use data for decisions about practice. For instance, some districts went beyond what was required by their state accountability systems to identify low-performing or at-risk schools. A Texas district identified "priority" schools that could be classified as low-performing under the state accountability system the following year, since the state annually raised its performance requirements. Although most districts tended not to include progress on measured outcomes in their formal teacher or administrator evaluations unless the state required it, supervisors said they informally considered this information when they recommended dismissals, demotions, or transfers.

Two districts, Alpine and Sandalwood, were both strong promoters of data use and used similar school-based strategies of support. While the two districts do not offer radically different approaches to building capacity around data, they illustrate interesting complexities in the challenges of using data to drive instructional decision making.

Alpine: An Example of Moving Beyond Test Data

Alpine is a medium-sized, suburban district located in a state that only recently had begun to phase in and publish state testing results at the school and district levels. District leadership actively embraced the view that these data would spur improvement and established new managerial structures and strategies to support schools' data use. They required schools to create Student-Focused Action Teams (SFATs) for areas that the data revealed to be problematic. Team members had to conduct research on the problem, collect additional data, and develop a work plan. The district also required each school to select at least one in-house data analyst. The district's professional development department, in conjunction with a local university, provided these individuals with 3 years of data analysis training, and the district paid them a stipend for performing this work. Finally, the superintendent offered additional support and used informal incentives to focus schools' attention on data. For example, although neither the state nor the district formally identified low-performing schools, the superintendent actively managed these schools. She assigned additional district staff to work with them on improvement plans, removed one principal, and encouraged another to voluntarily apply for Title I school improvement status.

The schools we visited there were working hard to use data. One principal required *all* of his teachers to be involved on one of the SFATs, hoping to nurture an understanding of and commitment to data. They went beyond student achievement data to identify problems and develop solutions. For example, they decided to have all third- through fifth-grade teachers count missing homework assignments from the beginning of the schoolyear. The school then created a detention center for students who did not turn in assignments. Further analysis of the data revealed that 33 students were doing 65% of all detentions and that high proportions of them had special needs. The school also noted which teachers were sending the largest numbers of students to detention and began working with them to improve their practices. Finally, the school developed a mentoring program for the students with these problems. Another school in the district had quite a different experience using data. This principal talked about their confusing, and quite painful, struggle to interpret and use data. This confusion led them to jump each year from one strategy and one subject to another as they tried to fix problems the data seemed to uncover.

Sandalwood: An Example of Hard Data, Hasty Decisions

Sandalwood is a very large, high-poverty urban district in a state with a well-established testing and accountability program. Leaders there also strongly emphasized interpreting and using data and research as a change engine. As the superintendent noted:

> There has been a major change in the culture of the district. We are now a data-driven district. Data can be our best ally. It has not always been considered that way, but it is hard to dispute the data regarding student achievement. The data can be compiled in such a way to create a sense of urgency that I felt was necessary to bring about change.

Like Alpine, this district gave the responsibility for interpreting and analyzing data to specific staff members—in this case, an "instructional guide" housed at each school—to help with the development of school improvement plans and with the interpretation of state outcome data. Other central office staff, especially the testing division, also helped schools analyze the information. The superintendent also highlighted the importance she placed on data in her interpersonal interactions with administrators. For example, she visited every school during the year to query how they interpreted and used data in their planning processes.

Sandalwood also illustrates how the "facts" of data, in the eyes of some, can lead to hasty or unwise decisions. Since a study found that the University of Chicago School Mathematics Program (UCSMP) was one of the few programs that reflected high standards and was correlated strongly to its state and national standards, the district mandated the program for all schools as part of its efforts to improve poor student achievement. District leadership fully anticipated that student test scores would decline initially, as is customary when a new program is adopted, and tried to prepare its schools and community. Many felt, however, that the district's decision to mandate UCSMP after a period of decentralization and substantial teacher autonomy was undertaken without sufficiently securing teacher buy-in. So, when student achievement data did in fact show a decline, the teacher union used this evidence to overturn the UCSMP program. District officials were dismayed.

Implementation Issues: School-Level Responses to Districts' Data-Use Strategies

Although districts took steps to improve knowledge and skills about data interpretation and use, many of our district and school administrators pointed to the need for more and better training on these topics. First, as in Alpine and Sandalwood, much of the training targeted building administrators or a select group of teacher leaders. These strategies assumed that this select group would easily be able to direct others in what course of action to take. They also assumed either that the general population of teachers did not need to know how to derive data implications for their day-to-day instruction or that they already knew how. But others saw a compelling need to make the feedback loop between data and practice more explicit. In one of our Kentucky districts, administrators realized teachers did not understand how to use tests to diagnose problems. In their estimation, teachers viewed data gathering and analysis as interference with the "real" work of schooling.

Deriving data implications, however, is not a simple task in the complex school environment. Late returns of state assessment scores often stymie local ability to make effective changes before students or teachers move to new venues. The assessments generated by states and supplemented by districts, schools, teachers, and others often create an overwhelming amount of information to which teachers and administrators are expected to respond. While many argue that no single indicator accurately measures students' knowledge and tout the notion of "multiple measures" to evaluate performance, using these various data creates a major intellectual challenge. The various tests frequently are not aligned and offer competing views of student achievement.

Finally, as was clear with one school each in Alpine and in Sandalwood, using data to drive decisions could lead to rapid-fire shifts in focus. Critics would say such shifts are too quick to produce any meaningful improvement. Others would argue that these interpretations of the data effectively shook up complacent bureaucracies and encouraged them to pursue new strategies for improving achievement. The answer probably lies somewhere between these two extremes: finding data-driven solutions that balance the need for continuity, in order to allow changes to take root and mature, with a feedback mechanism that allows for adjustments or removal if, after a time, success is not forthcoming.

CONCLUSION: WHAT AN ANALYSIS
OF THESE STRATEGIES SUGGESTS

In this chapter we highlighted three important strategies district leaders used to improve schooling: increasing professional knowledge and skill; strengthening and aligning instructional guidance; and using data to guide instructional improvement efforts. Districts approached these tasks in different ways, depending in part on the availability of financial, human, and institutional resources inside and outside the district; the way leaders or others defined the critical problems of improvement; and how they marshaled support and understanding for their strategies.

The major professional development strategies were handled differently in the large urban and smaller rural or suburban districts, due in part to size and availability of fiscal and human resources. But the sites also diverged from each other in how their leaders defined the problem of building knowledge and skills (see also Chapter 9, this volume, on this point). Barton perceived its primary knowledge challenge to be the lack of a uniform and clearly specified curriculum to undergird professional development. To Livingston's leaders, the problem was in providing teachers and others with a solid subject-matter-oriented foundation in pedagogy and in fostering a culture of professional learning. While Hazelcrest and Midview both chose to build instructional capacity through curricular reform, Hazelcrest administrators defined their instructional problem as a lack of alignment—of school and district curriculum and pedagogy with the requirements of their state's assessment, and of teacher practice with the district's new instructional guides. In Midview, teachers identified the need for instructional change after exploring new approaches to teaching language arts. Administrators subsequently supported these changes through curricular revisions and professional development opportunities.

Interviews about districts' capacity-building strategies suggest that teachers prized consistency and focus, wanted sufficient time and support to implement changes in practice, and sought relevance to practice. The focus of district initiatives could be content (e.g., Livingston's basic literacy training), curriculum (e.g., Barton and Hazelcrest), and/or pedagogy (e.g., Midview), as long as teachers saw the implications for improving their practice and affecting students' learning. Principals in Alpine valued the district's focus on data as long as they could discern its relevance for curriculum and instruction. After failed attempts to decentralize professional development, Barton teachers welcomed the new district focus on centralized curriculum. Teachers also valued initiatives that persisted over time and gave them multiple, extended opportunities to learn about changes they were expected to make. Phasing in new curriculum gave teachers time to become familiar with new teaching approaches and to participate in related professional development. Multiyear professional development programs provided an opportunity to build, and build on, a common, consistent foundation in content and pedagogy. In some sites, school-based assistance and learning communities fostered and supported instructional change.

Regardless of the district capacity-building strategy, teachers needed to see the relevance of the district initiative to their daily work. Teachers in Midview, for example, had to experience firsthand that they could substitute projects for workbooks and trade books for basal readers before adopting the Reading/Writing Workshop. Hazelcrest's curriculum guides provided teachers with more specific outcomes, while leaving them the flexibility they sought to teach to these outcomes. Livingston teachers had begun to see the power of school-based study groups to support their practice. In contrast, teachers in Barton and Wilder saw little value in their school-based resource teachers, perhaps because they worked with only a subset of teachers or took on other responsibilities.

Finally, learning to use data to drive decisions about curriculum and teaching is an increasingly significant piece of many districts', and many states', capacity-building agendas. Data publication and analysis have risen to the top of school administrators' concerns. Our cases suggest that schools can make promising use of data, especially when they move beyond student achievement numbers to identify gaps and weaknesses in instructional support. And the effort to network schools to break the cycle of low expectations for certain groups of students is also a promising turn of events. But to turn data into a meaningful exercise for instructional improvement will require a long-term agenda that reaches deeply into the training received by teachers and other school staff.

NOTES

The research reported in this chapter was funded by grants to the Consortium for Policy Research in Education (CPRE) by the U.S. Department of Education's National Institute on Educational Governance, Finance, Policymaking and Management (Grant #OERI-R308A60003); The Pew Charitable Trusts; and the Annie E. Casey Foundation. Opinions expressed in this chapter are those of the authors and do not necessarily reflect the views of the funders or of the institutional partners of CPRE. Kirsty Brown, Connie Keefe, and Elliot Weinbaum of CPRE/University of Pennsylvania assisted in the analysis of the teacher, school, and district data.

1. Alignment is not a new concern for districts (see Rowan, Edelstein, & Leal, 1985). The few districts in our sample that did not express concern over alignment felt that it had already been achieved.

CHAPTER 4

The District as a Professional Learning Laboratory

MARY KAY STEIN AND LAURA D'AMICO

More than at any time in recent history, the professional development of teachers is being viewed as the key ingredient to the improvement of our nation's schools (Darling-Hammond & Sykes, 1999). The perceived importance of professional development is directly related to the ambitious nature of the reform goals and standards that have been put into place over the past decade by subject-matter organizations (e.g., National Council of Teachers of Mathematics, 1989, 2000), state departments of education, and professional boards (e.g., National Board for Professional Teaching Standards, 1989). It is now widely accepted that meeting these goals and standards will require a great deal of learning on the part of practicing teachers—learning that is transformative in nature and requires wholesale changes in deeply held beliefs, knowledge, and habits of practice (Thompson & Zeuli, 1999).

Districts have had difficulty planning and carrying out the kind of professional development that is demanded by intellectually ambitious reform agendas. Recent surveys of district programs suggest that teachers, on average, receive fewer than 8 hours of professional development per year and that those experiences tend to be uncoordinated and unfocused (U.S. Department of Education, 1999). District staff development typically consists of a menu of training options (workshops, special courses, or inservice days) designed to transmit a specific set of ideas, techniques, or materials to teachers (Little, 1993a). Such approaches treat teaching as routine and technical (Little, 1993a) and encourage tinkering around the edges of practice rather than a total overhaul of practice (Huberman, 1993). In addition, they provide teachers with limited access to intellectual resources outside the teaching community and few oppor-

School Districts and Instructional Renewal. Copyright © 2002 by Teachers College, Columbia University. All rights reserved. ISBN 0-8077-4266-X (pbk), ISBN 0-8077-4267-8 (cloth). Prior to photocopying items for classroom use, please contact the Copyright Clearance Center, Customer Service, 222 Rosewood Dr., Danvers, MA 01923, USA, tel. (508) 750-8400.

tunities for meaningful collegial interactions within the teaching community (Little, 1993a).

New York City's Community School District #2 provides a counter-example to this undistinguished characterization of the role that districts can play as teacher educators. Located in Manhattan, District #2 is one of 32 community school districts in New York City. Community school districts are largely concerned with the education of elementary and middle school students, and the size and organization of the schools vary considerably. In District #2, 66% of their approximately 22,500 students are in kindergarten through fifth grade, while 34% are in sixth through eighth grade.

The district is diverse, encompassing affluent neighborhoods on the Upper East Side as well as diverse midtown and lower Manhattan neighborhoods that include both middle-class enclaves and neighborhoods with substantial concentrations of lower-income families and recent immigrants (Elmore & Burney, 1997b). The diversity of these neighborhoods is reflected in the wide variety of school composition within the district (D'Amico, Harwell, Stein, & van den Heuvel, 2001). The number of students eligible for free or reduced-price lunches ranges from as few as 10% in some schools to as much as 99% in others. Likewise, the number of students with limited English proficiency in each school ranges from less than 1% to just over 30%. Ethnic composition of the schools also varies broadly, with some schools consisting largely of Asian students (e.g., 93%), others of White (e.g., 79%) or Hispanic students (e.g., 66%), and still others with highly mixed populations.

Despite wider school variation than that of any other community school district in New York City (Harwell, D'Amico, Stein, & Gatti, 2000), District #2 has been committed to improving instruction and learning in all classrooms within its purview (Elmore & Burney, 1997b). Recognizing that efforts to improve student learning ultimately succeed or fail inside classrooms, its approach to reform relies on a systemwide plan for professional development coupled with accountability and a focus on content-specific instructional improvement (Elmore & Burney, 1999). To this end, a variety of forms of professional development are offered within the district. The uniqueness of District #2's approach, however, lies not in these multiple forms of teacher assistance, but rather in the manner in which professional development is organized and enacted.

Elmore and Burney (1999) have described the ways in which professional development is interwoven into the daily activity of the district and tightly coupled with accountability functions. Their point of departure consists of the theories, actions, and endeavors of the district leaders as they interact with the other educators of the district. We begin our investigation of professional development *within the classroom*, revealing two significant elaborations: (1) the use of systemwide instructional frameworks in literacy and mathematics to shape the substance and process of professional development and (2) the identification and use of variation in teaching expertise as a resource for professional development.

This chapter outlines the district's professional development system for teachers and the role that it has played in instructional renewal. It describes the design and enactment of learning environments for teachers within the district's systemwide literacy initiative. The first part explores how the district's Balanced Literacy program not only forms the basis for a pedagogical program for children but also serves as a touchstone for the district's professional development program. The second part explores the manner in which teachers with varying levels and kinds of expertise are identified and used in the district's professional development program. Our central claim is that District #2 teachers' professional learning is catalyzed by their membership and participation in a fully developed community of practice—a community whose boundaries do not stop at their schools' perimeters but instead include the entire district.

METHODS

This study is part of a 5-year research and development project (the High Performance Learning Communities Project, 1996–2001) that seeks to understand, support, and disseminate the work of Community School District #2 (see Chapter 10, this volume). The study was designed to investigate the district's approach to systemic reform and its effects on classroom, school, and district learning communities. The findings reported in this chapter are based largely on the data collected in school and classroom learning communities during the second year (1997–1998) of the study (Stein, D'Amico, & Israel, 1999); however, they are strongly informed by the associated wider data set.

Our data include a review of documents pertaining to literacy and the Balanced Literacy program (e.g., from District #2 and from the wider literature); formal interviews and informal conversations with teachers, principals, and professional developers; and observations of teacher meetings, professional development sessions, and classroom instruction. Specifically, we observed six mornings of literacy instruction in the classrooms of 12 moderately to strongly skilled elementary teachers spread across three schools for a total of 72 observed mornings. Also, we observed a variety of school- and district-based meetings and professional development sessions associated with the three schools.

INSTRUCTIONAL FRAMEWORKS AS A TOUCHSTONE
FOR PROFESSIONAL DEVELOPMENT

The failure of uncoordinated, 1-day workshops to have a positive impact on teachers' overall development has been well documented (Little, 1993a; Loucks-Horsley, Hewson, Love, & Stiles, 1998). When teachers' learning is not centered on day-to-day instructional practices, teachers quickly forget the lessons once they return to their classrooms and schools. From the perspective of the school or district, the simultaneous existence of numerous reform programs—each of which is associated with its own training package—can lead to diffuse and conflicting efforts, no single one of which has the power or momentum to significantly influence teaching and learning inside the classroom (Bryk, Lee, & Holland, 1993; Bryk, Sebring, Kerbow, Rollow, & Easton, 1998). District #2's antidote to these difficulties has been to focus and consolidate professional development efforts and integrate them into classroom practice through the districtwide adoption of a single literacy program.

The program it has adopted (and adapted), Balanced Literacy, serves as both a guideline for and language of instructional practice. As such, it provides teachers with a framework to support their efforts at teaching literacy (Stein & D'Amico, in press) and serves as a common reference for observations, conversations, and negotiations about teaching practice among District #2 educators (Stein, D'Amico, & Israel, 1999). Below, we outline the program itself and then describe the benefits of its use as an anchor for teacher learning in District #2.

District #2's Balanced Literacy Program

From the start, District #2 leaders eschewed school improvement strategies that focused on developing "pockets of excellence" or heralding and replicating the practices that already existed in a handful of boutique schools. Rather, they wanted to develop an improvement strategy that reached into every teacher's classroom and raised the competencies of all students. To accomplish this, they searched for a common literacy program to anchor their work throughout the district. They chose an instructional model called Balanced Literacy (Fountas & Pinnell, 1995; New Zealand Ministry of Education, 1996) to form the core of that program. Balanced Literacy is practiced in a number of school systems throughout the English-speaking world. The description here and references to the program throughout this chapter describe the program as it is practiced in District #2.

Balanced Literacy consists of a number of components or instructional forms in which students interact with texts at varying levels of challenge in a variety of settings with different levels of support from the teacher. These settings translate loosely into the following:

- *Reading to the student* occurs during whole-class "read alouds" and serves as an occasion to develop oral language, new vocabulary, and new forms of literature. The teacher provides maximal support by reading the text *for* the students and helping them to interpret it.
- *Reading with the student* occurs when the teacher provides significant support to students as they read. Two different components of the program provide "reading with" support. First, *shared reading* involves the teacher reading fairly challenging text along with the students in chorus and helping the students decode and comprehend the text or focus on specific reading strategies. It is a time for the teacher and more capable students to demonstrate the appropriate use of general reading strategies. Second, *guided reading* involves teaching a small, carefully selected group of students reading strategies with a text that is challenging to them but not outside their reach. It is considered to be the heart of the Balanced Literacy program because teachers provide students with direct instruction in specific strategies tailored to their needs using carefully chosen text.
- *Reading by the student* occurs during *independent reading* when students read texts silently on their own. Students read books that are within their current proficiency level and are expected to apply strategies that they have learned in shared and/or guided reading settings. Typically, the teacher conferences with a few students during this time to review their reading proficiency and book choice.

The "balance" in Balanced Literacy is the balance between these differing levels of challenges and support. In addition to these reading components, Balanced Literacy in District #2 also includes a writing component and a word-study component. Word study was introduced into the program in order to focus students on the structure of words, spelling, and, in some schools, phonics (Bereiter et al., 2000; Pinnell, Fountas, Giacobbe, & Fountas, 1998; Snowball & Bolton, 1999).

Balanced Literacy is not a curriculum. Teachers do not receive a list of specific topics they must cover throughout the year. Instead, selection of texts and moment-by-moment instructional decisions are based on continuous teacher assessment of student needs and, thus, cannot be easily specified in a programmatic way. The instructional forms used require teachers not only to continually revisit their plans for meeting students' current learning needs but also to respond dynamically to those needs as they reveal themselves in the course of instruction. While experienced teachers

may be able to predict many of the difficulties and responses students will
have with a particular lesson or text, they can never predict them all. Such
just-in-time teaching is, by its very nature, improvisational. It is a challenging form of instruction to implement, and the district's professional development system is meant to support teachers' efforts at doing so.

Expectations for Program Implementation

District leaders expect *all* teachers to teach literacy in a manner that is con-
gruent with the goals and purposes of the Balanced Literacy program, not
only those who are the most motivated, experienced, or well prepared.
Given the nature of the program, the amount of teacher learning required
to achieve quality implementation can be daunting. In contrast to most
other programs intended for large–scale implementation, the core of the
Balanced Literacy program is a philosophy, not a method. Although some
structure is provided by its components (independent reading, guided
reading, shared reading, read aloud, word study, and writing workshop),
successful enactment of the program depends most heavily on teachers'
grasp of the theory and rationale underlying the recommended practices.

Despite selective hiring practices, most beginning teachers in the district are not prepared to teach in such demanding ways. "That's why we
have such a large professional development program," explained the district's director of professional development. "You take a chance in hiring
. . . really bright [new teachers] who are going to do a good job eventually,
. . . [and] then hope you can change the mindset . . . [through] an awful lot
of professional development."

One of the most formidable challenges for teachers who are new to
the program involves learning how to implement each particular component well and, at the same time, learning how to weave all of the components into a seamless, productive learning experience for children. When
one of the most experienced staff developers was asked what was at the
core of the Balanced Literacy program, she stated:

> The balance. It is the reading *to, with,* and *by* children everyday.
> That's the core. [Right now] I'm talking to teachers about planning.
> When you look at the spread of their week or just their day, [I look
> for] where have you included those three areas. They've got to be
> worked in there, in whichever way you think they fit best and suit
> you best, but are they there?

Making sure that all children are sufficiently challenged during read alouds,
are appropriately supported through shared and guided reading, and have

opportunities to practice and self-assist during independent reading requires tremendous skills of planning, pedagogy, and classroom management.

Provisions That Enable Teacher Learning of Literacy Program

District #2's professional development program benefits in many ways from this districtwide adoption of a common instructional framework. In particular, the Balanced Literacy program provides a starting point and a coherence to formulations of *what* teachers need to learn and *how* they need to learn it.

Creating a Common Language. Facilitating communication across organizational layers is part of the challenge created by districtwide improvement efforts. "Meeting children's needs" may mean one thing to district leaders, something entirely different to principals, and something different still to teachers. Such breakdowns of communications are particularly apt to occur when programs are ill specified, leading to variable and weak enactment of intended practices (Cohen, 1997). In District #2, the Balanced Literacy program and the various materials and professional development experiences that support it provide a common set of terms and meanings that anchor discussions among district leaders, principals, and teachers. Everyone in the district is familiar with the form and purpose of the program's components, and it is this set of common reference points that holds their learning community together (Stein, D'Amico, & Israel, 1999).

Keeping It Whole and Complex. Teachers are not introduced to the Balanced Literacy program component by component or teaching strategy by teaching strategy. They do not, for example, learn to become expert at guided reading and then, with that component under their belt, turn to independent reading. Rather, they are encouraged to work their way through all the components simultaneously, using the structure of the program itself as a scaffold. They have even created a set of guidelines for pacing the program, known as the *Literacy Block*. (See Table 4.1.)

Over the years, district leaders and staff developers have found that such a structure is exceedingly useful for inexperienced teachers. By providing a pacing template for the morning activities, it gives them the security of knowing when they should be doing what. More important, the structure allows teachers to keep the entire task of teaching children to read and the relationships between the various components in mind when planning their lessons.

Although district leaders expect even the most novice teacher to follow the Balanced Literacy structure and teaching strategies, they antici-

Table 4.1. Literacy Block Guidelines

Kindergarten	Grades 1 and 2	Grades 3 and 4
Class meeting	Shared reading	Independent reading
Reading practice	Word study	Shared reading
Shared reading	Guided reading and reading practice	Word study
Letter/word study	Read aloud	Guided reading and reading practice
Center time	Independent reading	Read aloud
Read aloud	Writing	Writing
Share time	Share time	Share time

Source: Community School District #2, 1999, p. 6.

pate that inexperienced teachers will not get it completely right at first. With time and assistance, however, the teachers' understanding of each component and its impact on student learning is expected to deepen. Likewise, their practice is expected to become increasingly proficient and student-centered. After teachers have implemented the entire program for a period of time, they may be encouraged to focus on a particular component in order to gain a deeper proficiency. However, focus on a particular component is always done with reference to the overall program and its relationship to that component.

Depending on the teacher's level of proficiency with the Balanced Literacy program, District #2 makes available different kinds and amounts of assistance. Teachers—indeed, all professionals—are never viewed as "having arrived," that is, as being finished with learning. Teachers continuously receive new forms of assistance in order to refine or elaborate particular aspects of their practice or to learn new forms of practice. Quality, or kind of assistance, is at least as important as quantity and varies according to teacher need. The kinds of assistance available mirrors those provided to students through the Balanced Literacy program. District-sponsored workshops that outline the underlying philosophy of the program and that teach the instructional strategies associated with the program demonstrate the nature of Balanced Literacy *to* the inexperienced teacher. Learning *with* assistance tailored to the teacher's needs is provided through interactions with a school-based staff developer or more experienced colleagues, as well as regular classroom observations and assistance from the building principal. And finally, *by* teaching the Balanced Literacy program day-in and day-out and *by* discussing instructional issues with colleagues during grade-level and other school-based meetings, teachers develop the ability to do the program on their own.

Embedding It in the Work. A closely related feature to keeping the learning task whole and complex is the extent to which District #2's professional development is embedded in the actual work of teaching as opposed to being comprised of "pull-out sessions" (i.e., off-site training that leaves it up to teachers to make their own connections to practice). As the director of professional development stated:

> It doesn't just happen from [a workshop]. You really have to be in the classroom. I mean, you can show a teacher how to do a running record, but do they understand all the implications behind it? Do they really know what they're looking at, what this tells them about the child? They don't know that just by teaching them how to do it. That comes with time, it comes with experience, and it comes with putting all of the pieces together in the classroom.

Rather than residing at the district's central office, staff developers are school-based so that they can work with teachers before and after school hours, during free periods, and in their classrooms during lessons. In more conventional accounts of professional development, these forms of teacher learning would be considered "informal" because they are not officially designed pedagogical occasions for imparting a particular idea or skill. In District #2, however, these forms of professional development are anything but informal or ancillary—they are the heart of support for improving practice.

Unlike other districts in which the assignment of a professional developer to a teacher's classroom signals a "failing" teacher, in District #2, classroom-based assistance is not viewed as a deficit model. Although some classroom-based staff developers do work with high-need teachers, others work with teachers who are following the normal developmental progression from superficial to more mature forms of practice. Still others work with teachers on deepening a particular aspect of their practice or introducing significant extensions to what is considered to be already high-quality practice.

Variation in Practice as a Resource for Professional Development

Classroom observations indicate that most District #2 classrooms have a similar look and feel—warm rooms filled with books and examples of students' written work, organized to provide spaces for small-group, whole-class, and individual work. The instruction in these rooms, however, varies widely in terms of both its quality and its alignment with the Balanced Literacy program.

Observations show that even within Focused Literacy Schools—those that, because of their historically low literacy achievement rates and high-poverty student demographics, are expected to stick most closely to the program's Literacy Block guidelines—there is a great deal of variability in literacy instruction. Half the teachers observed (six) conducted instruction that was of high quality and highly aligned with Balanced Literacy. Four teachers, while clearly attempting to align their instruction with Balanced Literacy, were not yet proficient enough to conduct such instruction well; their practice appeared mechanical. Two teachers did not align their instruction with Balanced Literacy. The instruction in one of these two classrooms was very good, despite not being well aligned with Balanced Literacy (we refer to this teacher as an "innovator"); the instruction in the other classroom was quite poor, and the teacher seemed to be floundering.

District leaders make no pretense that everyone is at the same level of competence. Instead, they deliberately use differences in instructional expertise as a resource when designing their system of professional development, treating all 45 schools as their learning laboratory. Believing that asymmetries in expertise spark learning, they pair those who are viewed as more expert in particular components of the Balanced Literacy program with those perceived as less expert.

Observing experts can serve at least two purposes. First, such observations can provide a vision of "the possible," a particularly critical experience for teachers who are struggling to understand literacy as an integrated whole. It is not uncommon for inexperienced teachers to become frustrated with "fitting it all in," often because they have become overly focused on the particulars and have forgotten to keep the big picture in view. These teachers need to pause, step back, and observe the "masters" of Balanced Literacy, teachers whose practice vividly illustrates the interwoven and seamless character of the program when executed well.

Second, observing experts who are "just beyond" the reach of visiting teachers can provide nuts-and-bolts ideas regarding particular pieces of the Balanced Literacy program. These kinds of professional development experiences pair apprenticing teachers with those who are fairly close in mastery level but who have noticeably better practice in particular areas.

Decisions regarding who a particular teacher will visit and why are made very carefully in District #2. As the director of professional development explained:

There is scaffolding that takes place for kids; there's scaffolding that takes place for teachers. You have to know where the teacher is on the continuum and what's going to help them move to the next step. It does, however, sometimes help for teachers to see what the end goal is, so you may very well send them to a place . . . where you have a really high level of teaching. . . . But in the scaffolding of teacher learning you want to send the person to someone who is closer to where they're at and able to take them to the next level.

The district leadership plays a critical role in this matchmaking process. A key part of the professional development and oversight that District #2 leaders provide to principals is through the regular WalkThroughs they conduct in each school (Elmore & Burney, 1999; Fink & Resnick, 1999). During a WalkThrough, district leaders visit each and every classroom with the principal. They then discuss the instruction seen and next steps to take with each teacher. District leaders bring to this discussion knowledge of all the other classrooms they have visited throughout the district; accordingly, they are able to recommend particular schools and classrooms that the teachers just reviewed may profit from visiting.

Often, the observation of expertise in District #2 is a short experience—a couple of hours in another teacher's classroom to see a particular lesson. A longer and deeper experience is through a program known as the Professional Development Lab (PDL). PDL offers "visiting teachers" the opportunity to work alongside an expert teacher (called the "resident teacher") in his or her classroom, day-in and day-out, for 3 weeks. The opportunities for learning in PDL, although in some ways similar to other forms of learning from experts, are more intense and personal.

Interviews with teachers who have experienced PDL point to the unique benefits associated with this personal form of assistance. Primary among them is the opportunity to gain an "insider's" perspective on a "day in the life" of an expert literacy instructor. Visiting teachers typically arrive in the early morning to do planning with the resident teacher, stay late to evaluate and reflect on the day's lessons with the teacher, and spend lunches pondering the needs of particular children.

In addition to imparting knowledge, skills, and the thinking behind Balanced Literacy, PDL performs another important function: Resident teachers serve as role models for visiting teachers. Because the visiting teachers come to know the residents well, they serve as realistic role models and individuals with whom the visiting teacher can identify. As one teacher who had just completed PDL said (paraphrase):

> I have observed [the resident teacher] leading a clusterwide staff
> development, and [I've thought]: "She's beyond [my] reach. I will
> never be able to do what she does." . . . But now that I've had the
> opportunity to work alongside her everyday, I've learned that she
> struggles, too. Everything is not easy, not even for her. Sometimes
> her lessons don't go well—at least, not as she had planned for them
> to go. We've had to brainstorm together how to redo certain things
> or how to change our approach in order to reach certain children.
> Now, I believe that I *can* be like her.

By gaining a vantage point on the "master at work," this particular visiting teacher has learned that struggle is part of the game. She has learned
that her own struggles are normal and do not signify that she is unsuited
for this community. Because she has a new vision of herself as "someone
who can do this kind of work," she may be less likely to dismiss Balanced
Literacy as "beyond" her capabilities when she runs into obstacles.

"Learning by doing" means making mistakes. What is important is
how those mistakes are viewed. District #2 leaders strive to have teachers
understand that mistakes themselves are opportunities for learning, rather
than indications of failure. Nevertheless, it is not uncommon for novices
to feel the need to do everything perfectly from the beginning. As one staff
developer noted:

> [Teachers] want every lesson to be so powerful that when a lesson
> doesn't go well, they feel very reticent to try to do that sort of thing
> again. . . . I think they need to just free themselves up a little bit,
> have a go [at it], see what happens, [and] know that the kids are
> getting something out of the lesson that they provided. It may not
> have been the very best lesson in the world, but [it results in teach-
> ers understanding] that they can refine their practice by allowing
> themselves to make mistakes and growing from that [knowledge],
> rather than wanting everything to be perfect and, when it isn't,
> feeling . . . disappointed.

Consideration of the motivational processes that accompany teacher
learning is absent or underdeveloped in most accounts of teacher development (Goldsmith & Schifter, 1993). Yet, as indicated by the above quo-
tations, teachers' feelings—about their competence, about their ability to
be successful, about the meaning of mistakes—have a strong impact on their
learning.

LESSONS ABOUT LEARNING FROM DISTRICT #2

Over the past decades, we have learned much about the qualities of professional development that are effective in developing teachers' capacities to enact high-demand curricula. Professional development must be focused on the content we want teachers to teach, it must be continuous rather than one-shot, and it must be connected to what teachers face day to day in the classroom (Loucks-Horsley, 1995). We know much less about how to deliver this kind of professional development on a large scale. Most districts face huge challenges as they undertake efforts to improve the capabilities of all of their teachers to deliver high-demand instructional programs.

District #2 provides some lessons regarding how to organize professional development for high-level teacher learning for an entire district. To overcome the challenges of building a coherent professional development system, the district has found important ways to align its expectations for students' and teachers' learning with instructional frameworks. To overcome the challenge of building teacher capacity across a wide range of teaching expertise, the district has found a way to make that variation a resource rather than a liability.

Building Coherence Through Instructional Frameworks

The district's Balanced Literacy program provides guidance and coherence to the district's professional development program in two ways. First, it outlines what teachers must know and be able to do. By providing a label for certain features of practice, the Balanced Literacy program serves as a language of practice that both guides teacher learning and facilitates conversations about instruction among educators across the district. Making certain this language of practice is accessible and interpretable to all educators in the system is the driving force behind the design of District #2's professional development system. The district continually offers professional development that overviews the program's theory as well as its components. Although teachers who have been implementing the Balanced Literacy program for a number of years often seek out professional development experiences that extend beyond the core components of the program, those experiences are monitored to assure that they harmonize with the philosophy and management of the Balanced Literacy program (Stein, D'Amico, & Israel, 1999).

Second, the Balanced Literacy program guides how teachers learn. Because Balanced Literacy is a theory-based framework, not a scripted program, learning how to enact it well carries with it all the challenges of learning complex tasks. Teachers cannot learn to implement the Balanced Literacy program by reading a manual or imitating another teacher. Rather, their learning opportunities must align with what is known about how high-level knowledge and skills are learned: through engagement with authentic tasks (i.e., teaching the entire Balanced Literacy program, not artificially segmented pieces), by receiving long-term assistance tailored to their needs (i.e., interacting with experts and near-peers around specific difficulties they are facing), and by participating in a community of individuals who share common goals and values. In this way, teachers' style of learning—*how* they learn—suits the level of complexity of what they are being asked to learn.

Leveraging Variation to Build Capacity

District #2's success is based on its ability to cherish diversity while simultaneously building common ground. It would be easy for a district of such widely varying school contexts to become a divided one. Instead, the educators in this community have worked hard to cross the boundaries of school walls and classroom doors. It might be expected that a district with such a strong central vision would view variation in the kinds and levels of instructional expertise in its teaching body as an impediment. In District #2, however, such diversity is leveraged as a resource for supporting professional development and building professional community. This combination of diverse individuals working together on common goals has given District #2's learning community its power and coherence.

The successful harnessing of variation can be directly attributed to district leaders' perceptiveness and strong instincts for the arrangement of successful learning environments for teachers. In order to use variation wisely, one must first identify where talent lies in the organization, who can be helped by what kind of talent, and how to make matches between those with talent and those with needs. District #2 leaders play a critical role in this process both by serving as mediators themselves and by crafting mechanisms through which principals, staff developers, and teachers throughout the system may connect with one another.

Because learning is continuous, the combinations of who can learn what from whom are constantly changing. District leaders' frequent visits to schools and classrooms allows them to gain the knowledge regarding teacher variation that they use to suggest pairings of teachers that are "just right." As noted, sometimes the goal is to see what the Balanced Literacy program looks like when masterfully enacted; at other times, the goal is to witness the nuts-and-bolts of a particular component as enacted by a teacher closer in experience level to the visiting teacher. District leaders also provide opportunities for principals and staff developers to share information about teacher knowledge and expertise across school contexts through districtwide principal conferences and staff developer meetings as well as smaller working groups from subsets of schools. Nonetheless, top district leaders are the only individuals who have access to a broad view of instructional expertise across the *entire* system, and so they work closely with principals and staff developers to provide insights this broad view affords them.

At the time of our data collection, District #2's literacy initiative had been in place for nearly 10 years. The Balanced Literacy program was the accepted model of early literacy instruction throughout the district, and teachers with varying amounts and kinds of expertise were peppered throughout the district. The maturity of the literacy initiative must be factored into our account of how District #2 assumed the role of teacher educator. As other districts have attempted to build on the experiences of District #2 (Hightower, 2001; Mehan, Quartz, & Stein, 1999), it has been important to keep in mind that the districtwide learning community that exists in District #2 did not spring into existence overnight. Developing the norms and range of expertise that allow districts to become teacher educators takes continuous effort and time.

We believe, however, that the arrangements for adult learning described in this chapter provide proof of the efficacy of districts in the ongoing professional learning of teachers. Moreover, the two features discussed in this chapter—common instructional frameworks and identification and use of variation in teaching expertise—can be consciously adopted and developed by other district leaders. With patience and persistence, teachers' professional learning will be catalyzed by their membership and participation in a community whose boundaries do not stop at their school's perimeter but instead included the entire district.

NOTE

Preparation of this chapter was supported by a contract from the High Performance Learning Communities Project at the Learning Research and Development Center, University of Pittsburgh, under research contract #RC-96-137002 with the Office of Educational Research and Improvement at the U.S. Department of Education. Any opinions expressed herein are those of the authors and do not necessarily represent the views of OERI. The authors wish to acknowledge the teachers and principals of District #2 for welcoming us into their schools and classrooms. We especially want to thank Bea Johnstone, Deputy Superintendent of Community School District #2, for the insight provided about the district's professional development program in endless conversations and interviews.

CHAPTER 5

San Diego's Big Boom: Systemic Instructional Change in the Central Office and Schools

AMY M. HIGHTOWER

This chapter details the radical approach taken by reformers in San Diego City Schools (SDCS)—the eighth-largest school system in the country—as they sought to orient district bureaucracy around systemic, instructional change. It is called "San Diego's Big Boom" because that is precisely how reformers believed wholesale change must begin in an entrenched district system: The system first needed to go "boom" and organizational norms had to be "jolted" before reforms and new support structures could take hold.

To focus their district on instruction, San Diego reformers began with an explicit instructional theory and ideas about how district administrators could best support teaching and learning in schools. Rather than falling into systemwide priorities by carrying out traditional district conventions and norms, San Diego reformers actively challenged the logic of their district's status quo. In most districts today, priorities are determined by the availability of resources for the status quo, which is little more than an accumulation of programs and funding sources, resulting in fragmented, unfocused district systems in which instructional matters get lost (Guthrie & Sanders, 2001; Meyer, Scott, & Strang, 1994; Miles & Guiney, 2000). Tossing aside standard operating procedures, San Diego reformers first identified systemwide instructional needs and then aligned district resources, structures, and policies to serve them. Accordingly, this chapter entertains the notion that systemic change in a large urban district may require strong, even bureaucratic, methods to transition the system into supporting a culture focused on instruction and learning.

The data for this chapter come from 3 years of fieldwork in San Diego City Schools, beginning in the fall of 1998 as the district started its reform

School Districts and Instructional Renewal. Copyright © 2002 by Teachers College, Columbia University. All rights reserved. ISBN 0-8077-4266-X (pbk), ISBN 0-8077-4267-8 (cloth). Prior to photocopying items for classroom use, please contact the Copyright Clearance Center, Customer Service, 222 Rosewood Dr., Danvers, MA 01923, USA, tel. (508) 750-8400.

initiative and ending in the summer of 2001, with the initiative still underway. Therefore, the story presented here captures the early years of an ongoing reform. The analysis weaves together semistructured interviews and focus groups with more than 150 people involved in or observing the reform. The primary informants were central office administrators (40% of the total), teachers (25%), and principals (20%). Interviews with union officials, relevant community members, and state policy makers also lend insight, as do observation data from nearly 20 district-sponsored events and an extensive document review, including Lexis/Nexis searches, district and union websites, the local newspaper, district policy and communications, and the union press.

SDCS is large and urban, encompassing both great poverty and wealth. Fifty-eight percent of the students qualify for free or reduced-price lunches, 28% are English-language learners, and more than 50 native languages are spoken. Across nearly 180 schools, the district served 142,300 students in 2000–2001, approximately one-third of whom were Hispanic, one-fourth Caucasian, nearly one-fifth African American, and the remainder Filipino, Indochinese, Asian, or "other."

CONTEXT DRIVING DISTRICT REFORM

San Diego City Schools has long been recognized nationally as having pockets of great innovation and success. Yet as a *system*, SDCS was plagued by student performance gaps among students of different races, ethnicities, and parts of town (Mehan & Grimes, 1999). In the mid-1990s, local business leaders and interested parties across California had come to believe that the district as a whole was "stuck" (Rosenholtz, 1989) in an organizational rut (Vigil & Carstens, 1998).

For years, multiple "area superintendents" had jurisdiction over feeder-pattern clusters of schools—a decentralized arrangement that one long-time observer of the district characterized as "autonomous, reactive, and competitive." District supervisors rarely interacted with one another or others outside their departments. Resources, information, and capacity were inequitably distributed across district clusters and organizational subunits, probably contributing to the persistent achievement gap among different categories of students (Mehan & Grimes, 1999). Trust between the local community and district had taken a tumble after a 1996 teachers' strike exposed an unresponsive side of the central office (Magee & Leopold, 1998). As one long-time board member commented: "The confidence of the community in the schools was pretty low, particularly in the business community. . . . I think there was the sense that the patients were running the asylum."

By the mid-1990s, the state of the district inspired the Greater San Diego Chamber of Commerce's Business Roundtable to actively pursue educational reform. Pointing to gaps in student performance, unqualified graduates entering the local workforce, and negative sentiments lingering from the 1996 strike, the Roundtable focused on changing the district's leadership. It helped elect school board members who would hire a reform-minded superintendent, perhaps even a "noneducator," believing that fresh ideas might help make the kinds of deep changes necessary for true reform.

In March 1998, a divided board appointed Alan Bersin, the local U.S. Attorney for the Southern District of California and Southwest Border, as superintendent. Bersin was locally and nationally well connected and was passionate about equity and social justice. But as one board member later commented, "It was pretty clear that he needed a partner"—specifically, a counterpart who knew how to focus a district instructionally. By the time he assumed office, Bersin had recruited Anthony Alvarado to the district as his chancellor of instruction and co-leader of reform. Signaling his intention to share the top district leadership role, Bersin negotiated a superintendent's salary for Alvarado.

Alvarado had spent 10 years as superintendent of New York City's Community School District #2 (Chapter 4, this volume), demonstrating how a district could "use professional development to mobilize knowledge in the service of systemwide instructional improvement" (Elmore & Burney, 1997a, p. 3). District #2's demonstration that districts can constructively support their members helped Alvarado develop a national reputation as a "change agent" with a keen ability to see district operations through an instructional lens.

Alvarado's views about teaching and learning came to drive San Diego's reform agenda. Based on research and his experiences in New York, he believed the best way to improve student learning was to concentrate on teachers' practice and focus district decision making on instructional needs. According to Alvarado's theory of action, student learning increases when interaction between students and teachers is improved; therefore, deepening teaching practice becomes an effective mechanism for increasing student learning. His theory further assumes that district administrators have particular roles in supporting learning in schools. In District #2, his theory had proved effective: During Alvarado's decade as superintendent, District #2's standardized reading test scores climbed from tenth to second in a region of 32 K–8 districts (Elmore & Burney, 1997a).

San Diego's emerging reform initiative embraced similar change principles. In what essentially became a shared superintendency, Bersin and Alvarado sought to orient the district's bureaucracy toward teaching and learning and to infuse sound instructional strategies throughout the system. While Bersin handled political, organizational, and business aspects of district leadership, Alvarado managed the instructional side of things; and the pair learned to collaborate when these realms overlapped. This joint leadership arrangement put the superintendent in an unusual situation whereby he came to define his role as support for what Alvarado was trying to accomplish instructionally.

STRATEGY SUPPORTING REFORM GOALS

In the summer of 1998, Bersin and Alvarado announced that the district's status quo was no longer acceptable. Early the following year, Alvarado reflected on the state of the district when he and Bersin arrived and where he saw the most immediate need for change:

> San Diego . . . was fractionalized; it was not coherent; different parts of the system were sending different messages; . . . a million policies . . . [meant] there was an overabundance of work to be done, . . . but people were doing everything [only] an inch deep. . . . So I think the differences [between the old system and what we're trying to establish] are: Try to get some focus, try to get some coherence, try to deal with instructional issues as opposed to operational . . . things, [and try to] create a structure that can . . . support [learning and] give people the capacity to do [their jobs].

Superintendent Bersin liked saying in public, "You can't cross a chasm in two leaps," and with this mentality he and Alvarado sought to bridge the apparent split between organizational procedures and student learning. With great force and purpose, they and a few advisers inside and external to the district quickly and publicly took on their organization's established logic. Outwardly challenging theories of incremental change (Lindblom, 1980) and bricolage—that is, to learn, an organization needs both an anchor to and a bridge from the past (Lanzara, 1998)—reformers sought to tame the district's bureaucratic structure by transforming and dismantling its various functions, roles, responsibilities, positions, expectations, and traditions that did not align with the tenets of a "learning organization." In their view, a learning organization values and uses research and data to make decisions, embraces communal and systemic thinking, and treats employees as individual learners who contribute to the learning of others and the larger organization.

Reformers felt that for SDCS to function as a learning organization, its bureaucratic structures and norms needed to be shaken. As Bersin reflected 1 year into his superintendency:

> There was no other way to start systemic reform. You don't announce it. You've got to jolt the system. I understood that. You've got to jolt a system, and if people don't understand you're serious about change in the first 6 months, the bureaucracy will own you. The bureaucracy will defeat you at every turn if you give it a chance.

Under new central office leadership, this sentiment fueled the districtwide reform initiative that began in the summer of 1998.

Reformers focused on changing both the central office and the schools to create an organizational system oriented around instruction that would increase student knowledge and achievement by investing strategically in teachers' work. Reformers set out to integrate into their system particular research findings about teaching and teacher learning (Darling-Hammond & Sykes, 1999) that argued for the following:

- Long-term, professional learning networks for teachers and principals (Evans & Mohr, 1999; Fullan, 1997; McLaughlin & Oberman, 1996)
- Opportunities for continuous reflection and refinement of practice in communal settings (Darling-Hammond, 1997a; Little, 1999)
- Organizational configurations and deployment of resources that advance a coherent reform agenda (Bodilly, 1998; Cohen & Ball, 1997; Goldring & Hallinger, 1992; Price, Ball, & Luks, 1995; Rosenholtz, 1989; Spillane, 1996)
- Challenging teaching and learning standards tied to assessment tools through which teachers could diagnose student learning according to the standards (Darling-Hammond, 1997b; O'Day & Smith, 1993)

Accordingly, district reformers sought to create a system that was grounded in principled knowledge about teaching and learning. This system would be (1) driven by standards, (2) focused on building the profession, and (3) tailored to the specific school contexts; supporting this system would be central office policies and practices that placed instructional needs above all else. Most educational organizations tend to favor one of these "strategies" over another (Darling-Hammond & McLaughlin, 1999). When pursued collectively, such strategies theoretically can wield significant power by affording organizational flexibility to pursue an agenda in reinforcing ways and maximizing benefits (and minimizing the weaknesses) of any strategy pursued in isolation (Darling-Hammond & McLaughlin, 1999; Hill, Campbell, & Harvey, 2000).

ESTABLISHING INFRASTRUCTURE AND CREATING NEW NORMS OF PRACTICE (REFORM YEAR 1)

Bersin and Alvarado felt the district had become a series of independent units that bred inequities in knowledge and power to the disadvantage of low-performing schools and students. Therefore, they sought to dislodge arrangements they felt contributed to the disconnects and to unite the district around one organizational purpose. As Bersin announced in the fall of 1998, "The mission of San Diego City Schools is to improve student achievement by supporting teaching and learning in the classroom." Within this goal was a focus on the lowest-performing students and schools as a means to raise the overall performance so as to build districtwide unity of purpose.

Initially, district leaders felt they could best leverage the reforms by redesigning the central office to better support learning across the district's schools. Therefore, reformers launched their initiative on two fronts: (1) building an infrastructure to support principals' learning and (2) restructuring the central office to better support efforts to improve teaching in schools. Action on both fronts rested on a common belief that learning and school change necessitated restructuring and reculturing the central office, and that principal instructional leadership could effectively introduce change into schools. Accordingly, in the first year of the new administration, Bersin focused on abolishing outdated structures in the central office and raising money for the district by engaging the business community around promising, research-based plans for reform. Meanwhile, his chancellor of instruction began to envision and build a structurally and culturally different suborganization within the district.

Building an Infrastructure for Principals' Learning

As Alvarado had learned in District #2, principals could serve as linchpins for change within schools if trained to provide the instructional supports teachers need most to strengthen practice. Accordingly, he placed priority on principals as change agents and sought to devise an effective learning structure for them. Since SDCS had nearly 180 principals (compared to 30 in District #2), he wanted to create smaller working groups so all principals could deeply engage in the learning process. Rather than using the existing feeder-pattern arrangement run by "area superintendents," reformers chose to abolish it, believing that it bred inequities and fiefdoms and lacked orientation to systemwide instructional needs. Instead, combing the district for talented instructional leadership, Bersin and Alvarado hired and trained seven principals to become districtwide "Instructional Leaders" (ILs). With Alvarado, these ILs formed and led seven "Learning Communities" of about 25 principals each, heterogeneously mixed by grade level, principal experience, and school achievement levels. This arrangement enabled principals to learn from both trained experts and peers about leading school staffs in high-quality instructional practices.

In contrast to former area superintendents, the ILs worked closely together, co-constructing their new roles and jointly planning their coaching work with principals. In addition, they collectively received specialized training by professional developers from the University of Pittsburgh's Learning Research and Development Center (LRDC), with whom Alvarado had worked in District #2. These ties with LRDC linked San Diego City Schools with a network of other urban school districts that were focusing their systems on instruction (Chapter 10, this volume).

Alvarado and the ILs devised structures through which principals could learn about exemplary instructional practice and ways to support teacher and student learning. Foremost among these were required, monthly "Principals' Conferences," sponsored by the district's newly created "Institute for Learning" and led by Chancellor Alvarado. These meetings established regular occasions for Learning Communities to convene and for principals and district administrators to discuss reform implementation. The format of the Principals' Conferences varied, including both interactive "fieldtrips" to local classrooms and discussions with experts on relevant topics (e.g., teaching techniques, principals' role as instructional leader). Sometimes, site and central office administrators jointly examined student performance data to focus attention on the lowest performers and the means of increasing their learning.

Among the first activities in which these groups engaged was to understand the district's new Literacy Framework and a set of instructional concepts developed by LRDC called the Principles of Learning, which provided the instructional backbone for the district's reform agenda. The institute expected principals and, through them, teachers to understand the Principles of Learning and each component of the Literacy Framework (Chapter 4, this volume) and to progress toward full implementation of the framework in stages.

A second primary mechanism for principal learning was called the "WalkThrough," a school accountability and review process adapted from District #2 to evaluate site progress and assist principals in identifying instructional support needs. About twice each semester, an IL would visit each school in the Learning Community to see, through analysis of teachers' practice and school and classroom environments, how principals were incorporating what they had learned at the monthly meetings. During these WalkThroughs, the IL and principal together would visit about 10 to 15 classrooms in 2 or 3 hours. Walking from classroom to classroom, the pair typically discussed their observations, then reconvened in the front office to share further what they had noticed and agree upon next steps for the school. The Instructional Leader would follow up each visit with a letter to the principal, specifying what was observed and what areas needed improvement by the next WalkThrough.

Community Engagement and Organizational Efforts

As Chancellor Alvarado's team engaged district leadership in instructional reforms, Superintendent Bersin focused on the noninstructional aspects of running a district, including communications, organizational, and fiscal matters.

Bersin led a communications initiative to explain the changes underway and gain legitimacy and financial support for his educational agenda. Early on, Bersin revamped the district's communications office, which took charge of his personal correspondence to parents and district employees, issued press releases to the community and local press about district initiatives, filmed districtwide events, updated the district's website, and began to document the reform initiative's evolution. Bersin himself met frequently with business groups to discuss the importance of public education and reform directions. The November 1998 passage (on the first try) of a $1.51 billion bond measure by a 78% vote signaled growing community confidence in the reform agenda.

In the fall of 1998, Bersin and his top advisers initiated a "functional analysis" of the central office to "inventory" all district office positions and reporting streams as well as identify slack and incoherence in the system. Each central office employee was asked "How do you support teaching and learning in the classroom?" and to detail his or her specific responsibilities. Those who could not respond adequately or whose roles were deemed unnecessary or redundant were given notice at the conclusion of the process. Bersin's chief of staff explained:

> As Alan says, there are two types of people in this [district] community. There are the teachers and those who support teaching. Alan and I are those who support teaching. And if you can't fit into one of those two categories, if you can't accept your role in one of those two categories, then you need to leave. Clear and simple.

As Bersin noted in his annual self-evaluation report, this process was conducted to "refine the organization of the district's infrastructure with the intent to be an organization which was both more efficient and more effective in supporting the improvement of student achievement." It also helped to identify internal funds that could be redirected for new instructional priorities and to reduce central office expenditures by at least 5% for the 1999–2000 budget—a directive the school board had given Bersin for his first year.

Expecting that reassignments would be massive and hoping to realize savings from the reorganization immediately, reform leaders negotiated with the board to abolish a long-standing district policy whereby individuals reassigned to a lesser-paid position would retain their former salaries for 1 year. District reformers cast the policy change request as one that would save jobs and make the reorganization less severe. In the spring of 1999, Bersin's reorganization team recommended that 104 central office positions be cut or consolidated.

USING BUREAUCRACY TO SOLIDIFY DISTRICT'S REFORM (REFORM YEAR 2 AND BEYOND)

Building on the first year's accomplishments, reformers in years 2 and 3 increased attention to schools and teachers while focusing on the system's role in supporting instructional needs. They devised a sophisticated instructional agenda for districtwide learning as well as policy mechanisms and creative financing through which this agenda could be implemented. Increasingly, the district's instructional and operational branches were intertwined. Accordingly, the district's mechanisms for resource allocation, agenda setting, and role assignments, among other areas, did *not* perpetuate the status quo, as in most districts; rather, they became a means for infusing instruction across the system.

Crystallization of Instructional Agenda

The district's instructional agenda was built on several cornerstones revolving around continuous professional development, intense literacy study, differentiated support for low performers, and high standards coupled with assessments to determine learning levels.

A centerpiece was the creation of a network of trained, highly qualified teachers—one for each school and more for schools with concentrations of new teachers or low-performing students. These "peer coach/staff developers" would coach other teachers and principals on pedagogical techniques aligned with the reform initiative and research-based strategies for learning. In this "train-the-trainer" model, Alvarado and colleagues from LRDC and District #2 worked with ILs, who worked with principals; the literacy department within the Institute for Learning worked with site-based coaches; and together, principals and coaches worked with teachers on deepening practice in each school setting.

Because this position was new, it required negotiations between the district and the teacher union—the San Diego Education Association (SDEA), which was concerned about reporting streams for these coaches, selection and placement processes, and the impact of their work on teachers' evaluations. After a bitter and public debate in the spring of 1999, a neutral third party negotiated an agreement establishing the position, with San Diego State University's School of Education screening and certifying applicants, the Institute for Learning providing ongoing training, and school-site councils interviewing and selecting from multiple candidates for the position.

By the start of the reform's second year, nearly 100 certified and trained literacy peer coaches blanketed two-thirds of district schools. Criteria including student performance, teacher attrition, and grade level determined which schools received full- or half-time coaches immediately and which would receive them a year later when the program added on 200 additional coaches. These coaches worked with principals and staff to design and implement professional development activities appropriate for, and approved by, teachers in each school and aligned with the institute's philosophy, pedagogy, and Literacy Framework. Coaches spent 4 days a week at the school sites. On the fifth day, staff from the Institute for Learning helped the coaches understand their roles and the instructional strategies that teachers were beginning to implement, learn coaching strategies, and develop ways to become accepted in a school community.

Elementary school peer coaches worked with receptive teachers, and those in secondary schools worked specifically with teachers implementing the new district-required Genre Studies course. Introduced in year 2, this two-period literacy course was required for all sixth-graders and ninth-graders below the 50th percentile on the spring 1999 Stanford Achievement Test (9th edition; SAT-9), or, in later years, who performed poorly on district-developed diagnostic assessments that replaced the SAT-9 in determining eligibility for Genre Studies. The course was designed to improve reading and writing skills while meeting the district's language arts standards. Based on preliminary success in raising reading proficiencies, the district expanded the Genre Studies concept in year 3 by creating 2- to 3-hour blocks of literacy and 1- to 2-hour blocks of mathematics for students beginning middle or junior high school and grade 9 students performing below grade level.

In addition to peer coaches and new curriculum, summer school became another way to simultaneously support struggling students and enrich teacher learning opportunities. Beginning in the summer of 2000, schools not undergoing facilities repairs held classes for students below grade level in all elementary grades and grade 8. Summers offered intensive learning opportunities for teachers as well. Teachers learned about literacy strategies through an array of paid, professional development courses offered through the Institute for Learning; with experienced coaches, they had opportunities to practice techniques during summer school classes.

In keeping with the tenor of the reform initiative, district leaders also offered extra resources and central office support to schools with the lowest-performing students. In eight extremely low-performing elementary "Focus Schools," identified through state rankings based primarily on the SAT-9, reformers gave first-grade teachers $8,000 for enhanced materials (first-grade teachers elsewhere got $5,000 for this purpose). Focus Schools also received another full-time peer coach, 24 more instructional days each year, enhanced parent training and involvement programs, and programs for preschoolers. Also, each Focus School received four mathematics specialists to work initially with fourth- and fifth-graders and later with third- and sixth-graders. Reformers identified 11 other low-performing elementary schools, which received an additional full-time peer coach and increased per-classroom allocations for enhanced first-grade materials.

Realizing that the SAT-9 was inadequate for diagnostic purposes, by year 3 district reformers had developed assessments for determining student progress and specified cutoff scores for promotion and retention. These assessments became interactive tools for teachers to assess students' vocabulary, comprehension, and reading skills as well as monitor their progress. The district later developed a corollary instrument for assessing mathematics.

Finally, focusing on principals as critical change agents, in year 3 the district instituted the Educational Leadership Development Academy (ELDA) and recruited Elaine Fink, deputy superintendent from District #2, to direct it. In addition to providing training for principals and ILs, ELDA established a program in which up to four full-time mentor principals and 20–25 coaching principals would individually mentor new or struggling principals or those wanting specialized support. Also, in collaboration with the University of San Diego, ELDA included an administrative training and credentialing program for a cohort of teachers, initially a dozen but expanded greatly in subsequent years.

Enacting Supportive Policy and Fiscal Arrangements

Most instructional reforms were implemented through a single policy package, created with public input during year 2 of the reform and called the

Blueprint for Student Success in a Standards-Based System. Enacted by a 3–2 school board vote in the spring of 2000, this plan articulated for the first time a specific instructional agenda under the new administration. It emphasized professional development and focused attention on low-performing schools and students, suggesting that doing so would "lift the base of instruction across the whole system . . . so [that] the academic achievement of all students . . . rises" (San Diego City Schools, 2000, p. 1). It set forth a revised plan for social promotion/retention, thereby addressing a state mandate and mounting public pressure to enforce standards. Moreover, it wove together a set of standards-based strategies that the district had pursued for the past 2 years.

The Blueprint solidified the district's reform agenda and engineered an elaborate reallocation mechanism involving federal, state, and local dollars to fund the costly instructional strategies. The big-ticket items included approximately 300 peer coach/staff developers, $5,000 for every first-grade class for extra books and materials, and extended student and staff learning opportunities through summer school and after-school programs. District finance officials determined that each peer coach alone would cost approximately $87,500 with benefits. Indeed, most of the changes cost some $62 million in 2000–2001, over 6% of the total operating budget, and were estimated at $96 million in 2001–2002.

The district drew from several funding streams to cover expenses, including Title I dollars ($19 million of $33 million), integration funds ($16.6 million), and various state-funded programs supporting school libraries and new teacher induction ($15 million). Also, Bersin redirected $4.5 million of $8.3 million, identified through central office reorganization, toward building the peer-coaching network. Annual central office reviews helped surface additional savings in redirected dollars ($1.7 million in 2000; $1.6 million in 2001).

Among these reallocations, Title I funds proved most contentious; ultimately 600 of 2,800 teacher aides were dismissed at the end of the 1999–2000 schoolyear (300 more aides lost work hours). Knowing their plan would spark controversy, district officials offered employment assistance workshops to those affected. They also actively sought state and federal approval, which was granted after the district explained how these funds would serve as supplemental assistance and be allocated to schools in proportion to the student poverty levels. The district's mandate regarding schools' use of categorical resources significantly reduced the discretionary resources available to the schools. For example, while formerly schools had complete discretion over Title I and integration dollars, under the Blueprint they were required to spend at least 80% of these funds on particular reform strategies.

RESULTS AND REACTIONS TO REFORM

By the end of year 3, principals, teachers, and central office administrators were engaged in genuine discussions about instructional change. School staff were applying these discussions to practice, facilitated by principals' work as instructional leaders and coaches' daily presence in classrooms. The district's efforts appeared to pay off, although the link to student learning is difficult to prove conclusively, especially in a short time period.[1] Nonetheless, district SAT-9 scores increased for 3 years in a row during the reform initiative (scores increased statewide during this period as well). In 2000, 16 more schools scored above the state average, and 5 more at state average, than in 1999. In 2001, scores were flatter (as was the case across the state), even though the district tested (rather than waived out) more low performers and more high performers had parental waivers from taking the SAT-9 assessment. In addition, Genre Studies performance data were promising: after 6 months in Genre Studies, sixth-graders showed 1.7 years' growth, while ninth-graders averaged a year's growth.

Not all outcomes and responses were positive, however. Vocal resistance to the reforms came from the schools and more subtle resentment from some central office staff. While few questioned the necessity for reform or the initiative's ultimate goals, consensus broke down over implementation strategy. Some principals and many teachers questioned the reform's speed, abruptness, and top-down character. The teacher union served as a rallying point for these feelings for both teachers and administrators. And two of the five board members were increasingly uncomfortable with the process undertaken by district reformers.

Evolving Culture of Learning Across Schools

Principals were mostly enthused about the changes, though wary of the increased attention on their position. Of approximately 30 principals interviewed, the vast majority said they appreciated their Instructional Leader, liked the Learning Community groupings, and valued other structured opportunities to talk with their peers, noting the monthly Principals' Conferences as a source of professional growth and inspiration and also an important conduit for information between schools and the central office. They viewed WalkThroughs as positive, nonthreatening opportunities to interact with the IL on a more personal, context-specific basis.

In addition, a majority of principals spoke enthusiastically about the reform's "equalizing" quality. They noted that everyone—not just specific schools or areas of town, as in the past—was getting the same message about effective teaching and learning strategies. One veteran elementary school principal explained:

> That consistency helps me to know that when I look at someone who's on the other side of town, they're trying to do the same thing I'm trying to do. And that's very reassuring, rather than to think: "Gosh, they've got the corner on the market for something I haven't even heard about." At least we're all in the same sailboat.

Principals also identified where the reform could be strengthened. Some noted that the Principals' Conferences failed to address differences in participants' needs and learning levels. A frequent request was to separate principals by grade level. High school principals were especially concerned that the reform initiative was "too elementary" and viewed the exclusive focus on literacy as antithetical to comprehensive high schools' mission. This request to treat high schools differently was honored by district officials toward the end of year 3; by year 4, most Learning Communities were homogeneous by grade level. In addition, while appreciating the renewed central office support for instruction, principals frequently lamented the lack of support for noninstructional, or "operational," matters. For many site administrators, a day off-site each month—sometimes more, when principals of a single grade level would meet for additional half-day sessions—created tension between on-site responsibilities and their professional learning.

Principals also spoke about feeling overworked and somewhat fearful about the pressures and consequences for principal and school performance under the new district administration. They often noted the high stakes attached to principal learning—a fact driven home the summer after the reform's first year (1999), when 15 site administrators were abruptly reassigned to classrooms for failure to demonstrate effective instructional leadership (Hightower, 2001). Prior to the Bersin administration, principals were rarely removed from their schools other than through voluntary transfers; and in extreme cases, questionable principals were placed in central office roles. Accordingly, the new administration's actions came as a shock, particularly to site administrators, many of whom wondered if they might be next.

Teachers' reactions to the district's instructional reforms were more mixed. In general, they appreciated the emphasis on professional development but disagreed with overall implementation, claiming the reform was "too cutthroat" (elementary teacher), "top-down" (elementary teacher), and "bureaucratic" (Genre Studies high school teacher). Elementary school teachers appeared more aligned with the reform principles and literacy focus than were middle or high school teachers, raising fundamental questions about the literacy initiative's relevance for all teachers, schools, and students. Furthermore, while many elementary teachers, in particular, noted how losing instructional aides through reallocation of Title I dollars made their job more difficult, about two-thirds indicated that peer coaches offered helpful support for their practice.

On the one hand, many teachers—particularly in elementary grades and the Genre Studies courses at the secondary level—offered examples of how the reform had changed and deepened their own practice. Even those who resented the top-down nature of the reform described ways in which they were incorporating many of the strategies in their classrooms. On the other hand, teachers had concerns about: (1) a lack of curriculum materials to accompany the literacy focus; (2) the homogeneous tracking of the lowest performers into Genre Studies, which appeared to contradict some research on learning; and (3) subject-matter distinctions limited to literacy. Some teachers also complained that the reform had eliminated "successful" programs underway within a school. Others noted incompatibilities with their personal conceptions of good teaching. As the reform unfolded, teachers increasingly demanded to see the research upon which the strategies were built. They also expressed interest in reading about District #2 and learning about its structure and operations. Additionally, they wanted to see research and cases of exemplary practice from *within* SDCS, where policy and professional contexts were immediate.

Changes in the Central Office

In the central office, budgeting and operational managers learned to collaborate with instructional administrators to specify and prioritize educational needs and direct district dollars toward instructional priorities. Both instructional and operational administrators commented on a shift *away* from letting the available money guide program and policy decisions, and *toward* having districtwide, articulated, instructional needs govern the budget. Alvarado described the shift as getting "operational departments [to] become the handmaiden of instruction." The district's chief financial officer—self-described as the "chief administrator of the Blueprint"—noted, "It was a daily process and a daily collaboration on how to get the resources behind the strategies that were being identified." Alvarado summed up this change accordingly:

> The Blueprint . . . created a group of people working together for the first time in which the . . . instructional issues drove [things],

and the budget people and the operational people knew that their job was to make the budget thing happen. That's a *very* important thing to happen in districts. It almost never happens.

These central office changes focused the organization on instructional priorities; however, they also came at a cost to the system's emerging culture of learning. The 100 positions eliminated in 1999 during the first functional analysis, and smaller eliminations in subsequent years, caused some ripples of fear in the district community. Remaining central office administrators lost trusted colleagues with whom they had worked for decades. Some were angry and confused over particular individuals who were reassigned. Others felt that because of their position they were having to implement someone else's tough decisions. One district administrator wrote the teacher union president a note, published anonymously in SDEA's newsletter: "We work in an environment here of hostility and/or fear of retribution and ostracization if we are not part of that 'inner circle'. . . . Morale here is at an all time low" ("Classified Partner," 1999, p. 1). A top-ranking, exiting administrator predicted this massive reorganization would mark the beginning of an 18-month "era of intimidation" characterized by fear of the new administration, distrust among those making changes, and the formation of deep alliances among those affected by the reform.

CONCLUSION

San Diego City Schools is an unusual case of reformers using strategies grounded in research on teaching and learning to align a large urban district's organizational structures and norms toward the improvement of instruction. Their initiative differed markedly from most districts' efforts in three respects. They (1) built and nurtured new instructional supports that reflected effective practices, (2) sought changes within the central office and at school sites, and (3) followed an unabashedly directive change process to move beyond traditions they believed did not support learning. Building on the New York District #2 "existence proof" that central offices in modest-sized districts can be agents of instructional change (Elmore & Burney, 1997a), the San Diego reform story extends this notion to the seemingly intractable, large, urban district central office, heretofore known for impeding rather than instigating change.

Simultaneous efforts to dismantle and build within the district, coupled with an expectation for systemwide change, underlay this comprehensive approach to district reform. At points, however, reformers walked a thin line between focus and chaos, acting swiftly to direct change but failing to adequately engage all employees and members of an increasingly resentful teacher union. And at times, reformers unintentionally allowed fear to invade the district community as they abruptly dismissed and reassigned staff—sometimes without warning or perceived due cause. Complicating matters, a deeply split school board gave reformers a narrow one-vote margin on which to act. By year 3 of the initiative, reformers had refocused district bureaucracy on instruction—but in a way that was politically unstable.

While urban district central offices are themselves particularly unlikely objects of change (Meyer et al., 1994), it was the targeted central office changes that facilitated San Diego's instructional change initiative. Quickly and with great force and purpose, the district's reformers reoriented their bureaucracy to focus on instruction and bring coherence across programs, policies, and instructional agendas. They simultaneously attended to instructional quality across their system of schools *and* to the district-level details that reinforced the system's instructional vision. Adherence to specific, rational rules and a prescribed order gave the district a structure within which learning could occur. This structure included formal roles and functions, budgeting procedures, accountability mechanisms ensuring that members upheld their responsibilities, and a division of labor reflecting instructional priorities. Reformers simultaneously created a districtwide professional learning culture in which members interacted with others around research, performance data, and teaching practice and through which the larger system learned to incorporate the feedback it received.

Moreover, the San Diego case surfaces nuances about *catalyzing* large-scale change initiatives and suggests a reciprocal relationship between centralized action and principled knowledge grounded in research on instruction. San Diego's top-down, nonincremental approach provided an *enabling* condition for principled knowledge to take hold systemwide. Only through going "boom" *first* in San Diego—and immediately launching specific support structures to reinforce the changes—did reformers have a chance of establishing instructional design principles about instruction throughout the system. Had they waited for organizational buy-in, the reforms likely would never have come to fruition because too many forces were at work to stabilize the district and return it to its former state. Equally, the principled knowledge underlying the change initiative legitimized reformers' centralized approach. The case of San Diego City Schools illustrates how top-down change initiatives can center on the core of teaching and learning. Nonetheless, questions remain about the reform's longevity amid an uncertain reform climate: Going "boom" and sustaining reform may prove a difficult combination in the long run.

NOTES

The work reported here was conducted for the Center for the Study of Teaching and Policy, supported under the Educational Research and Development Centers Program, PR/Award Number R308B70003, as administered by the Office of Educational Research and Improvement (OERI), U.S. Department of Education. However, the views expressed in this chapter do not necessarily represent the positions or policies of the sponsors.

1. It took a decade for the District #2 (New York) patterns of test score improvement to be attributed to the reform strategy on which the San Diego reform is modeled.

CHAPTER 6

New Haven Unified School District: A Teaching Quality System for Excellence and Equity

JON SNYDER

This chapter describes New Haven (California) Unified School District's teaching quality system with specific focus on the role of its personnel office. New Haven is located in the San Francisco Bay Area, midway between Oakland and San Jose. The district serves more than 14,200 students of diverse backgrounds (28% Hispanic, 24% Caucasian, 17% Filipino, 16.5% Asian American, 12.5% African American, 1% Pacific Islander, and less than 1% Native American) across its schools. Thirty-one percent received free or reduced-price lunches in the 1998–1999 academic year. All 12 conventional schools (8 elementary, 3 middle, and 1 high) have received state or national recognition in recent years. However, 30 years ago New Haven was the lowest-wealth district in the county and had a reputation to match. The school board was in turmoil, and the public was known to throw chairs at members during meetings. School-savvy families avoided moving into the district. Today, while still a low-wealth district, New Haven has earned a well-deserved reputation for excellent schools. Whereas 20 years ago their students went elsewhere, today the district has to close its doors to out-of-district transfers because the schools are bulging at the seams.

Of the many factors contributing to the district's success, a key one is its early recognition of the essential role of teachers and its support of quality teaching. This chapter analyzes the components of New Haven's teaching quality system, identified as (1) standards for teachers; (2) recruitment and retention; (3) teacher development; (4) rewarding of knowledge and skill; (5) organizing of schools for student and teacher learning; and (6) standards for students. The chapter ends with an Epilogue, which discusses recent changes in the district since this case study was first written in the late 1990s.

School Districts and Instructional Renewal. Copyright © 2002 by Teachers College, Columbia University. All rights reserved. ISBN 0-8077-4266-X (pbk), ISBN 0-8077-4267-8 (cloth). Prior to photocopying items for classroom use, please contact the Copyright Clearance Center, Customer Service, 222 Rosewood Dr., Danvers, MA 01923, USA, tel. (508) 750-8400.

Data for this chapter were collected during 18 months of fieldwork completed between the fall of 1997 and the winter of 1998. Four data sources were used. Document review included district and school websites, state and grant reports, district policy documents, presentations and papers by school and district personnel, and local newspapers. Semistructured interviews were held with district and school leaders, school-based teacher educators (pre- and inservice), beginning and experienced teachers, university-based teacher educators, and state officials. Observations were made of mentoring sessions, school board meetings, workshops, and classrooms; in addition, district and school personnel were shadowed. A fourth data source was collaborative presentations. As a result of relationships formed during the research, the author and a district administrator presented papers at several conferences together. In the spring and summer of 2001, follow-up interviews were conducted both with existing school and district personnel as well as with several of the retired leadership team.

HIGH STANDARDS FOR TEACHERS

Twenty-five years ago, leadership in New Haven "got real" about teaching standards by establishing high expectations right off the bat. The former superintendent recalls:

> The presence of . . . teachers who did not perform to high standards lowered academic achievement of students and ultimately led to lower morale among other teachers. . . . One of my first acts as superintendent was to tighten the teacher evaluation process and implement procedures that allowed for due process while still enabling the district to remove teachers who simply were not able or willing to address deficiencies in their performance. . . . Now, with performance standards in place and clear expectations as to the need to exceed them, teachers respect the district's effort to maintain high instructional standards, and rarely is a teacher terminated. Furthermore, the district's reputation in this regard draws high-achieving teachers, deters those who are not as committed, and generally elevates the status of the teaching profession.

The district held administrators accountable for assessing teachers and for providing necessary supports to meet expectations. New Haven put together thorough evaluation procedures requiring the systematic collection of data—no more "drive-by" teacher observations. In addition, the district abolished the infamous "shuffle of the incompetents" whereby teachers "counseled out" of one school await placement in another. This move drew criticism from some teachers, administrators, and community members: The former superintendent recalls being called "Little Caesar"— and not always behind his back. It sent an unwavering message, however, that the district was serious about assuring students the teachers they deserved.

Today, in coordination with the union, New Haven has adopted a Professional-Growth Assessment Process (P-GAP) for experienced teachers. P-GAP is a collaborative process for exemplary tenured teachers built on peer and personal assessment of knowledge, skills, and abilities related to high teaching standards accompanied by personal growth plans. P-GAP shifts the system's focus away from underachieving teachers and toward supporting exemplary teachers.

The standards New Haven uses for the evaluation process and P-GAP are closely aligned with the California Standards for the Teaching Profession. The standards are accompanied by a narrative description of what they mean and look like in practice; a series of statements covering the elements of that standard; and sets of questions to guide thinking about one's development in each of those elements. Since the district's Beginning Teacher Support and Assessment (BTSA) program uses these standards, New Haven provides teachers with a clear and explicit set of expectations as well as structures and processes that support their development toward meeting those expectations.

RECRUITMENT, RETENTION, AND ENABLING TECHNOLOGY

The responsibility for assuring the caliber of all teachers in all schools was a powerful incentive for making good initial hires. Making good hires required the district to revamp its recruitment and retention strategies to guarantee that qualified candidates would know about, wish to come to, and want to stay in the New Haven district.

Thirty years ago, New Haven did what many districts continue to do today: wait until the last minute and see which teachers are available. New Haven learned that even in a buyer's market, this approach is shortsighted. The district began to seek out exceptional teachers, simplify the application process, make decisions, and offer contracts in a manner that was timely and respectful of candidates.

Over time, the district built support systems and teaching conditions to retain exceptional teachers; eventually, it became immersed in preservice teacher education. Today, the district can afford to be choosy, recruiting with an eye toward teachers with the skills and dispositions to grow within the teacher learning environments the district supports. Because of its low attrition rate of new and experienced teachers, New Haven does not have annual, large-scale recruitment crises. The district's hiring needs come from enrollment increases rather than from vacated positions.

Traditionally, the teacher labor market is a local affair expanded by district administrators going to prospective teachers at job fairs held on college campuses. Such recruiting trips typically yield few bites, especially as recruiters move farther away geographically. New Haven's approach is to attract prospective candidates through its interactive website (http://www.nhusd.k12.ca.us) and to invest recruiting resources once there is a "hit." Granted the prestigious C. S. Robinson Award by the American Association of School Personnel Administrators for exemplary use of technology in recruiting, New Haven's website expands recruitment to a national pool of exceptional teachers who are drawn to the district's remarkable technological infrastructure. One first-year teacher noted, "I had several offers, including one in the district where I had always planned to teach. But I saw the computers [in New Haven] and took the job the same day." The director of personnel feels that an electronic lure actually humanizes the recruitment process: "The Web . . . reaches a lot of people we wouldn't otherwise reach . . . I've become more personal with applicants because of e-mail. It used to be form letters and 2 to 3 days' turnaround time. Now it is personal and immediate."

The district also uses a computerized applicant-tracking system. After applicant data are entered into the system, applicant files can be searched based on multiple criteria and on a ratings scale of 1–100. For instance, a principal can request a search of active candidates with a set of desired characteristics, and the computer will instantly sort out applicants possessing those characteristics. If a principal needs a teacher with a physics and biology credential and 10 years of experience who can coach women's volleyball, this system can identify candidates with these specific qualifications.

More recently, district administrators have employed video technology to interview candidates from any place in the world without ever leaving the office. The district now has the technological infrastructure to hold an interactive videoconference in which six principals, sitting at their desks, can interview an applicant sitting in a Kinko's in Kansas.

New Haven supplements recruiting technology with the face-to-face touch of nonelectronic communication methods. One beginning teacher remembers getting most of her information via the Web and e-mail; then, however, she said:

> I met the principal at the interview and she offered me a job. I said I needed some time. [She] said, "OK, take two weeks, but come visit

before you make up your mind." [The school's induction program support provider] took me on a tour of the school, and I accepted the position that day.

There is easy allure in the idea that all a district needs to do to be like New Haven is go to the local software store, buy a couple of application programs, and hire a few consultants from the business community to demonstrate how to do it right. Would that it were so simple. First, New Haven administrators are quick to caution: "Don't do anything without input from the people who will be using it." Second, quality educational applications do not currently exist—not for lack of need, but because programmatic adaptations are tricky and because few vendors focus on the education market. New Haven administrators have had to seek out their own solutions. As one administrator explained: "What business is using can be applied. . . . But you can't buy it. You have to know your own business and what you're trying to accomplish—then get ideas that you can rearrange and make work [for your situation]." One key technological support has been New Haven's charter membership in the California Educational Computer Consortium, an association with other school districts throughout the state that offers (at significant savings) the advantages of several different users applying the same software. This consortium helps New Haven in terms of solving problems and developing enhancements.

TEACHER DEVELOPMENT

New Haven personnel realized that if they wanted good teachers, the district would have to collaborate with a teacher education program and enter into the business of teacher development from recruitment to retirement. They understood that a core component of teacher development is assessment and evaluation and that "development" implies movement toward a goal. To determine and support that movement, they defined the goal by adopting standards, accurately assessed the whereabouts of a teacher in terms of those goals, and used that assessment information to support development toward those goals. Accordingly, the district's approach to teacher development was supportive of its existing core function—enhancing quality teaching and learning in the district.

Preservice Teacher Education

In 1993, with the advice and support of California State University, Hayward (CSUH), New Haven designed the Single Subject Partnership Program (SSPP), an innovative, combined preservice and internship teacher education program housed in district secondary schools. The SSPP simultaneously educates teachers and provides a quality education for students.

The SSPP combines elements of internship and traditional preparation routes for preparing credential candidates to meet high teaching standards for secondary school teaching. The curriculum is jointly planned and delivered by university professors and district faculty to provide for close articulation of district, school, and university activities. Most of the academic coursework is delivered in the district for candidates' convenience. Beginning a month before school starts, a cohort of about 30 credential candidates work closely together and with partner teachers for an entire year. Each candidate is welcomed as a full member of the school faculty. The program, which melds theory and practice, offers the following:

- A common, clear vision of good teaching, articulated in well-defined standards of practice and performance that are used to guide and evaluate coursework and clinical work
- A curriculum grounded in substantial knowledge of children taught in the context of practice (e.g., linking lesson designs and classroom environments with understanding of development)
- A careful screening process for interns prior to the assignment of limited teaching responsibilities (not all credential candidates become interns)
- Strong relationships, common knowledge, and shared beliefs among school- and university-based faculty

Hard questions must be asked of any internship program that allows untrained or minimally prepared individuals to assume the role of teacher of record. Most specifically, what protections are in place for the students so that having interns teach does not constitute an educational disservice? In New Haven, children are protected by the following:

- Providing multiple levels (school, classroom, and university) of support and supervision for the intern
- Avoiding placement of interns such that students would be taught by an intern for 2 years in a row or for 2 periods in the same year
- Placing minimal load and preparation demands on interns (i.e., interns have only one or two courses and do not have multiple preps)
- Basing selection on documented experience with students and on performance during the intensive summer session
- Providing ongoing, intensive learning opportunities as a major part of every schoolday

- Pulling the intern back from two periods to one or returning the candidate to an entirely traditional student teaching experience if children are not being well-served or if the intern is not meeting all preparation program requirements at an exemplary level

Commenting on the district's hiring of interns, the former associate superintendent for personnel argues that concern for children requires all educators to engage in the larger preparation and guided entry of individuals into the teaching profession, noting that "we hire interns . . . as a response to our concerns about beginning teachers and the needs of our children."

The district offers a significant amount of faculty expertise to its preservice partnership with CSUH. Recognizing that teachers who become teachers of teachers have their own needs, the district provides paid supervision seminars for master and partner teachers.

The former chair of CSUH's Department of Teacher Education said of their collaboration with New Haven:

New Haven identifies teacher preparation as part of their reason for being, as much as teaching third-graders how to write in cursive. . . . This is the Shangri-La of partnerships. . . . A lot of districts criticize IHEs [institutions of higher education], but not so many are willing to say, "Let's make it better." New Haven has walked the walk for decades. . . . They do not have a "gimme gimme" attitude. They ask and they offer. . . . They deliver. You know that . . . every cooperating teacher, every supervisor, every support provider will be properly oriented and trained.

Induction Support

District personnel never thought of teacher education as something that ends before a teacher begins his or her career. They knew and acted on the belief that a teacher is not something one becomes but something one is always becoming; they knew and acted on the fact that good teaching requires, and good teachers demand, continual education. Thus, New Haven was one of the first California districts to implement the state's Beginning Teacher Support and Assessment (BTSA) program, which provides support for teachers in their first 2 years in the classroom.

All teachers new to New Haven participate in a 5-day, district-sponsored orientation that includes work with veteran teachers at the school site, technology workshops, and preparation time before the arrival of students. In addition, first-year teachers receive BTSA support in four ways—a support team, professional development opportunities, release time and financial support for supplies and materials, and monthly support meetings.

At the time of hiring, principals assign each beginning teacher a two- to three-member support team of a partner teacher, the site mentor, and/or the BTSA specialist, with possible additional members as deemed appropriate. Speaking of the support team, one first-year teacher reflected: "You never had to look for help—it was always there. It is so different with friends I talk with from other districts who are always being told 'Don't be a pest.'" Partner teachers teach at the same school and in the same grade level or subject area; they also receive release time to work with the new teacher. Site mentors teach at the same school and receive release time (the amount depending on the number of beginning teachers at the site) to use their special training and skills with partner teachers and beginning teachers. BTSA specialists tend to be full-time, district-employed teacher educators. The district pays the support team with a combination of state BTSA funds ($3,000 per new teacher) and district funds (a minimum of $2,000 per new teacher). All teachers who serve as BTSA support providers participate in a 3-day training session. The district pays for the participants' and trainers' time; the state provides "trainer-of-trainers" workshops for district-based workshop providers.

First-year teachers have opportunities throughout the year to attend and receive professional development credit for a variety of inservice sessions, some specifically for beginning teachers and others for all who wish to attend. They also attend monthly after-school support meetings with other beginning teachers. In addition, New Haven beginning teachers receive a small stipend to purchase classroom materials. Of more worth, according to beginning teachers, are the two release days they receive to observe other teachers, to collaborate with their partner teachers, or to work on their own BTSA growth portfolios.

Second-year teachers ("BTSA 2s") continue work on their Individual Induction Plans (IIPs) with the same support team and process that were used during their first year. BTSA 2s continue to do classroom-based research on their own practice, but it is documented in more sophisticated portfolio entries. Formal observations guided by the California Standards for the Teaching Profession conducted by trained partner teachers and BTSA specialists continue to support second-year teachers. In addition, BTSA 2s can choose from a variety of workshops (called the "BTSA 2 Academy") designed specifically for them. The district decides on workshop topics based on results of a questionnaire completed by first-year teachers each June. Second-year teachers receive credit on the district's salary scale for participating in the after-school workshops.

New Haven is not alone in offering a partner teacher, half-day workshops, and a portfolio process. What distinguishes New Haven from most districts is the way the three link together to provide effective professional development through sustained learning opportunities connected with continuous coaching. The workshops come from the self-identified, practice-based strengths, interests, and needs of beginning teachers. Through its first-year BTSA process, the district provides guidance and support to help teachers base those self-identified strengths, interests, and needs on data—particularly classroom-based observation data and student achievement data. In the second year, workshop content is supported both by continuing portfolio inquiry and support from more experienced site-based teachers.

In its integrated entirety, New Haven's BTSA program enhances educational outcomes for children in several ways:

- It provides grounded, standards-based support for beginning teachers to continue to become better teachers.
- It keeps highly qualified and highly committed teachers in the profession.
- It provides opportunities for experienced teachers to become better teachers while simultaneously taking up the professional responsibility to assure that the people entering teaching maintain and expand the care and competence with which they began their careers.
- It builds expertise and shared norms of practice.
- It breaks down the isolation that is anathema to the teaching that children deserve and communities require.

REWARDING KNOWLEDGE AND SKILL

New Haven keeps quality teachers in classrooms by rewarding knowledge and skill, both tangibly and intangibly. One intangible thing the district provides teachers is broad-based community support of schools and of teachers. Community support also shows up tangibly—the last two bond levies passed by 80%, showing that the community puts its scarce resources where its pride is.

Like the community, the district also puts its money where its pride is. Salaries in New Haven range from $37,604 to $70,373—the highest in the Bay Area and in the state's upper echelon, despite New Haven's historic standing as one of the lowest-wealth districts in the state and county. New Haven's total spending per ADA (a measure of per-pupil expenditure) is $4,103, approximately the fifth percentile in the state and $2,337 per student below the highest per-pupil expenditure in the county.

The district also understands the reward of creatively and flexibly staffing classrooms. New Haven gives teachers opportunities to have their knowledge and skill rewarded both financially and professionally, without having them abandon their classroom work with children. Teachers enact the internship program and the BTSA program; develop curriculum; design technological supports; and create student standards, assessments, and indicators of student learning. Using a combination of release time, after-school workshops, and extensive summer institutes, the district involved more than 100 teachers (nearly two-fifths of K–4 teachers) in its language arts and mathematics standards committees during the 1996–1997 year. During the summer of 1997, approximately 65% of the district's certified teachers participated in district-sponsored staff development activities.

When not compensating teachers for their time directly, the district pays for courses leading to additional certification in hard-to-staff areas such as special education, math, science, and bilingual education. This coursework counts toward increments on the salary scale; ultimately, through such coursework, teachers reap ongoing financial benefits. Not surprisingly, teachers report that free is better than paying. They also report that district-sponsored coursework is better education for them than other course offerings because its content is designed specifically for New Haven and because the teacher cohort consists of teachers they have worked with before and will be working with again in the schools.

The associate superintendent for instruction is responsible for curriculum, staff development, pupil personnel, family services, and special education. During the 1997–1998 year, her office hired four teachers on special assignment to work on class-size reduction, technology, assessment and accountability, and language development. She believes that "the teachers in this district do all the work. We don't have a massive central office staff. . . . If we didn't have these teacher specialists, we would be in real trouble." She also believes that the way the district rewards teachers with the opportunity to share expertise while remaining in or returning to the classroom is an essential component of the district's success with students:

> Unless somebody focuses on what teachers and students do with
> this (*she gestures around her office, which is full of curricular materials,*
> *and out toward the district's central technology lab*) in the classroom,
> it's pretty meaningless. It is really important that they keep working
> with students.

The district invests resources in qualified and supported teachers while minimizing resource allocations to pull-out programs and administration. New Haven is not a rich district, and its teachers' salaries for the most part come from the basic state funding package. It can afford quality because its overhead is low (e.g., by maintaining fewer but larger school buildings); it has flattened the traditional hierarchy of district and school bureaucracies (with 771 teachers and 50 "managers," nearly 94% of certified personnel work with children); it spends categorical funds in classrooms; it allocates resources, including technology, to support and build teaching capacity; and it has created multiple hybrid professional roles that enrich teacher learning while enhancing district policy and practice.

ORGANIZING SCHOOLS FOR STUDENT LEARNING

In any human endeavor, one often overlooked reward is the opportunity to do what one is capable of doing, which in education means working in an organization designed for student learning. New Haven schools, especially the high school, are purposefully somewhat large and, at first blush, incongruent with what we know about how small schools support learning through personal knowledge and sustained relationships. Several factors, however, make New Haven's large schools very personal places to learn.

One factor is that the district used a personalized approach to making the decision to have one large high school. A second key factor is that its high school clusters its 4,200 students into three "houses," creating student cohort groups of approximately 1,400 students each within the larger physical facility. Another factor is the school's use of clubs to personalize relationships between teachers and students. These clubs bring students and teachers together around common interests and passions on a regular and ongoing basis.

A parent of two New Haven children (one "gifted" student and one special education student) noted: "Extracurriculars like the clubs and teachers make it personal. I am not sure how they do it. Even though it is crowded, it is so safe. I think it may be because of the availability of teachers in and out of the classroom." With simple eloquence, the special education student, who may not go to Berkeley but who will graduate with his class, meeting all graduation standards, commented, "I am not real good at school, but I really like my teachers."

Technology in the Classroom

While the district's initial uses of its technological infrastructure were administrative, district personnel believe and are committed to the notion that the major impact of technology is classroom-based. The district focuses on providing students and teachers with up-to-date technology that helps students learn and that assists teachers in supporting student learning.

To date, the best evidence of the district's success is available to anyone with access to the Web. Log on to the New Haven website and click on "School Sites." Choose any one of the schools, and you can be transported to a gallery of student work, communicate directly with students, or gain "virtual" access to classrooms.

Extended-Day Program

In September 1997, New Haven implemented a districtwide extended-day program. The impetus to extend the piloted program came about as a result of discussions during the 1996 Youth Summit held at the high school. At that time, community members raised concerns about the lack of affordable and supervised activities for youth in the community—especially activities that were both educational and enjoyable. Today, the schools are open from pre-dawn to dark, providing educational experiences connected with the school program as well as the more traditional enrichment activities and clubs. Fees for the K–8 program are charged on an ability-to-pay basis.

The extended day offers supervision at an affordable price, keeps children out of trouble, helps make sure that their homework is done, and helps them get to school on time. More than providing day care, this program focuses on community development as well. While programs vary from school to school depending upon parent and student choice, activities in all the schools address recreational, academic, social, and psychological needs of students beyond school hours.

ORGANIZING SCHOOLS FOR TEACHER LEARNING

Schools organized for student learning must also be places in which the adults who work with students learn and in which teachers can use their learning in the service of children and families. No matter how wonderfully qualified teachers are, their capacity to support student achievement is limited if they are not allowed to use the knowledge, skills, and dispositions they earn, learn, and possess. A teacher may be well qualified to construct a science lab that engages students in hands-on, minds-on learning; however, if the lab is not available for lack of space and materials or the necessary time is not available because of a school's schedule, students' opportunities for learning are diminished.

The district's approach to technology is evidence of how it recognizes and acts on the relationship between opportunities for teacher learning and student learning. With the philosophy that "machines do not teach—people do," New Haven supports people using machines in the interests of children and their families. In 1992, a broad-based community effort assured passage of a school bond measure, making New Haven one of the most technologically elite districts in the nation. However, the district foresaw that without comprehensive professional development, teachers and administrators would not grasp the possibilities inherent in the technology, nor would the technology have much impact on classroom practice.

At the center of the district's efforts stood one high school math teacher who, in the early 1980s, became interested in computers. In 1984, he became the district's director of information systems. As early as 1986, the district began networking all school offices for attendance, grading, and e-mail. When the bonds began passing in 1992, the district faced a wonderful challenge: Now that we have some money, what do we do? The district used two guiding principles. First, the system should be focused around students' needs and work that teachers want them to be doing. Second, the district should support people to use the machines well. That support factor is not merely a matter of helping people learn a few new tricks; it is also a matter of unlearning old tricks and of opening up to a world of possibilities. The director of information systems points out that "technology is an agent of change, and change is always difficult." To make matters more difficult, as this administrator notes, "Technology doesn't save any money; it costs money. But it is much more efficient and safe. It is more efficient because we can access and manipulate much greater amounts of information."

The school district took up these challenges and provided an ongoing support and training model, built around program and department needs, that does the following:

- Encourages and models the use of technology
- Provides staff with a variety of ways to learn how to use technological resources as part of their regular tasks, functions, and routines
- Provides documented software, hardware, and network connectivity
- Provides inservice support by site or department based upon needs
- Implements a trainer-of-trainers model within each department and at each site

STANDARDS FOR STUDENT LEARNING

In 1998, New Haven piloted a comprehensive K–4 standards and assessment system that was to serve as a prototype for all grade levels. This districtwide system consisted of the following:

- Clearly articulated performance standards with clear descriptions of seven different performance levels (from pre-readiness through independent) tied to grade-level expectations

- A standards- or criterion-based parent reporting system that all K–4 students, including special education and second-language learners, receive
- A three-stream assessment structure
- A database system that pulls together assessment, demographic, and intervention information for analysis and use in program planning and targeting student assistance

According to information the district has received from the U.S. Department of Education and the RAND Corporation, the model is one of the few comprehensive standards systems in the country to incorporate a learner-centered developmental perspective with the more traditional accountability features of standards-setting efforts.

The key to the standards and assessment system is not so much the testing as it is the web of supports activated by the assessments. Perhaps the most fundamental use of the standards and assessment system is as a tool for classroom-level instructional planning. For example, each August every teacher receives a printout of the levels of each of his or her students' performance in reading, writing, and mathematics. Teachers initially use this information to design guided reading groups, target computer software, and assign home reading levels. Ongoing authentic assessment (e.g., running records of reading) against the standards helps teachers continually modify these groupings. In addition, teachers use this assessment information to identify students needing tutoring during the after-school, extended-day program and/or homework support. On a more personal level, the database also helps maximize the match of primary-age students and intermediate-age reading buddies. At the school level, educators use the system to guide changes in just about every educational arena, including staffing, instructional programming, allocating resources, and configuring classes.

Such a program puts a major responsibility on teachers—what one elementary school principal calls "a seachange in teaching." It is no longer sufficient simply to assess whether or not a child is meeting a grade-level expectation. What children know and are able to do must be clearly documented through both student work and teacher observation. This documentation requires more than presenting information; it involves an expectation that the content of the standards be accessible to, and learned by, students at all performance levels. The purpose is not to label a child but to develop a program that facilitates that child's development.

New Haven enacted its teaching quality system for one reason: to make a difference in the lives of the community's children. The district began not by saying all children should learn X, Y, and Z because these are endpoints. Rather, the district began by getting serious about and upholding standards for teachers. The student standards and assessments grew out of good teaching and knowledgeable teachers. The district simultaneously developed in two areas: (1) recruiting, retaining, and rewarding quality teachers, and (2) creating educational environments—both pre- and inservice, and both in and out of school—that provided opportunities for the quality people who have been recruited to continue to grow as teachers. With this teaching quality system in place, New Haven personnel have created a district that does more than just announce what students should learn— they have created a district in which educators can see to it that students do learn.

EPILOGUE

Since 1996–1998, when the data for this chapter were collected, time has not stood still. California elected a new governor who actively promulgated educational policy; three members of New Haven's longtime district leadership team retired; and the local real estate market skyrocketed. These contextual changes have influenced New Haven's teaching quality system.

State Policy Changes

At the urging of the governor, California instituted a testing system that ranked schools and attached cash rewards for schools that performed well on the tests and consultants from a state-approved list for those that did not perform well. Initially, the school performance "index" used only scores from the SAT-9 exam, which was not aligned with the new state standards approved by the state board of education. In addition, the California student content standards were conservative, while New Haven's emerging student standards were progressive. In short, with the stakes attached to the SAT-9, the locally developed standards and assessments for students described in the chapter have taken a backseat. Several longtime employees of the district feel the results "of obsessing with the state testing system" are a "dumbed-down curriculum," with teachers knowing "less about their children and what they are learning than what we did before." With a state-mandated graduation exit exam looming, high school teachers in particular report feeling increasing pressures to teach to the test.

The state also invested in Cal State Teach, a web-based teacher–district matchmaking service that now provides other districts with some of the technological wherewithal that historically has given New Haven a recruiting edge. In addition, the state legislature voted to offer augmentation funds to districts to raise beginning teacher salaries. Finally, California fully funded its BTSA program so that such support is now potentially offered to every new teacher in the state. The net result of these state efforts to enhance teacher recruitment and retention is that other districts around the state are "catching up" with New Haven. These state efforts helping other districts emulate New Haven's successful approaches can be viewed positively in the big picture. In fact, New Haven personnel were key in developing Cal State Teach and helping other districts offer beginning teacher support and assessment programs. In the small frame, however, they have taken away some of New Haven's competitive advantages.

Leadership Changes

Within 2 years of the writing of the case study, New Haven lost three members of the administrative leadership team that had been together in the district for more than two decades: the superintendent (first) and then two associate superintendents who had been responsible for personnel and for technology. As one teacher put it, after 23 years of stable leadership, "New Haven teachers are not used to dealing with change." Complicating matters, the previous superintendent was "a mythical figure when I left. . . . All of a sudden I was without sin. I know that wasn't true."

The retired leadership team spent considerable time talking with educational colleagues prior to making decisions—"talking days on end with the cabinet" and meeting with every member of the staff at least twice a year. At least initially, some faculty members felt the new leadership team waited to listen to concerns until after decisions were made. As one teacher put it, "It was the leadership team's connecting to those of us who know before making decisions that made for better decisions and served as leadership development. Fewer of those connections are happening now." In addition, some changes were reversed when they did not work as designed. These reversals, while probably sound decisions, reduced confidence in the district as well as increasing "personal" faculty concerns (e.g., "in what building will I be teaching next year?"). One longtime teacher mentor put it this way: "As support providers get more personally concerned, they use more energy just to focus on what is going to happen to them and to their students. You can't help others if you don't know what is going to happen to you."

Demographic Changes

Traditionally, New Haven had been a working-class community. However, a third recent contextual change is the doubling of housing costs in the area, with new homes priced in the $500,000 to $1 million range. As the dot.com world spread north, the community began changing to a younger, wealthier group with fewer children. Yet today, with the dot.com market dropping, many of the homes remain vacant. This change portends potential peril to the schools' role as community centers for a diverse population. Unless the district consciously combats typical trends and makes difficult decisions, attendance areas could end up segregating the district and exacerbating economic isolation.

More immediately, the student population of the district has diminished recently. In addition, acting on the findings of a professional demographer, the district asked all nondistrict students to leave its schools in anticipation of a space shortage. When the enrollment predictions proved inaccurate, the district found itself with significantly reduced enrollments. Because state aid is dependent on number of students, the net result has been a decrease in funding for the district. Predicting the future is always a tricky business; however, some feel that "this never would have happened" with the previous superintendent. With his context-specific knowledge of education and the community, he did the enrollment predictions himself and used out-of-district transfers as a safety valve to ensure his predictions were met.

Thus far, the district has avoided making deep programmatic cuts. The personnel office, however, has taken a hit—losing 2.8 full-time equivalents and downgrading the head of personnel's role from an associate superintendent with a continuing contract to an assistant superintendent on a year-to-year contract.

The housing market has also influenced New Haven teacher retention, many of whom marry, want to have families, and try to buy a home. "Our people are staying in teaching but leaving [the area] because they can't afford to live here." Despite these challenges, the district retains a commitment to teaching quality. The new superintendent still sees teacher support as a priority, especially for beginning teachers. For instance, she personally visits every new teacher's classroom and has continued to fund the district's teacher education program when traditional external sources dried up. According to one school-based teacher educator:

> Through the climate changes, we are still as strong as we were. We have actually gotten better, even more powerful, in terms of encouraging inquiry into our own teaching, pressing our teachers to self-assess and look at their own practice, to teach from the inside out. It is not about the standards; it is scaffolding those standards and how we are in community in our classrooms and in our schools.

CHAPTER 7

Constraints and Opportunities in Changing Policy Environments: Intermediary Organizations' Response to Complex District Contexts

PATRICIA ELLEN BURCH

Despite surging interest in how district policy enables instructional reform, limited research exists on how school reformers—who are positioned outside the central office or in an intermediary position—actually experience and make sense of central office policy developments. A growing body of literature documents the important role that district policies typically play in setting the standards for instructional change and unleashing the resources that allow changes to be sustained (Elmore & Burney, 1999; McLaughlin & Talbert, 1993). Other studies have investigated how district policies respond to, rather than direct, school-level agendas (e.g., McLaughlin & Talbert, 2001; Wechsler & Friedrich, 1997).

While shedding light on district actions and on the incentives for change these actions establish, these lines of research have ignored the influence of intermediary groups, such as professional development organizations or teacher support networks, which in the largest districts form a vital part of the "infrastructure" supporting teachers' learning. These groups interpret district policies through their interactions with schools. As central office activity related to accountability intensifies and as schools come under pressure to demonstrate progress, understanding the role of these groups becomes critical.

Adopting a sense-making frame (Weick, 1979) on implementation, this chapter investigates the role that professional development organizations can play as mediators between changing central office policies and schools' efforts to help teachers move toward student-centered instruction. It ex-

School Districts and Instructional Renewal. Copyright © 2002 by Teachers College, Columbia University. All rights reserved. ISBN 0-8077-4266-X (pbk), ISBN 0-8077-4267-8 (cloth). Prior to photocopying items for classroom use, please contact the Copyright Clearance Center, Customer Service, 222 Rosewood Dr., Danvers, MA 01923, USA, tel. (508) 750-8400.

amines the response of professional development organizations (PDOs) to swift policy changes in the Chicago Public School District during the late 1990s.

The chapter draws on case studies of four professional development organizations collaborating on a 3-year initiative, commencing in 1995, to move teachers toward student-centered approaches to instruction. Case studies of the organizations involved repeated structured and semistructured interviews and observations with nine professional development staff and ten school leaders across four schools that had partnered with the organizations in the reform. Interview data were combined with observations of professional development activities and a review of documents pertaining to the district, schools, or consortium activities (see Burch, 2000, for a more complete description of study methods). The four schools were similar in size but varied in terms of their experience with instructional reform and their record of academic achievement.

FRAMING IDEAS

Institutional theory in organizational analysis serves as the theoretical anchor for the study. New institutional theory encompasses a broad range of thinking about change within organizational environments (Scott, 1995). Three core ideas proved central to understanding professional developers' experience implementing reform within the Chicago Public School District.

Role of Intermediary Organizations in Sense-Making

Much research on districts focuses on the formal policy system and does not attend to the vast terrain of private and nonprofit organizations, such as subject-area networks, reform organizations, and foundations, that collaborate with schools and the central office on instructional improvement. Over the past decade, the activity of these "nonsystem actors" has intensified (Rowan, 2000). Especially in decentralized school districts, schools often deal directly with outside organizations for services, such as staff development, rather than looking exclusively to the district for support. Intermediary organizations thus can have an important influence on policy dynamics in a district and schools' progress toward instructional improvements.

Role of Sense-Making in the Process of Policy Implementation

The role of these organizations is particularly critical in a reform climate in which schools bear the onus of figuring out how to translate broad accountability pressures into concrete instructional changes. These outside organizations can become in effect part of the support system for schools and a means by which schools make sense of the district policy environment. Over the past decade, a growing number of studies in education have emphasized the role of sense-making in the process of policy implementation. As defined here, sense-making is a central organizational activity through which individuals seek to interpret unexpected changes in their environment and to reconcile them with existing practices and beliefs (Weick, 1979). These studies adopt the perspective that the individuals directly involved in teaching and learning often confront policies that are ambiguous and contradictory (Lipsky, 1980). Therefore, enacting policies involves deciphering the underlying meaning of policies and figuring out what, if anything, to do differently given policy priorities. Based on this perspective, this chapter examines how and why the staff of four professional development organizations as well as collaborating teachers and principals made sense of evolving central office

Reciprocal Influences in Sense-Making

As individuals interpret district policies based on collectively or individually held beliefs, they influence how others view the policies and their relationship to existing reform agendas. In this sense, the process of policy implementation is reciprocal, as policy interpretation shapes policy response, which can generate new understandings about policy intentions. Drawing on this perspective, this chapter examines how sense-making by intermediary organizations helped teachers and others locate strategic opportunities within district flux and shifted teachers' responses to policy changes.

THE PROFESSIONAL DEVELOPMENT ORGANIZATIONS

The research focused on an initiative known as the Chicago Consortium for Teacher Professional Development (pseudonym), hereafter referred to as the Consortium. Through this period, the Consortium comprised four professional development organizations, each with expertise in a distinct content area: Writers' Workshop, History Center, Arts in Action, and Math Matters (pseudonyms). In 1995, the Consortium was awarded a four-year grant to provide middle-grade teachers across 12 schools with multiple venues for teacher professional development.

The four professional development organizations resembled each other structurally. They were comparable in size and, even before their collaborative work on the grant, held similar organizational goals. These shared goals reflected research on effective learning environments and the conditions that support student and teacher growth (Bransford, Brown, & Cocking, 1999). For example, each PDO believed in providing students with hands-on learning opportunities geared toward students' authentic interests, which the Consortium termed "student-centered practice." In addition, each PDO advocated teacher-led and/or classroom-based staff development as an alternative to the generic, one-time workshops typically offered by the district. As part of their work on the grant, PDOs' focal professional development strategy for the 1996–1997 and 1997–1998 schoolyears involved ongoing classroom-based support for three-member teacher teams, known as "pathfinders."

In the summer and fall of 1996, each PDO hired the equivalent of one full-time classroom consultant with in-depth knowledge of a particular content area to provide intensive classroom-based support to middle-grade teachers. For the 1996–1997 and 1997–1998 schoolyears, consultants were assigned to work 1 day per week, or 40 days per year, in each of five schools.

PDOs held similar visions regarding the format of good professional development. This approach emphasized making professional development accessible to teachers. Professional development opportunities included school-based workshops, extended inquiry, public exhibition of students' work, classroom visits, cross-school networking meetings, a teacher leadership course, and a week-long summer institute. PDOs also agreed that professional development should be scheduled flexibly to meet teachers' needs, in settings that included classrooms, project offices, teachers' lounges, college campuses, high school auditoriums, and, in one case, a park. Professional development activities primarily targeted teachers, but in several instances parents, principals, and students also were invited to participate.

THE DISTRICT POLICY CONTEXT

In the summer of 1995, the district appeared to be a welcoming and supportive context for the reform. The Chicago School Reform Act of 1988 had decentralized decision making authority and identified school communities as the locus of change. Heralded as one of the most dramatic and far-reaching decentralization reform experiments, the Chicago School Reform Act established local school councils composed of teachers, parents, community representatives, and the principal. The local school councils were given responsibility over setting school policy concerning school improvement, budget, and curriculum. The law also devolved control of state Elementary and Secondary Education Act funds to the school level, thereby raising the amount of discretionary resources available to each school.

In the years preceding the act, a handful of school advocacy groups had documented the problems of the Chicago Public Schools. When Education Secretary William Bennett labeled the city's schools the "worst in the nation," he was echoing what many Chicagoans already believed (quoted in O'Connell, 1991, p. 1). The act and the political organizing that preceded it galvanized a cross-section of the community, including business leaders, community groups, academics, city officials, parents, and teachers. The directors of the Consortium's professional development organizations were active participants on decentralization task forces. In separate interviews, each director referred to this period as a time of great optimism. Even though, by 1994, the decentralization reform had begun to develop a growing number of critics who were forecasting its demise, other members of the reform community, including Consortium PDOs, remained hopeful that Chicago schools were on the road to improvement (e.g., Consortium on Chicago School Research, 1993, 1995, 1996; Hess, 1995).

In its planning proposal, the Consortium identified the presence of the decentralization reform (then in its sixth year) and its vision of school-based accountability and building-level change as the ideal architecture to support the grant's emphasis on school-driven professional development. For PDOs, the reform had introduced a vision of accountability consistent with their own ideals about teacher and principal expertise.

Initial Compatibility with District Curricular Frameworks

New curricular frameworks adopted by the district central office seemed especially supportive of the Consortium initiative. The PDOs' initial design preceded a nearly identical curricular framework mandated by the district, called Pathways to Achievement (Chicago Public Schools, 1994). The Pathways model, which appeared in every key document across the system, asked teachers to emphasize activities and materials that "engage students' intellect and stimulate them beyond acquiring facts, toward analyzing and understanding a subject to hypothesize, to discover meaning on their own" (Chicago Public Schools, 1994, p. 7). From the Consortium's perspective, the Pathways model aimed to reconstruct teachers' practice in exactly the ways encouraged by its reform.

The district's vision for staff development also appeared to mirror the Consortium initiative's design. The Pathways model described good staff development as having five key ingredients: (1) active experiential activities that stress new approaches, (2) more in-school time for professional development, (3) more opportunity for teachers to focus on the local concerns of each school and faculty, (4) collaboration among teachers and the development of team approaches, and (5) reflective dialogue and professional conversation. The Consortium proposal affirmed all five as integral to its approach to professional development.

PDOs viewed the district curricular frameworks as signifying support for the Consortium's goals. The district's standards and curriculum guidance, developed in response to state standards, seemed to further legitimize the Consortium's own reform plans. Explained one PDO director:

> [F]or example, the [District's] sixth-grade social studies standard of comparing and contrasting religious beliefs in different cultures, the math goal of laying out spaces and using lines and curves to figure out geometric relationships, and how they handle different themes in different cultures as a language arts goal . . . are three areas required by the city that resonate in reality with what we really want to do, that fit with this project.

Similarly, the standards' emphasis on real-world learning gave new credibility to the Consortium's focus on having students learn by doing. Stated one PDO director, "You cannot get these things from skill-and-drill instruction. So you can really make a case here about teaching to the new standards; if you want to reach higher standards, you got to teach a different way."

In this context, the PDOs had been able to secure interest and support for their initiative from high-level central office administrators. Not only were district administrators cosigners on the grant, but also the director of the district staff development unit had attended planning meetings for the grant and pledged in-kind support. Furthermore, the district made it possible for the planning committee to host meetings in their offices, and district staff have been active participants in these meetings.

The Sudden Shift in the District's Agenda

Anticipating continued support, the Consortium was caught off guard by sudden, dramatic changes in the emphasis and mechanism of the district accountability agenda. In the spring of 1995, anticipating a district budget shortfall of $150 million, Governor James Edgar passed legislation that changed the governance structure of the school system, expanding the authority of the mayor in school matters. A core management team directly appointed by the mayor—the Chicago School Reform Board of Trustees—was given expansive new powers over low-performing schools and the district's general operations. The mayor's appointees took swift and highly publicized action to increase the stakes associated with standardized tests, in particular the IOWA, a basic skills norm-referenced test. Under district chief executive officer (CEO) Paul Vallas's leadership, the test was increasingly identified as the primary source of information for judging school and teacher performance.

In October 1996, the board placed 109 of the city's 557 schools on academic probation for IOWA test scores, firing principals and closing high schools. School officials announced that teachers who failed to follow improvement plans at probation schools could be removed without standard procedures, including an evaluation, warning, and remediation period. In the winter of 1997, the Reform Board instituted a new promotion policy that required students in third, sixth and eighth grades to meet test score targets or the school would face probation and possible closure. Students in those same target grades who did not achieve minimum requirements in reading and math had to attend a 6-week summer school, the Chicago Bridge program. Teachers participating in the program attended 2 days of inservice and received prescribed lesson plans. According to four Consortium teachers who were part of the Bridge program, district staff developers made surprise visits to classrooms to ensure compliance with scripted lessons. The national and local press applauded most of these changes and pointed to evidence of overall improvement in test scores as a sign that the district was finally improving (Katz, Fine, & Simon, 1997).

These policy developments altered central office priorities. Under new district leadership, the central office repeatedly repudiated student-centered practice as contrary to the back-to-basics, test-driven focus endorsed by district leaders. During the Consortium's first summer institute, for example, the district CEO made public statements contrasting the substance of direct instruction with the "fluff" of progressive teaching and learning methods. In his first year in office, the CEO also made a strong push for a back-to-basics approach emphasizing phonics for beginning readers, and he introduced direct instruction in 25 schools.

As central office intervention in low-performing schools intensified, the district's vision of staff development ceased to align with that of the Consortium. For example, both the Consortium and the former district approach framed staff development as a necessary condition for professional growth, to which all teachers in the system were *entitled*. Actions taken by new central office leadership, in contrast, treated staff development as a form of remedial action for schools and teachers deemed in need of improvement. Schools on probation were *required* to contract with an external partner to develop corrective action plans that, among other, things *mandated* teachers to attend workshops and be regularly observed in their classrooms.

THE PROFESSIONAL DEVELOPMENT ORGANIZATIONS' RESPONSE TO THE CHANGING POLICY CONTEXT

These changes in the district policy—which constituted a state of policy flux that is typical in urban districts—had an immediate yet unpredictable influence on Consortium PDOs' implementation strategies as well as teachers' and other reform partners' engagement in the work. PDOs' response reveals how the policy flux can create both constraints and strategic opportunities for reformers. While policy flux initially posed obstacles to work in schools, the Consortium assumed an important intermediary role by helping teachers and principals find new meaning in an apparently adverse policy environment, balance competing reform pressures, and learn ways to expand support for their work.

District Policy Flux as a Condition for Reform Work

The experience of the Consortium professional developers illustrates how dynamic central office policy can be and how the volatility of the policy environment evokes new sense-making activity on the part of all participants. Not only did district policies change unexpectedly; the changes were added to existing policies, rather than replacing them. In this case, the initially supportive policies remained in place throughout the period of the Consortium initiative: the decentralization reform, which gave schools more discretion over instructional practices and budgets; the district's new curricular frameworks, which endorsed higher-order thinking skills that the PDOs also encouraged in their work with teachers; and the collaborative agreement with the district's staff development office.

    Layered onto these arrangements, the new accountability policy posed a major uncertainty for Consortium members, thereby creating an occasion for them to make new meaning of their environment and relationship to it. PDO liaisons, who less than 12 months before had characterized the local policy context as supportive and secure, now viewed it in more negative and dynamic terms. One director described policy developments as "a counterrevolution to what we expected—the major emphasis right now is standardized tests, and the current administration will let nothing, including this so-called decentralization reform, get in the way of that." Another director commented, "Suddenly, there is less open discussion throughout the district; people are just more afraid to talk—and this in a city where people have generally been very vocal about their ideas." These perspectives were repeated by each of the other directors interviewed as well as all but one of the consultants.

The Consortium steering committee assumed new importance as a safe venue for PDOs to make sense of new district pressures. Originally, the steering committee was charged with grant oversight. With changes in the district, monthly steering committee meetings were rescheduled on a weekly basis to devote time to discussing district policy flux and strategies for dealing with the flux. Exclaimed a PDO director at one such meeting, "My board suddenly wants evidence of how what we are doing leads to improved test scores. Should we make a case for this or suggest other ways of measuring student progress?"

Challenges to Collaboration with Teachers and Principals

Changes in central office policy shifted dynamics between schools and the PDOs enlisted by schools (independent of the district) to help with instruction. First, testing pressures undercut teacher and principal participation in professional development. Second, new sanctions linked to standardized tests made teachers and principals more wary of having *any* outsiders in their building, including professional developers with whom they had already established relationships.

During the 1996–1997 schoolyear, all four principals and all six teachers reported that they simply had less time than anticipated to participate in professional development activities. In the view of three of the four principals, teachers' work on the project either had little connection, or else conflicted, with instruction linked to district test pressures. One principal explained:

> It would be nice if the test scores went up [as a result of participation in the project] you know . . . if there was some carryover, but it's been my experience that projects like this don't always have a direct connection to standardized testing. So the kids might do this student-centered instruction well, but when it comes to standardized testing, that's a whole different mindset. For teachers, it's a whole different way of thinking about what you have to do.

Three of the six teachers in the spring of 1996 had suspended all student-centered instruction until after the test had been administered, while three others reported that the demands of testing and the mandated curriculum largely determined the focus of their classrooms. For example, a fifth-grade teacher who had spent several months working intensively with the consultant from the writing PDO had become eager to try out new strategies such as literature circles and had rearranged the desks in her classroom (from rows to clusters of desks) to better support student-centered activities. Shortly thereafter, she moved her desks back to the original row position. When queried, the teacher reported that she would move the desks back and resume group work once the standardized tests had been administered.

In the view of nearly all participants, the lack of time and constraints on participation could be directly traced to an environment discouraging activities that did not contribute directly to test score improvement. The Consortium's 1997 annual report to project funders noted:

> The pressures inherent in Chicago at this time place many demands on principals in our partner schools. Our original proposal suggested the formulation of a principal network in Chicago to hold monthly meetings as forums for issues. We have found that the tensely charged climate this year in Chicago had made these meetings difficult for principals to attend.

A reduction in time or willingness to participate in Consortium activities was not the only consequence of the change in district policy. Explained one director, "Schools have become suspicious of any outsiders; that makes it difficult for even those of us with insider relationships to come in." Apparently, testing pressures had made teacher and principal leaders wary about taking any leadership or ownership for the project. As one PDO director put it, "The last thing a principal needs in the present climate is to be lionized as a supporter [of] student-centered practice." One principal, who was experienced in student-centered instruction and had agreed to act as a mentor to other principals in the network, decided to "lay low" as testing pressures intensified, given that "the new [Reform] Board has a mission from the mayor . . . [to] get it done the way that he sees that it can be done, and Chicago Consortium for Teacher Professional Development is not what they're talking about."

To summarize, by 1997, student-centered practice had moved to the margins of the district's policy agenda. With shifting district priorities, resources upon which PDOs had counted, such as teachers' trust and principal leadership, grew scarce. These changes rocked PDOs' original sense of the district as a supportive backdrop and propelled them toward new strategies for interacting with the central office and for sustaining interest in their initiative.

Shift in PDO Strategy

The PDOs responded by becoming more strategic intermediaries between school agendas and district pressures. They shifted the way in which they tried to align with central policy and interact with district-level staff. They drew connections to central office policies still perceived as supportive. For example, the Consortium designed workshops that used the district standards as an organizing framework for teaching higher-order thinking. By the spring of 1998, two of four PDOs had expanded their repertoire of after-school workshops to include sessions on integrating standards-based instruction into student-centered reform. PDOs also worked to help teachers make sense of district pressures in ways that emphasized compatibility with reform. In particular, consultants modeled ways in which teachers could integrate inquiry-based instructional approaches with test-oriented student assessments. One consultant, for example, demonstrated the use of journal writing as an alternative to drill-and-skill word lists to build students' vocabulary. Two other PDOs introduced workshops aimed at helping teachers use student-centered strategies to improve test performance in reading.

As testing pressures mounted, some PDO directors also initiated contacts with staff outside of the district staff development office, the unit from which PDOs initially sought central office support for their work. While originally thinking it unnecessary to collaborate or inform other central office administrators about the project, by the summer of 1997 all four directors reported contacting other central office staff and high-ranking city officials to inform them of the Consortium's work. These contacts included inviting members of the mayor's education staff to participate in professional development workshops and sending press clippings and videotapes to central office staff. For example, the director of the arts PDO developed a relationship with the central office representative to the city's cultural affairs department—initially through meetings to explain further the scope of the PDO's work, and subsequently through an invitation to attend professional development activities and serve as a co-presenter in a citywide conference on the arts' contribution to other areas of student learning.

PDOs thus sought not only to inform but also to deepen central office staff's understanding of their work. They did this by both involving staff in professional development and conducting professional development explicitly designed for central office staff. For example, in 1997 the director and five other staff members from the district Office of School Leadership Development attended a week-long retreat organized by the Consortium that included workshops for interested policy makers from inside and outside of the state. The previous year, PDOs' only interaction with the Leadership Development Office had been to send them a copy of their annual project report.

Expansion of PDO Support Networks

At the outset of the initiative, the four PDOs had laid only sketchy plans to collaborate with one another or with other reform organizations. As testing pressures mounted, PDOs began to view these relationships as more important and in turn deepened their investment in them.

First, PDOs intensified collaboration with other reform organizations. During the 1996–1997 schoolyear, PDOs jointly hosted three conferences in collaboration with other professional development reform networks, although only one such conference had originally been planned. Two additional networking meetings, planned collaboratively with other reform organizations, were added the following year. During the 1997–1998 schoolyear, individual PDOs also partnered for the first time with other kinds of local institutions, outside of the central office, which had interest in their work, including a popular blues club, a natural history museum, and a local arts council.

Second, over the course of the initiative, PDOs also increased their collaboration with one another. The original Consortium design had offered PDO staff few opportunities to learn about one another's work. With changes in district policy context, nearly all consultants and directors reported spending more time meeting with one another to talk about one another's work, participating in workshops led by other PDOs or co-leading workshops at the school level. At the outset, PDOs considered learning about one another's work to be an "extracurricular" and secondary aspect of the project. But, as one director noted, shifts in central office priorities moved PDOs to

> formalize [their own collaboration] by, among other things, setting up some sessions in which the different consultants train each other in their knowledge base. That it isn't always about serving teachers. That we may need to service each other. And that there's a synergy that comes from that.

Professional developers explained their shift toward more collaborative strategies as a direct response to central office policy flux. Directors described efforts to increase collaboration with other reform partners and one another as a means of expanding support for their work beyond the central office. As a result of meetings with other reform groups, one director reported:

> We [PDOs] are starting to get a better handle on our methodologies; . . . we're starting to articulate what they are; . . . the teachers are starting to be able to articulate what they are. In other words, rather than just trying to market our wares to as many schools as possible, I find [that] an environment like this allows us to be a think-tank, and [we] start to surface our pedagogy.

Similarly, another PDO director reported that by developing relationships with well-known cultural organizations outside of typical reform circles, the project had created a reform network that could anchor PDOs' credibility in a shifting district policy context. The professional developers shared their new perspectives on the importance of collaboration with teachers and principals. The flyer distributed to teachers participating at one reform networking activity stated: "We all are connected. By linking together, we can grow a progressive alternative for city schools."

In this way, shifting central office policies created strategic opportunities as well as constraints for PDOs. As testing pressures placed central office policy support in question, PDOs pursued strategies aimed in part at strengthening other networks and aligning their work with wider reform agendas.

New Understandings for Teachers and Others

PDOs' responses to district pressures were not just good coping strategies. They generated new understandings on the part of the teachers, principals, and other reform partners about how to engage in the work and sustain it once the grant's direct funding ran out.

By the spring of 1998, three of the four principals had moved from seeing improvement or maintenance on test scores as the bottom-line goal to viewing support for teachers' work with the Consortium as equally important. For example, one principal who had argued in the summer of 1996 that the project should primarily help schools improve student test scores ultimately came to see central office and project priorities differently. After viewing an exhibition of student art and writing that PDOs had organized in partnership with the state arts council, he commented, "We used to do stuff like this all the time. And we've become so focused on the test that we've forgotten that the kids need to do this, too."

Similarly, teachers' first response to the district policy change was to rely heavily on traditional drill-and-skill teaching in the months preceding what they saw as a basic skills test. By 1996–1997, four of six teachers reported or were observed integrating inquiry-based lessons with textbook reviews and worksheets and using the standards as a framework for creating student-centered units. For example, one teacher described how she integrated basal readers and journal writing into her language arts program. On certain days of the week, the teacher used basals to work on students' comprehension. The journals, which she described as "something new that I'm working on this year," were aimed at "motivating the students to write more."

Five of six teachers were also observed adopting the networking strategies modeled by PDOs. Three teachers led workshops on student-centered instruction for their own faculty or teachers in other schools. Two teachers arranged to visit faculty in other schools identified as experienced in student-centered instruction. Four teachers sought support from their principal to enable them to develop new student-centered curriculum with teachers at other grade levels and in other areas of expertise. By 1998, teachers involved in these collaborations not only displayed greater confidence and comfort with the goals of the project but also identified themselves as playing a leadership role to support the spread of student-centered ideas throughout the school district. For example, the teacher who reorganized the furniture in her room during the test preparation season (from cooperative groups to rows) ultimately assumed a leadership role in the project, co-teaching a course on literature circles for teachers from other schools and talking with more reluctant teachers about how to integrate the work into classroom practice.

In addition, PDOs' attempts to reach out to new district personnel and other reform organizations generated new sense-making and engagement on the part of these partners. By 1997, PDOs were collaborating with a total of five new organizations, all of which had agreed to provide in-kind support for the project after the initial grant had concluded. None of these organizations had previously been involved in public schooling or student-centered approaches. While not formally part of the district or its programming, they assumed a place in schools' support infrastructure.

PDOs' efforts to forge new contacts with district leaders helped these leaders' develop a deeper understanding of Consortium's work. One director explained:

> Now we have some friends in and outside the central office, which we didn't before. We got this woman who actually was sympathetic to our work out to the national conference. So here was an African American woman who had some Black colleagues to talk to, who were excited about this sort of work. And I think it has made it safe for her as a Black educator to speak up for this work in the district.

Likewise, after participating in the Consortium's summer institute, a high-level district administrator brought a PDO partner to the central office to provide a workshop for district staff developers. The administrator was extremely pleased with the professional development and expressed hopes to continue the collaboration in the future, commenting that the PDO liaison "was a starter for this . . . and we wanted to infuse this collaborative into our everyday conversation and let the schools know that we're working with [these PDOs] and that we were partners in this program."

EMERGING ISSUES AND IMPLICATIONS

The experience of reform organizations working in the midst of policy upheaval in Chicago demonstrates how important sense-making is to the progress of instructional reforms. Rather than static backdrops for reform, urban school districts are dynamic settings that create both challenges and strategic opportunities for schools and the intermediary organizations that work with them. The behavioral orientation of much district policy research has meant that how schools and reform partners interpret this upheaval has not received close attention. In a site-based district where schools had come under increasing pressure to generate improvements on standardized tests, the professional development organizations emerged as critical intermediaries between changing district expectations and teachers' ability to engage in student-centered instructional reforms.

Ironically, district flux created new incentives for PDOs to become more exact about the points of intersection between their own vision of reform and district priorities. The substance of their sense-making involved sharing these perspectives with teachers in the context of professional development strategies. These strategies aimed at providing teachers with the tools to balance short-term accountability pressures with longer-term instructional reforms and to build professional community within and outside of the district. PDOs' attention to school-level understanding of district pressures left teachers with an expanded repertoire of instructional tools as well as the know-how to sustain the work in the face competing reform priorities.

These findings have implications for how intermediary organizations such as PDOs try to support school-level instructional reforms in large urban school districts. Professional development organizations can certainly play an important role in helping teachers learn new instructional strategies (Consortium on Chicago School Research, 1993). They may also build schools' capacity to understand and manage policy change and to marry school-level reforms with complementary agendas beyond school walls. In this sense, intermediary organizations should be viewed as central rather than peripheral to the broader policy dynamics of school reform.

The roles of PDOs and other reform partners in supporting teachers as interpreters and sense-makers of district policy is particularly important to examine as policy activity around accountability intensifies. Accountability involves a clear set of rewards and sanctions linked to student performance outcomes. Teachers often receive mixed messages about how to achieve these outcomes. Intermediary organizations such as PDOs can help teachers make sense of district accountability policies and connect the district's message with work already underway in classrooms.

More research is needed on the ways in which policy makers at different levels of the system share responsibility for making sense of dynamic district environments and jointly developing strategies in response to them. Teachers and principals helped alert PDOs to the ways in which district policy changes were influencing their work. In this sense they served as important partners in moving district issues to the foreground of the reform agenda. Like PDOs, district-level staff can also play an important role in the policy sense-making process. As outsiders interacting with schools, district staff can help teachers make sense of district policy and find compatibility between agendas that might otherwise be viewed as dichotomous.

The experience of the Consortium identifies a central dilemma faced by reformers collaborating with schools around these instructional agendas. Sustaining reform requires helping principals and teachers explore new practices *in the midst of* (*rather than in spite of*) local policy changes. Particularly in large urban settings where policy flux and politics are the norm, intermediary organizations can play an important role in helping school communities align their work with compatible policies and to build alternative networks of support where central office policies may seem in conflict.

PART III

Building Better Frameworks
for Inquiry and Action

Provocative cases such as those presented in the preceding part beg to be understood deeply, from the vantage points of both scholars and educational leaders. Strong frameworks underlie that understanding and help guide further inquiry and action. New work is emerging that contributes directly to this need, including the four chapters in this part, by Grossman and colleagues, Spillane, Resnick and Glennan, and McLaughlin and Talbert. Typically rooted in closely studied district settings, in which leaders have experimented with the district's role in instructional renewal, such writings bring powerful concepts and theoretical frames to the task of analysis.

The four chapters construct and apply empirically grounded frameworks for this purpose, drawing on ideas from cognitive learning theory, sociocultural theories, research on teaching and teacher learning in particular subject matters, and work on organizational development and learning. While they do not exhaust the possibilities for such frameworks or the range of settings to which the frameworks might be applied, these works, in conjunction with other chapters in the volume, offer a set of mutually supportive ideas for understanding what districts can do to assume a more potent presence in instructional renewal and how they can do it.

CHAPTER 8

Focusing the Concerns of New Teachers: The District as Teacher Educator

PAM GROSSMAN, CLARISSA S. THOMPSON, AND SHEILA W. VALENCIA

As beginning teachers look for jobs, they think mostly of the schools and classrooms in which they will work. The school district looms distantly on the horizon, barely in focus after they are hired. Once ensconced in the classroom, new teachers may not realize the power of the district to affect their teaching and professional learning. New teachers are not the only ones to overlook the influence of districts. Traditionally, researchers have also ignored the power of the district in studies of educational change, with schools seen as the most influential units (Knapp & McLaughlin, 1999). However, a growing body of research suggests that districts can play pivotal roles, both in fostering and inhibiting effective policy implementation and teaching practice (Massell & Goertz, 1999). This role is perhaps most powerful in the lives of beginning teachers, as they struggle with the daily decisions about what and how to teach.

Our study set out to examine the role that districts and district policy environments play in the lives of beginning teachers. We ask: How do policies at the district level affect first-year teachers' instructional and curricular decisions and classroom practice? What role do district policies play in shaping the learning opportunities for beginning teachers?

SCHOOL DISTRICTS, POLICY, AND PRACTICE

Teachers work within many different policy contexts. For example, policies designed to improve teaching quality can come from institutions as

School Districts and Instructional Renewal. Copyright © 2002 by Teachers College, Columbia University. All rights reserved. ISBN 0-8077-4266-X (pbk), ISBN 0-8077-4267-8 (cloth). Prior to photocopying items for classroom use, please contact the Copyright Clearance Center, Customer Service, 222 Rosewood Dr., Danvers, MA 01923, USA, tel. (508) 750-8400.

seemingly remote from the classroom as the state or federal government, or from places closer to home, such as teachers' school districts, schools, or even subject-matter departments within schools. Teachers often experience the impact of these policies as an array more than as individual policies. As these policies converge on teachers' working lives, they may interact with one another in ways that are consequential for teachers' practice (Knapp, Bamburg, Ferguson, & Hill, 1998).

Districts have a number of different strategies for using policy as a means for improving teaching quality within the system. As such, districts are both interpreters and originators of teaching-related policy (Knapp & McLaughlin, 1999). The district can also be a site for creating opportunities for learning about policy.

As an interpreter of policy, districts play a pivotal, "nonmonolithic" role in facilitating the implementation of other, remote policies (Spillane, 1998b). Their responses to state policies span the entire range from deliberate and thoughtful implementation to actions that undermine a state's intention (Firestone, 1989b; Spillane, 1994, 1996). For example, how districts communicate about the policy, their understanding of the policy, the resources they provide, and the leadership exerted to coordinate change all influence how state policies about standards and learning find their way into the classroom (Firestone & Fairman, 1998; Spillane, 1998b; Spillane & Thompson, 1997).

In their efforts to improve instruction, districts also create their own policies, some of which expand on state initiatives or establish structures that facilitate their implementation (Fuhrman & Elmore, 1990; Spillane, 1996). Other times, district leaders develop policies based on a vision they have for good instruction across the district. For example, districts can create local policies about professional development, mentoring, restructuring, curriculum, and assessment.

A third role that school districts can play with regard to policy and instructional improvement is to provide opportunities for learning about and from policy. Cohen and Barnes (1993) describe policy itself as a curriculum, arguing that opportunities for learning are a necessary part of the policy enactment process. Before policy can influence practice, people at all levels of the system require opportunities to understand these policies, what they are about, and what it might mean to enact them. The school district can create these opportunities in several different ways.

Districts can cultivate instructional leaders at all levels of the system, who in turn can help teachers use existing policy to improve their classroom practices (Nelson, 1999; Spillane & Thompson, 1997). Similarly, districts can create roles and structures for teachers and administrators that support conversation about teaching and how to improve it, such as providing teachers time for collaborative work or supporting the creation of professional communities of practice (Elmore & Burney, 1999). Districts can also offer professional development that relates to what teachers are doing or are asked to do in their classrooms. For example, districts can provide workshops on how to teach a specific subject or how to make sense of the standards teachers must use to assess student learning.

In sum, school districts can serve as powerful links between policy and practice and, as a result, can exert enormous influence on teachers' thinking and instruction. Facing the challenges of the first year of teaching, new teachers are likely to experience district policies in unique and perhaps unexpected ways.

THE STUDY

This chapter draws on a larger longitudinal study of teacher learning in the language arts (Grossman, Smagorinsky, & Valencia, 1999; Grossman et al., 2000). Through classroom observations and teacher and administrator interviews, we documented the experiences of ten teachers in eight districts from their last year of teacher education (1996–1997) into their first 3 years of teaching, as well as the district policy contexts in which they worked.

We focus here on the experiences of three of the first-year teachers in two medium-sized suburban districts in Washington State. We selected these two districts because they represent contrasting policy environments in terms of the focus of their reform efforts, the ways in which reform was enacted, and their policies regarding beginning teachers. In this sense, they represent a strategic contrast for this research.

As is true of all districts in Washington, both districts are affected by the state reforms, which include a set of curriculum frameworks (the Essential Academic Learning Requirements, or EALR); statewide assessments at grades 4, 7, and 10 to assess whether students are meeting standards (the Washington Assessment of Student Learning, or WASL); and, beginning in 2008, an accountability measure that will tie high school graduation to passing scores on the state assessments. While 2008 may seem far off, the accountability measure has forced districts to take the results of the WASL seriously and has contributed to an environment in which schools are focusing their attention on the improvement of student performance on the WASL. Despite these similarities, the districts differed in their policies regarding curriculum, professional development, and mentoring—differences that ultimately affected the experiences of these new teachers.

In the next section, we briefly describe the teachers and the districts in which they work. These sketches illustrate both what these first-year teachers experienced and what districts provided in terms of language arts curricular and instructional policy.

WATERSIDE SCHOOL DISTRICT: ALLISON

Waterside (all names in this chapter are pseudonyms) operates 11 elementary schools, 2 middle schools, and 2 high schools. Of the 10,000 students served, 72% are Caucasian and 28% are students of color; 15% receive free or reduced-price lunches. At the time of our study, the district was in a transition, motivated in large part by the state reform. It invested heavily in interpreting state policy for teachers and administrators, trying to understand what the state-level assessments meant for students, teachers, and classroom practice. The district was also becoming more centralized, as it sought to create common assessments and curriculum guidelines across schools. For example, a district assessment team, created several years earlier, received training around the WASL and assessment issues in general. They were then responsible for training others in the district. Allison, our participant who worked in Waterside, was hired primarily to teach seventh-grade language arts, although she also taught one section of foreign language.

Curriculum

In spite of Waterside's shift toward greater centralization, the district continued to leave curricular decisions and implementation in the hands of schools and teachers. Allison relished this freedom to create her own curriculum. The school had a set of textbooks available for her use and a range of novels "articulated" for seventh grade by the district, but there was no formal curriculum she needed to teach. Drawing on resources from the school, department members, resource books, and the Internet, Allison developed several curriculum units in her first year. She shared these units with other department members and also borrowed and adapted units from colleagues. She remarked that her department was "trying to just put all of our stuff together, too, so that we can have a compilation put together for any new teachers who come in." An atmosphere of collaboration characterized the department, as well as a desire to provide new teachers with the curricular resources they often so desperately needed.

State Reform

Although Allison had a great deal of freedom in her curricular choices—freedom she appreciated—she recognized that she was responsible for teaching toward the district and state curriculum frameworks. She talked at some length about her role in addressing the EALRs in her classroom; in addition, she was acutely aware not only of the state reform efforts but also of her district's curriculum frameworks. Her sense of the importance of these goals and objectives was directly attributable to her district's efforts. Waterside had elected to rewrite the state standards for the district, making them more appropriate for its own needs, weaving in references to particular district curricula, and filling in specific benchmarks for each grade. Allison remarked that "everyone is always talking about the [district version of the state standards] now, and how they look as compared with the state essential learnings."

The Waterside district actively tried to help teachers learn how to connect their own curriculum and instruction to the state standards and assessments. Allison possessed a variety of state documents addressing the relationship between several different policy pieces, including the EARLs and samples of the state assessments (WASL). She was as familiar with the state test as she was with the learning standards. She described the enormous emphasis the district placed on the test: "It seemed like we were just WASLed out; we were constantly talking about the WASL and pulling out our WASL notebooks and doing practice tests in our staff meetings and familiarizing ourselves with the WASL."

Mentoring

The district provided Allison with a mentor teacher within her department. As part of the district's mentoring program, Allison and her mentor went to a districtwide meeting at the beginning of the year. At this time, they were introduced to, among other things, the district curriculum frameworks and the predictable ups and downs of the first year of teaching. Although Allison and her mentor did not share a common planning period and had difficulty meeting on a regular basis, Allison did borrow materials and ideas from her mentor. Allison's department chair also played an active role in her professional life. She sent Allison to several district workshops, including workshops on writing assessments, which Allison used extensively in her classroom. Throughout her first year, Allison spoke frequently of the exchange of materials that occurred in her department. When Allison had a question or concern about teaching language arts, help was close at hand.

PROSPECT HARBOR: FRANK AND NANCY

Prospect Harbor serves approximately 15,000 students in 16 elementary schools, 8 middle schools, and 6 high schools. Almost 69% of the students are Caucasian, while 31% are students of color. Approximately 18 percent of the students qualify for free or reduced-price lunches, although the range across schools is substantial (e.g., 3% to 46%). In recent years, the district has become increasingly diverse and, at the time of this study, was definitely a district in transition. A new superintendent had arrived a few years earlier and his charismatic personality, combined with the changes he initiated, made him a strongly felt presence in the district. Under his auspices, and in keeping with the district's move from site-based management to more centralized decision making, Prospect Harbor undertook a major effort to adopt new materials and align curriculum across schools and grades.

Frank was a seventh-grade middle school teacher in Prospect Harbor. Hired because he was able to teach both foreign language and language arts, Frank found that his first-year teaching schedule included those two subjects as well as social studies and an elective course. Nancy, who had an undergraduate major in English and a minor in psychology, was hired to teach both those subjects at a high school in Prospect Harbor. During her first year of teaching, she taught three sections of tenth-grade English, an American literature class, and a social science class.

Curriculum

Prospect Harbor was in the midst of its new curriculum adoption and alignment process when Frank and Nancy were hired. Consequently, while both teachers were left almost entirely to their own devices in terms of what to teach, they heard a lot of talk about the lack of curriculum and the impending arrival of district-mandated texts. As they began their work as teachers, Frank and Nancy felt frustrated and anxious about what to teach and how to structure their curriculum. Frank said that his language arts/social studies block class "has some guidelines you need to sort of touch on this kind of stuff, but otherwise it's very nebulous." Similarly, Nancy said, "It would have been nice if the English Department as a whole had a set curriculum so you knew what you were supposed to be teaching."

In response to the superintendent's concern over the variability of curriculum across the district, Prospect Harbor was actively adopting districtwide curriculum for all subjects and grade levels. During this year, social studies teachers, including Frank, piloted a new textbook series, while language arts teachers developed common course titles and sequences and decided on common texts for each grade level.

State Reform

Frank and Nancy both felt that the state frameworks did not affect what they were doing in their Prospect Harbor classrooms. While Nancy considered herself fluent with the EALRs, based on her student teaching experience in Waterside, she believed that Prospect Harbor was at least 2 years behind Waterside in designing a curriculum that addressed the state frameworks. She said, "I don't think half the teachers know what they are." Frank was uncertain about what the state reform might mean for his classroom, believing that his difficult schedule and the lack of curriculum forced him to make certain sacrifices. Instead of state reform, standards, and assessments, Frank was most concerned with the absence of curriculum and his search for materials. He assigned low priority to the WASL and felt no pressure from the school or district to emphasize the WASL or the EALRs. According to Frank, there was a sense that teachers should "try and keep those test scores up, but they don't lean on us or anything like that."

Mentoring

During Frank's and Nancy's first year of teaching, Prospect Harbor was just beginning a new mentoring system. Frank, in particular, was eager and willing to have a mentor. Unfortunately, because the system was new, Frank and his mentor did not establish a relationship until November. Early on in the schoolyear, he lamented the lack of a mentor and talked about the district's old system, which might have assigned him, as a mentor, a language arts teacher from his own school. Under the district's new system, Frank's mentor was responsible for mentoring all of the new middle school teachers, across all subject areas. While Frank and she developed a good relationship, and he looked to her for help in locating curriculum resources and for moral support when he became frustrated, she was not a language arts teacher. Consequently, she was not able to give him the subject-specific curriculum help that he sought.

Nancy also established a relationship with a mentor, who was responsible for all the district's new high school teachers. While Nancy was frustrated about the district's lack of curriculum and curriculum guidance, she was not experiencing as much difficulty as Frank. She noted that her mentor did not visit her school very often because he believed that she and the other new teacher in the building were "doing fine." Nancy also acknowledged that the conversations with her mentor centered on classroom management rather than subject-matter issues. Her mentor, a former math teacher, was not necessarily able to help her with the curriculum dilemmas she faced in language arts.

FOCUSING CONCERNS: DISTRICT POLICY AS LENS

Looking up from the classroom, we were able to track the ways in which these districts helped focus the concerns of beginning teachers. Working in a district and school that were "living the WASL," Allison spent more time than any other teacher in our study talking about the impact of the state curriculum frameworks and the WASL. Coming into a district that was abuzz with talk about the lack of curriculum and the impending required curriculum, Frank and Nancy worried about curriculum. In contrast, Allison, who had a similarly unspecified curriculum, relished the opportunity to construct her own.

Much of the literature on the concerns of beginning teachers has developed within a psychological framework, looking to the individual as the explanatory factor (Berliner, 1986; Fuller, 1969; Kagan, 1992). Although individual factors play some role in shaping the concerns of beginning teachers, our cases suggest a more sociocultural perspective on how such concerns develop. The contexts in which teachers work, including the district context, help draw the attention of beginning teachers to certain issues rather than others. Districts can provide a variety of lenses to focus teachers' attention on particular issues—through direct policies, including curriculum policy, standards, or assessment; and through implicit policies and learning opportunities they provide for new teachers. The particular design of mentoring programs, for example, may focus teachers' attention on issues of management or on issues of subject-matter instruction. Similarly, the content of professional development opportunities, and how individuals come to attend particular workshops, teaches teachers to pay attention to certain issues to the exclusion of others.

Although district policies provide a lens to focus teacher concerns, we also need to look at the degree of magnification provided by these lenses. In most of our cases in the broader sample, the districts provided relatively weak lenses for looking at teaching. These lenses, including the state curriculum frameworks or the policy of adopting a common set of texts for language arts, focused teachers' attention on the more superficial aspects of the language arts. One example of a relatively weak lens includes the state and district curriculum frameworks. Allison, the first-year teacher in Waterside, felt these frameworks were little more than common sense:

> When I read it [EALRs] now, I feel like "duh" . . . it seems so
> commonsensical, and I wonder if that's just because . . . these are
> the things I would think were important to teach anyway or if it's
> because I've been so inundated with these, that they're so ingrained

in my mind, after hearing them so much, I think . . . of course I would do that.

Because she saw the curriculum frameworks as common sense, they do not require her to question her own practices or to think deeply about what or how she teaches. The EALRs, for example, require that "students will learn to use the writing process"; the framework goes on to list five stages from prewriting through editing. This requirement, however, does not distinguish among more or less effective versions of engaging students in the writing process. In addressing this EALR, Allison adopted a formulaic unit plan on writing that did indeed lead students through all the steps of the writing process, but in a rather lockstep fashion. Students participated in prewriting of several kinds, drafting, revising, and editing. However, the plan allowed for very little student engagement with the writing, nor did it provide a meaningful context for writing. Allison never addressed the content of the papers during this unit, nor did she provide an audience or purpose for the essays. Using the EALRs as a lens for looking at writing instruction does not necessarily focus teachers' attention on these elements of their classroom practice. Since the EALRs do not provide conceptual definitions of the various writing stages, such as prewriting or revising, or address how these stages might be recursive rather than linear, they did not help Allison critique the version of the writing process represented in curriculum materials. The curriculum frameworks were so broad that they could not necessarily focus new teachers' attention on some of the key issues and dilemmas in the teaching of writing.

Similarly, Prospect Harbor's policy on curriculum addressed only what books to teach, not how to teach them. As a lens on practice, this policy focused teachers' attention on the selection of texts rather than on how those texts might be taught in the classroom. The policy seems to suggest that *which* texts are taught matters more than *how* the texts are taught. Such a lens on practice ignores the enormous variation in what students might learn from different approaches to instruction. What does it mean for student learning that all eleventh-graders read *The Scarlet Letter* rather than *The House on Mango Street*? From the perspective of curriculum enactment, how either book is taught makes all the difference in what students learn. Either book could be used to teach students the elements of fiction or to allow students to develop interpretive strategies. Students could be taught to look at texts from a historical or cultural perspective, or they might be taught that a text must stand on its own. This particular curriculum policy does not focus either on tasks for students—what students will do in the classroom—or on classroom interaction and discourse, two concepts identified by Spillane and Jennings (1997) as critical to looking at curriculum implementation. The district's decision to focus on core texts, absent a framework for thinking about goals for student understanding in literature and how instruction could support such goals, again provided a weak lens on classroom practice.

While district policy can serve as a lens to focus new teachers' concerns—teaching them, in effect, what to worry about—the lenses provided in these two districts drew teachers' attention to more superficial aspects of practice. A higher degree of magnification would have been required to help new teachers learn in more depth about the writing process or about the teaching of literature. In another one of our cases, a beginning teacher in a neighboring district was assigned to teach the Pacesetter curriculum, a curriculum designed as a capstone language arts course for high school seniors (Scholes, 1995). The decision to adopt the Pacesetter curriculum in this teacher's high school provided a stronger lens for looking at the teaching of language arts. Described as an "integrated program of standards, instruction, professional development, and assessments," the Pacesetter curriculum addresses a broader array of issues, including what to teach, how to teach it, and why one would even teach such a curriculum in the first place. The curriculum also comes with ample professional development opportunities that, in turn, are focused specifically on implementing this curriculum. Pacesetter focuses teachers' attention on more aspects of teaching—curriculum, instruction, assessment, and purposes for teaching language arts—and provides greater depth in its learning opportunities (Ball & Cohen, 1996). Other curriculum materials adopted by these districts, including portions of 6-Traits for the teaching of writing and First Steps for reading, both commercially prepared curriculum materials, did not specify much about the nature of instruction.

While leaving instructional decisions to teachers may be appropriate in many instances, if district policy is meant to influence student learning, it cannot entirely ignore issues of instruction. Research in math reform, for example, highlights the need to attend simultaneously to issues of curriculum and instruction. Adopting reform-oriented curriculum materials, without helping teachers understand how to enact such curriculum in their classrooms, is unlikely to change teachers' classroom practice in significant ways (Cohen, 1990).

Mentoring programs also differ in how they focused teachers' attention and the opportunities they provided for teacher learning. Generic mentoring programs, almost by definition, focus new teachers' attention on issues of classroom management and general survival, while subjectspecific mentoring programs focus teachers' attention on issues of teaching the language arts. We explore this issue in more depth below.

CHANNELS FOR SUBJECT-SPECIFIC LEARNING

These two districts differed in the opportunities provided for first-year teachers to learn about issues directly related to the language arts. While Allison had ample opportunities to get the curricular and instructional help she wanted for teaching language arts, Frank, with greater need, had much less opportunity. The difference in these teachers' opportunities to learn reflects district and school structures that channeled or thwarted subject-specific conversation. These structures included roles and responsibilities within the districts, lines of communication across the district, the design of mentoring programs, and the organization of teachers within schools.

In Waterside, several people were responsible for overseeing language arts instruction and were linked in various ways. The district employed a language arts coordinator who saw his job as working closely with school department chairs to provide information about district activities and to gather information about teachers' concerns and needs. The district also provided new teachers with mentors who were selected to be both subject- and site-specific. As a result of this policy, Allison had as her mentor an experienced English teacher at her school site, who provided her with curriculum resources and a ready ear. When Allison struggled with teaching prepositional phrases, she knew just where to go. The department chair of Allison's school, in turn, played an important role in the district. She had been an active participant in the district's work on standards for language arts and had served as a link between the district and the school. Because she had worked on the district curriculum frameworks for language arts, she served as a school-based resource for questions about district standards. She also provided informal mentoring for Allison and made sure that she attended workshops in the teaching of writing. The department as a whole was a supportive environment that encouraged the sharing of materials and ideas.

Frank's situation provides a stark contrast. At the height of site-based management, Prospect Harbor had eliminated curriculum specialists. At the time of our study, the district was in the process of resurrecting the role of language arts curriculum developer. The first person they hired did not have a history in the district and was weakly connected to the schools and department chairs. She saw her primary responsibility as overseeing the adoption of a districtwide curriculum. Department chairs, in turn, played a minor role in district affairs. While department chairs might be informal leaders in their schools, the district did not intentionally designate chairs to serve as instructional leaders, nor did it deliberately tap them to lead district reforms. Mentoring in this district was generic rather than subject-specific. Frank's assigned mentor was an experienced middle school teacher who had never taught language arts. Although his mentor tried hard to provide support, the curricular help Frank desperately needed for teaching language arts was beyond her scope. Because Frank's middle school was organized into cross-subject matter teams, rather than by department, Frank did not share Allison's ready access to language arts colleagues. Even the school's physical structure worked against him, since he worked on a hall populated primarily by social studies teachers. By the end of his first year of teaching, Frank was ready to abandon language arts for social studies, even though his college major had been English.

The cases of these first-year teachers indicate that their access to resources for teaching language arts was dependent, in large part, on school and district structures that channeled opportunities for learning to teach language arts. Waterside had a cohesive policy environment around the language arts; administrators were generally in agreement about a broad vision for the language arts, and professional development opportunities generally focused on frameworks for the teaching of reading and writing that were consistent with this larger vision. Curriculum specialists were teachers, located in schools. From this locale, they had an immediate sense of classroom teachers' needs as well as the kinds of resources available at the district level. The curriculum specialist in language arts, a former department chair himself, met regularly with the department chairs, providing another channel for information to flow both ways, from department to district and back again. Finally, at Allison's school, the department chair was seen as an instructional leader within the school and district, providing another channel for information to flow back and forth.

The channels in Prospect Harbor were less clearly organized around subject matter. The role of curriculum specialist had been newly resurrected and, in the year of our study, existed primarily to oversee the adoption of a common curriculum. The district did not invest in department chairs as instructional leaders, and chairs were only loosely connected to district activities. Frank's middle school did not have a functioning language arts department through which he might have received support. Even at the high school level, Nancy's department chair felt her position was only nominal. Finally, the structure of generic mentoring did not support subject-specific conversations about teaching and learning. As Nancy's and Frank's experiences illustrate, the mentoring program emphasized issues of classroom management and general support more than curriculum and instruction. Although this picture of generic professional development in Prospect Harbor is markedly different from that in Waterside, the situation may be more the norm than the exception: Even when the funds allocated to professional development increase significantly, there is some indication that neither the supply nor the demand for content-specific professional development seems to grow (Columbia Group, 1997; McDiarmid, 1999).

Channels connecting district and schools in Waterside flowed along subject-specific routes—from district, through language arts coordinator, through department chairs, to teachers. Just as importantly, these channels flowed both ways; the department chair and language arts coordinator were able to communicate subject-specific concerns and needs of teachers back to the district, even as they communicated district expectations to teachers. In contrast, the channels for subject-specific conversations in Prospect Harbor were continually deflected. The district designed few intermediate structures, such as department chairs or subject-matter specialists, to promote subject-specific conversation. The channel that did exist flowed only one way—downstream—from the central office to the schools.

This analysis suggests the importance of looking at intermediate structures within a district and how these structures are interconnected (Fullan, 1994). By taking a perspective that looks from the classroom up, it may be easier to see how intermediate structures bridge district policy and classroom practice.

THE DISTRICT AS TEACHER EDUCATOR

Much of the existing research on districts has looked at districts' roles in the lives of experienced teachers (e.g., Spillane & Jennings, 1997). Our analysis suggests that districts may play a particularly important role in the lives of new teachers. Unlike experienced teachers, for whom district reforms may require reconstruction of well-worn routines, new teachers are at the very beginning stages of constructing their classroom practice. The policy problem differs, in this respect, from the problems of attempting to change the knowledge, beliefs, or practice of very experienced teachers.

Districts can play powerful roles as teacher educators for beginning teachers, even if the teachers are only dimly aware of formal district policies. The tasks they assign to new teachers, the resources they provide, the learning environments they create, the assessments they design, and the conversations they provoke all have consequences for what first-year teachers come to learn about teaching the language arts and about teaching more generally. For example, one of the primary tasks set for teachers in Waterside was to become familiar with state and district curriculum frameworks. Much of teachers' professional development time was devoted to understanding and using these frameworks. Both through her own engagement in these efforts and the sustained involvement of her department chair, Allison developed a clear understanding of the district frameworks and incorporated them into her classroom curriculum. Prospect Harbor did not engage teachers in such a task. Instead, the district involved teachers in discussions of a common curriculum for the district, a conversation that both heightened these beginning teachers' concerns about their lack of existing curriculum and suggested that "curriculum" meant a common set of texts or textbooks. In both of these instances, the tasks assigned by the districts taught teachers a way to look at teaching and learning.

Mentoring programs serve as an important resource for beginning teachers. In fact, such programs could be viewed as curriculum for beginning teachers. Mentoring programs specify, both implicitly and explicitly, what beginning teachers should learn about teaching and provide resources to support that learning. To analyze this particular resource, however, it is important to look at how the curriculum is enacted, in part by looking at the conversations occurring between mentors and new teachers. Our analysis suggests that how mentoring programs are designed, particularly with regard to subject-matter specificity, may result in quite different opportunities for teacher learning.

Our analysis suggests that districts can play a critical role in fostering the learning of new teachers. By focusing their attention on substantive issues in the teaching of subject matter and by providing opportunities to address the subject-specific concerns of new teachers, districts can support beginning teachers as they struggle to meet the needs of all learners.

CHAPTER 9

District Policy Making and State Standards: A Cognitive Perspective on Implementation

JAMES P. SPILLANE

Districts matter. They matter because the response of local government agencies to state and federal policies influence implementation at the classroom level (Berman & McLaughlin, 1977; Firestone, 1989a). Implementation failure is not solely a function of local school districts' inability or unwillingness to carry out state and federal policy. It is, in part, a function of district leaders' understandings of policy messages and the manner in which they communicate these understandings to teachers. Drawing on a study of nine school districts' responses to state mathematics and science standards, this chapter examines the district's role in the implementation of state standards.

SITUATING THE WORK: THEORETICAL UNDERPINNINGS

The complex changes in instruction pressed by recent reforms will require substantial and focused learning on the part of local district leaders. Drawing from ideas about the "pedagogy of policy" (Cohen & Barnes, 1993), this chapter illuminates how district leaders—district administrators, curriculum specialists, and lead teachers, who, by virtue of formal position or informal role, develop and implement district policies—both learn from policy and "teach" it, or what they understand of it, to school administrators and teachers. Several lines of theory provide lenses for viewing what happens in these transactions.

School Districts and Instructional Renewal. Copyright © 2002 by Teachers College, Columbia University. All rights reserved. ISBN 0-8077-4266-X (pbk), ISBN 0-8077-4267-8 (cloth). Prior to photocopying items for classroom use, please contact the Copyright Clearance Center, Customer Service, 222 Rosewood Dr., Danvers, MA 01923, USA, tel. (508) 750-8400.

Learning from State Policy

Recent scholarship investigates the role of implementing agents' cognition in the implementation process, underscoring the fact that the instructional ideas that implementing agents construct from policy are critical in understanding their enactment of that policy (Cohen, Spillane, Jennings, & Grants, 1998; Lin, 1998; Spillane, 1999; Yanow, 1996). From a cognitive perspective, a key dimension of the implementation process concerns whether, *and in what ways*, implementing agents change their minds in response to policy (Spillane & Reimer, 2001). District leaders must decipher what a policy means to decide whether and how to ignore, adapt, or adopt it into local policies and practices.

Cognitive theory suggests that people use their prior knowledge and experiences to construct new understandings. Coming to know involves the reconstruction of existing knowledge rather than the passive absorption of knowledge (Anderson & Smith, 1987; Confrey, 1990). Moreover, cognition is influenced by the social, physical, and cultural contexts of the person (Brown, Collins, & Duguid, 1989; Resnick, 1991). Applying these ideas to policy implementation, implementers *construct* what a policy asks of them, and it is these understandings they respond to in implementing policy. Thus, the policy stimulus is not all that matters: Implementing agents' beliefs, knowledge, and experiences as well as their situation also influence the ideas they come to understand from policy (Spillane, 1998a).

District Policymaking as Teaching

School districts are not only interpreters of state and federal policies but also makers of local policies and programs designed to guide teachers' instructional practice. District leaders must figure out whether and *how* to communicate their understandings of the policy message(s) to schools. Classroom teachers' learning from and about state policy will depend *in some measure* on district leaders' approach to teaching them.

Teacher learning can mean different things depending on one's conceptual perspective. Three perspectives on learning—quasi-behaviorism, the situative-sociohistoric view, and the quasi-cognitive view (Greeno, Collins, & Resnick, 1996)—help frame this exploration of district leaders' thinking about teacher learning. The behaviorist perspective, associated with B. F. Skinner, is concerned with actions (behavior) as the sites of knowing, teaching, and learning, and transmission as the instructional mode. To promote transmission, complex tasks are deconstructed into component subskills that must be mastered sequentially from simple to complex

(Gagne, 1965). Learning is externally motivated and involves developing correct reactions to external stimuli.

The situative-sociohistoric perspective (Hutchins, 1995; Lave, 1988; Resnick, 1991) regards individuals as inseparable from their communities and environments and views knowledge as distributed in the social, material, and cultural artifacts of the environment. Learning involves developing practices and abilities valued in specific communities and situations. With respect to motivation, learning opportunities need to be organized to encourage participation in inquiry and learning, support the learner's identity as skilled inquirer, and enable the learner to develop the disciplinary practices of discourse and argumentation.

From the cognitive perspective, knowledge includes reflection, conceptual growth and understanding, problem solving (Newell & Simon, 1972), and reasoning. Learning involves the active reconstruction of the learner's existing knowledge structures, rather than passive assimilation or rote memorization, with learners using personal resources including prior knowledge and experiences to construct new knowledge (Anderson & Smith, 1987; Confrey, 1990). The motivation to learn is intrinsic. Learning activities engage students' interest and prior knowledge, sequence their conceptual development, and introduce students to the core principles of a domain.

This chapter primarily draws on interview data that were coded along theoretical lines. These data reflect instructional policy making in nine Michigan school districts and the effects of national, state, and local policies on mathematics and science teaching or instruction (Spillane, 1999; Spillane & Zeuli, 1999). Districts were selected to represent variation in geographic location in the state, size and urbanization, student social and ethnic demographics, and reputation for instructional innovation (see Table 9.1). Data collected from 1994–1995 included interviews with local leaders, board members, and parents, as well as local policy documents such as curriculum guides, annual reports, policy statements, and listings of professional development workshops. (For additional methodological information, see Spillane, 2000a, in press; Spillane & Callahan, 2000.)

Making Sense of State and National Standards at the Local Level: A New Vision for Mathematics Education

Many national and state standards urge a reconceptualization of school mathematics and what counts as worthwhile mathematical knowledge. These reforms argue that school mathematics involves understanding central mathematical concepts and that "principled" mathematical knowledge, as distinct from "procedural" knowledge, should receive more attention

Table 9.1. Characteristics of School Districts

District	Student Enrollment	Students Eligible for Free or Reduced-Price Lunches (%)	Ethnic Minority Population (%)	Community Type
A	19,000–26,000	50–65	40–50	Mid-sized city
B	19,000–26,000	50–65	More than 60	Mid-sized city
C	1,000–5,000	50–65	More than 60	Mid-sized city
D	10,000–18,000	5–10	Less than 5	Suburban
E	5,000–10,000	10–20	5–10	Suburban
F	1,000–2,000	10–20	Less than 5	Rural
G	500–1,000	30–40	Less than 5	Rural
H	500–1,000	70–80	20–30	Rural
I	Less than 500	40–50	Less than 5	Rural

(Greeno, Riley, & Gelman, 1984; Lampert, 1992; Leinhardt, 1985). While procedural knowledge centers on computational procedures, principled knowledge focuses on the mathematical concepts that undergird these procedures. Reformers also propose that students learn to appreciate doing mathematics as framing and solving mathematical problems and reasoning with others about mathematical ideas (Lampert, 1992; National Council of Teachers of Mathematics [NCTM], 1989, 1991).

The NCTM (1989, 1991) captures these substantive changes in mathematics education under four themes—mathematics as problem solving, mathematics as communication, mathematics as reasoning, and mathematical connections. According to the NCTM, problem solving should permeate the entire mathematics program, providing a context for learning both principled and procedural knowledge. Similarly, mathematics as communication should also be central because students need to appreciate mathematics as a way of representing ideas; they need opportunities to "speak mathematics" so that they can clarify their thinking and appreciate different ways of representing mathematical ideas. The Michigan Department of Education's standards for mathematics education, although not elaborated to the same extent as standards in some other states, were reasonably compatible with national standards (Goertz, Floden, & O'Day, 1995; Thompson, Spillane, & Cohen, 1994).

The School District Response

All nine districts in the study had either revised their existing curricular policies or were in the process of putting in place policies that specified topic coverage that was consistent with the mathematics reforms (Spillane, 1999; Spillane & Thompson, 1997). Still, as argued above, the mathematics reforms sought more than a revision of the coverage and sequencing of mathematics topics. Hence, topic alignment alone can be considered as a low level of implementation. Local school districts had made much less progress in aligning their local policies and programs with the more fundamental changes in what counted as mathematical knowledge and doing mathematics. Indeed, we found evidence of substantial moves toward these more fundamental changes in only three districts—two suburban and one rural. For example, in six of the nine districts, district reform initiatives did not reflect several central themes of the mathematics reforms, including communication and reasoning. Despite considerable local district attention to and efforts to implement the state and national standards, only three districts had high levels of implementation (i.e., they were implementing the standards in ways that resonated with their core elements).

District Leaders' Learning from Standards

One explanation for this variation in implementation involves the sense district leaders made of the standards. District leaders' accounts of what it meant to "do the mathematics reforms" suggest that they tended to miss the intended functions of the reforms, focusing instead on their forms. Form-focused understandings refer to pedagogical forms such as learning activities, students' work, instructional materials, and grouping arrangements (Gearhart, Harding, Saxe, & Troper, 1997; Saxe, Gearhart, Franke, Howard, & Crockett, 1999). Functional understandings center on what counts as mathematical knowledge, doing mathematics, and learning and knowing mathematics. From this functional view, collaboration, problem solving, and using manipulatives—ideas that figured in district leaders' talk about the reforms—enable students to develop understandings of principled mathematical knowledge and to appreciate doing mathematics as more than computation.

Sixty-five of the 82 district leaders interviewed (79%) expressed form-focused understandings that centered on using manipulatives to teach mathematics, new grouping arrangements, and more real-life story problems. These forms of instruction were understood in terms of existing pedagogical functions, thereby preserving the conventional view of mathematics as procedural knowledge. Hence, district leaders' understanding of the mathematics reforms shifted the focus of the reforms to a reconfigured means to a familiar end. Consider some examples.

While most district leaders recognized problem solving as representing change for mathematics education, their understandings were mostly form-focused. One sort of understanding focused on the form of the mathematical problems and involved the development of more realistic story problems and problem situations connected to real-life situations. From this local perspective, the mathematics reforms involved changing the form of the story problems without making any changes to what counted as mathematics in the K–12 curriculum. Their understandings were firmly grounded in a procedural conception of mathematics and a computation-focused perception of doing mathematics. For these district leaders, problem solving did not involve placing greater emphasis on principled mathematical knowledge.

The situation was similar with respect to district leaders' understanding of "hands-on," the most prominent descriptor they used to describe the standards. A common perspective of hands-on mathematics involved the use of manipulatives. Hands-on activities were perceived as important because they increased student retention, interest in, and enjoyment of mathematics. A district leader, for example, argued, "We're finding that [student] retention is better and teachers and students are liking it better, and that's why we started to go with the manipulatives." Another leader remarked, "I'm hoping that it really catches on and, you know, with the hands-on type of thing, I think it is a little better, you are going to remember a few more things with it, I think." For these district leaders, manipulatives reinforced a procedural understanding of mathematics. Even when probed, they said nothing to indicate that hands-on mathematics represented any change in the mathematical content of the K–12 curriculum.

While representing instructional change, these form-focused understandings miss a core element of the mathematics reforms. Reformers are clear that problem solving involves more than making problems more interesting and relevant to everyday life. Problem-solving, in their view, means making the mathematics problematic so that students can explore why things are and consider different conjectures (NCTM, 1989, 1991).

There was a striking relationship between district leaders' understandings of the mathematics reforms and level of implementation by their district. Specifically, district leaders in the three high-implementation districts were more likely to hold function-focused understandings of the reforms.

Of the 17 district leaders who expressed function-focused understandings, only 3 (18%) worked in one of the 6 low-implementation districts, while 14 (82%) worked in the high-implementation districts. Fifty-one of the 65 district leaders who expressed form-focused understandings worked in one of the 6 low-implementation districts (78%). While a causal relationship cannot be inferred, our analysis does suggest that district leaders' understanding of reform is an important explanatory variable in the implementation process.

DISTRICT LEADERS' PERSPECTIVES ON TEACHER LEARNING

District leaders' ability to support teachers' implementation of the standards also depends on how they communicate their understandings of the policy message(s) to teachers. District leaders' beliefs about and knowledge of teacher learning and change also are important considerations. The study's nine school districts used four formal channels to shape classroom teaching and learning: curriculum guides, curricular materials, student assessment, and professional development. Leaders in some districts also used informal strategies to press for instructional changes, including recruiting teachers and encouraging them to participate in state curriculum committees. The analysis here, however, goes beyond the structural features of district professional development, such as format and duration, to explore district leaders' theories about teacher learning.

District leaders' theories about instructional change and teacher learning fell into three categories: the quasi-behaviorist, the situated, and the quasi-cognitive. This analysis focuses on a subsample of 40 district leaders—ranging from 4 leaders in smaller districts to 6 in larger districts—who took a central role in selecting or designing learning opportunities for teachers. Of these leaders, 10 were district office subject-matter specialists; 19 were district office assistant superintendents, directors, or coordinators with responsibility for curriculum and instruction (including professional development); 6 were school administrators; and 5 were classroom teachers.

The quasi-behaviorist perspective was the most prevalent, with 34 of the 40 district leaders (85%) supporting this perspective. (District leaders did not use terms such as *behaviorist*, *situated*, and *cognitive*, but instead less technical language in talking about teacher learning.) Five of the 40 district leaders (13%) expressed a situated perspective, which featured prominently among those responsible for reforming mathematics instruction in one rural district. One district leader expressed a quasi-cognitive perspective, though there was some evidence that this perspective was emerging among three or four other district leaders. This next section compares these perspectives in four domains: ideas about teaching teachers, teacher learning, the curriculum for teacher learning, and teachers' motivation to learn.

Ideas About Teaching Teachers

District leaders in the quasi-behaviorist category understood teaching teachers as the transmission of knowledge from expert to novice. A district curriculum specialist explained, "We filter the information down to them . . . we can disseminate the information down to the teachers." Similarly, another district leader remarked, "Teachers . . . need to have some new ideas brought in and demonstrated in their classroom . . . and have someone else do the demonstration." Another noted, "I think teachers will become receptive when they see that it works. And it is a matter of bringing to them a picture of it working." District leaders primarily instructed teachers through "show and tell," treating knowledge as a commodity that could be deposited in teachers' minds. Transmitters of knowledge for instructional change included external consultants, district specialists, and teachers who had received specialized training. As one district leader noted, "I think probably what I need to do is to get one of those individuals in here out of California someplace to talk with the group so it's more firsthand."

In contrast to district leaders in the situated category, who identified local and outside experts as important agents in the teacher learning and instructional change process, quasi-behaviorist leaders accorded local teacher leaders a central role in the education of their peers. For example, one district leader commented:

> You have to have teacher leaders who will . . . confront one another and who will question one another in a positive, professional way and say, "What are we doing? Is this working? Why are we doing this?" And talking [sic] about the things that go on in the classrooms every day.

These district leaders believed that lead teachers were important because they simultaneously were situated in teaching practice and had in-depth understanding of the reforms, a combination that enabled them to help other teachers translate reform ideas into practice. They also understood the exchange of ideas among regular classroom teachers to be an important occasion for teacher learning. Unlike the quasi-behaviorist focus on transmission, knowledge was something that learners constructed. A district leader explained:

I would push for teachers to have release time to go watch one another, push for the conversations to happen. . . . It all goes back to the culture . . . as a classroom teacher when my door is closed, I do what I wanna do. And that's the culture we're trying to change. No, we are a community of learners just like your classroom is a community of learners.

Conversations among peers provided opportunities to grapple with and develop an appreciation for the meaning of reform proposals for practice.

For the district leader in the quasi-cognitive category, teaching teachers involved getting them to reflect on existing knowledge, experience, and practice; challenging their current thinking; and guiding them toward new understandings. In contrast to the situated perspective, thinking and reflection was an individual rather than a social process. This district leader understood her role as "peeling the layers back" so teachers could develop an appreciation of their learning needs to revise their science teaching.

Ideas About Teacher Learning

For district leaders in the quasi-behaviorist category, learning involved remembering and following advice. Teachers as learners were understood chiefly in terms of their preferences for professional development. One district leader noted how teachers began to come up with topics they thought were important for professional development, and she then organized professional development on some of these topics. While district leaders in the quasi-behaviorist perspective focused on engaging teachers as learners on the level of their preferences, the district leader in the quasi-cognitive category focused on the level of their prior knowledge, beliefs, and experiences. In her view, teachers' learning depended on their reconstructing their existing knowledge and beliefs, rather than memorizing new knowledge. Teachers' prior knowledge and practice were central to their learning.

From the perspective of those in the situated category, learning communities that fostered conversations among peers were central in teacher learning. A teacher leader in this category recounted an experience with a mentor, remarking, "He was always focusing on the kids. . . . 'What do you think went well today?' 'Who do you think was insightful and what is your evidence?' 'And who do you think is struggling and what is your evidence?'" The teacher leader noted how this experience helped her to see aspects of instruction not previously noticed and to listen to students' ideas: "As I started to listen, there were two things that happened. I found out my kids knew a lot more than I thought they knew, but they also had a lot more gaps than I realized they had, things that I had taken for granted that weren't there." Listening to students helped the teacher leader learn about and change mathematics instruction.

Thus, for district leaders in the situated category, learning focused not only on understanding reform ideas but also on translating these ideas into practice and figuring out how to manage the practical challenges that emerged in the process. Participating in discussions about practice, teachers were active agents in one another's learning. Learning involved teachers participating in inquiry and reflection about their practice and in solving pedagogical problems that were meaningful to teachers as learners.

Ideas About the Curriculum for Teacher Learning

For district leaders who expressed a quasi-behaviorist perspective, the curriculum for teacher learning included workshops and in-class demonstration lessons conducted by either external or local experts, videotapes of teaching, and curricular materials. Curricular content included an array of topics that were integrated only at a very general level, including content knowledge; pedagogical knowledge; generic teaching strategies; and knowledge of materials, technology, and the content of the teacher learning. According to one leader:

> We've done . . . cooperative learning. We've worked 'em [teachers] in outcome based education. . . . We're looking at . . . going into authentic and performance-based assessment, and really the object is to have the teachers as the trained assessor[s] and using the teacher as the primary assessment tool for instruction.

The curriculum for teacher learning consisted of a melange of discrete topics, and district leaders never discussed how these different components might be integrated into a coherent body of knowledge about teaching for teachers. Curriculum coherence was mostly understood at a very broad level, such as professional development that helped teachers learn about preparing their students for taking the mathematics component of the Michigan Educational Assessment Program (MEAP). For those in the quasi-behaviorist category, then, knowledge was treated in separate chunks, broken into different categories, often by external professional development providers. There was also little acknowledgment that teachers might need help in integrating these different pieces.

There were at least two differences between the quasi-behaviorist perspective and the situated perspective with respect to the curriculum for teacher learning. First, those in the situated category designed curriculum to support teachers' learning about the reform ideas as embodied in experts' proposals *and* to support their learning about translating these ideas into practice. Second, unlike their counterparts, they understood classroom curricula, daily teaching practice, and students' work as central components of the curriculum for teachers' learning. A lead district teacher explained, "She [mentee] came in my class a lot . . . I kept saying whenever you can, come into my room and we can talk about it." Even when these opportunities for teacher learning were organized outside the school, teaching practice and students' work were central components. One district leader said:

> The kids are there for 2 hours during the training and then the rest of the training, we do . . . a lot of talking about what we've just done . . . we talk about . . . the actual materials . . . and the teaching techniques. . . . We do a lot of talking about the NCTM standards . . . and the research . . . and . . . try to integrate all of those.

The curriculum for teacher learning enabled ongoing inquiry about the ideas advanced in reform proposals *and* implications for day-to-day mathematics practice.

Similar to the situated perspective, the district leader who supported the quasi-cognitive perspective believed that the curriculum for teacher learning should be integrated around the classroom curriculum and cover subject-matter and pedagogical knowledge. The curriculum for teacher learning was developed from teachers' needs as expressed by teachers and observed by the science coordinator, not just their general preferences for professional development or a consideration of the reform proposals for science education.

Ideas About Teachers' Motivation to Learn

District leaders in the quasi-behaviorist category believed that external motivation through the use of rewards and sanctions was important for teacher learning. One district leader commented, "Well, there is a certain amount of resistance at times. Many of them will indicate that they are interested; however, in actuality, very little change takes place in the room." Others identified inertia as one of the chief barriers to changing practice.

District leaders in this category believed that a variety of policy levers were essential in motivating teachers to learn and change, including monitoring instruction, state assessment, and resource allocation. One district leader noted, "Right from the beginning we [said our district] will support strong educational practices and that they will be monitored. One of our problems is, I think, [as with] with many districts, we have the curriculum, [but] if it isn't monitored, it isn't taught." State assessment instruments and the materials and professional development opportunities available to classroom teachers were other ways of motivating teacher change and learning. A district leader noted, "If I see a purchase not relating to what we are supposed to be doing, or if I have an opportunity to buy something that promotes, ah, the content things that we are talking about, then I can do that." These district leaders used extrinsic motivators.

In contrast, district leaders who expressed a situated perspective understood the motivation for teachers to learn and change as more social and intrinsic to teachers' local communities of practice. Motivation was about teachers' developing and sustaining identities as knowers and learners in their school communities. An administrator remarked, "We have strong teacher leaders in mathematics in each of our buildings . . . who push it [reform] all the time. That is one huge factor." A critical mass of teacher leaders helped convince other teachers that the new ideas about mathematics education were legitimate and important for students. Commenting about how a critical mass is formed, one teacher noted that another teacher "dragged us along" initially; in time, they started "dragging [in] others. I guess because, you know, it was a teacher-initiated kind of thing and teachers are willing to get busy and get involved in it." Peer encouragement motivated teachers to reform their practice.

Implementing new ideas in their practice—and observing the students' responses—introduced another incentive for teachers to change. Teachers noticed changes in students' learning, and they reported that these changes altered their expectations for what students were capable of doing. One teacher remarked, "I see it with the kids. They just come up with things that years ago, we probably wouldn't have thought they were capable of. They have . . . a lot more mathematical sense than what we give them credit for." Another teacher said, "They [students] can feel confident [about mathematics] and . . . I do see kids that are not necessarily the best students, but still they feel confident and aren't afraid to take the challenge on, even if they don't necessarily succeed at it 100% or whatever." Undertaking changes in teaching within supportive communities of practice motivated teachers to learn from their students' talk and from work with peers. Observing students' interest in and success with mathematics change also inspired teachers to continue with their reform efforts. Nevertheless, these district leaders did not ignore extrinsic motivation, applying pressure to teachers who continued to resist reform.

For the district leader in the quasi-cognitive category, engagement with learning involved a combination of extrinsic and intrinsic motivation, with extrinsic motivators seen as a way of activating teachers' intrinsic motivation to learn and change. Delivering "ready-to-use classroom materials"—student readings, handouts, pre- and post-tests, equipment and consumable supplies necessary to teach a particular science unit to teachers' classrooms—this district leader created incentives for teachers to revise their science teaching. While teachers were not required to use the materials, they were required to cover the same conceptual material, to meet the same district and state objectives, and to document the materials and methods they used to meet these objectives. Because the units were designed to meet these objectives, teachers who used the kits could show compliance by completing and signing a checklist included with the materials instead of generating their own documentation—creating an added incentive to use these units. This district leader believed that these extrinsic motivators would give way to intrinsic motivation as teachers began to change their practice.

DISTRICT LEADERS AND INSTRUCTIONAL CHANGE: INDIVIDUAL AGENCY AND SOCIAL STRUCTURE

The predominance of the quasi-behaviorist perspective in part reflects dominant societal conceptions of teaching as telling and learning as remembering (Cohen, 1988). An extended "apprenticeship of observation" (Lortie, 1975) in school, the home, and other institutions reinforces this perspective for most individuals, including district leaders. Furthermore, district leaders' work is structured in particular ways. These structural arrangements constrain their thinking about instructional change and help account for the predominance of the quasi-behaviorist perspective. The two aspects of structural arrangements that are especially relevant are relations between the district leader and the classroom teacher and the fragmentation of district leaders' responsibilities and functions.

The Structure of Relations Between Teachers and District Leaders

The teacher–student relationship is fraught with tension (Cohen, 1988; Jackson, 1986; Lortie, 1975). Similar tensions are evident in the way relations between district leaders and classroom teachers are structured. District leaders who want to facilitate teacher learning and change, especially those using a situated or cognitive approach, have to gain the confidence of teachers if they are to understand teachers' learning needs and build learning opportunities on teachers' prior knowledge and experience. At the same time, district leaders are also often placed in the position of evaluating teachers and instructional change, and monitoring the implementation of reform initiatives. Therefore, teachers often have good reason not to confide in district leaders, covering up their failure to understand new instructional approaches and camouflaging their implementation failures.

Recent policy developments exacerbate these tensions, especially the press by state agencies for accountability and tangible results in the form of student test scores. State accountability mechanisms having tangible sanctions for failure to comply put district leaders in the position of pressuring school principals and teachers to show results. One district leader summed up the situation:

> They [district administrators] really are putting [on] pressure— especially on the principals. The principals are feeling most pressure and . . . they need to come up with strategies . . . that will improve the [state test] scores at their building level, or they may find [them]selves in big trouble. . . . You know, when your back is up against the wall . . . you gotta do something . . . administration puts pressure on the principal, the principal [puts it] on the teachers.

In putting pressure on principals and teachers to show results, district leaders are less likely to gain the confidence of their teachers/learners. These circumstances work against the use of situated and quasi-cognitive approaches to teacher learning and promote a quasi-behaviorist perspective that does not require district leaders to gain in-depth understandings of teachers' existing knowledge and beliefs. State timelines for compliance also complicate matters for district leaders. Pressed to meet these timelines, they often hurriedly put together programs to support teacher learning. Whether teachers learned and the depth of their learning were often secondary to compliance with state regulations.

An additional challenge complicates relations between district leaders and teachers. Getting the sustained attention of the teacher as learner was not an easy task given the multitude of instructional changes in mathematics, science, literacy, and social studies that teachers were expected to undertake. A suburban mathematics coordinator remarked:

> But one of the things that slows us down . . . is that we've had in the last 5 years . . . just a lot of things happen. . . . It's just that 15 things are coming at 'em [teachers] at the same time. . . . And all of a sudden they [teachers] say, "wait a minute, you know. I can only handle so many of these things at the same time." . . . If you get too many things—positive things—happening to you, you're overwhelmed.

Teacher overload complicated district leaders' efforts to focus and sustain teachers' attention on a particular topic.

District Leaders' Responsibilities

Relations between district leaders and classroom teachers were affected by the fragmented nature of leaders' work, which, in effect, promoted a quasi-behaviorist perspective of teacher learning and instructional change. An analysis of the interview transcripts of the study's 40 district leaders suggests that most had a variety of responsibilities, including writing grants, procuring curricular materials, organizing and carrying out professional development, developing curricular materials, and completing regulatory paperwork. In smaller districts, local leaders often also had a full-time classroom teaching load. One explained:

> In a small school system you become a little bit of everything. You're . . . a leader for the staff, and you should be a model for the students, and at times, you're a custodian and a janitor and a little bit of a counselor. . . . It's my job to facilitate student learning and professional development for staff.

Even in larger suburban and urban school districts where mathematics and science specialists were more common, these district leaders were responsible for diverse functions. District leaders reported that, because of their diverse portfolios, the task of educating teachers often fell below their other priorities. As one district leader said:

> My real passion is working with teachers, so when I have to be in here [district office] and coordinate stuff and can't get out there . . . I miss that part of the job. . . . And you can't do that kind of training and do coordinating, too, because time doesn't allow it.

A quasi-behaviorist approach enabled district leaders to tackle these tasks in a way that reduced the time and energy burden. A situated or cognitive approach to this task would have required much more time.

To complicate matters, the ratio of district leaders to teachers, in most districts, was high. Typically, district leaders had hundreds of teachers to inform about change. One local leader remarked:

> Part of my job is to go in and provide demonstration lessons, and that sometimes is difficult because . . . I'm one person working in the area of language arts with approximately a 100 [teachers]. And

to be really effective . . . it would be nice if I could work with that teacher on a Monday and then perhaps go back in on a Wednesday and follow it up. That really isn't possible with the number of teachers we have at this point.

Under these circumstances, tailoring instruction to the learning needs of particular teachers was difficult. A quasi-behaviorist approach was more manageable than either a situated or cognitive approach because it allowed local leaders to package knowledge so it could be taught more efficiently by one or two consultants to many teachers.

CONCLUSION

This account illuminates the cognitive dimension of the implementation process, underscoring that what district leaders learn from and about policy and how they teach what they learn from and about policy to school-level actors are critical dimensions of the implementation process. Although district leaders understood the mathematics reforms as representing change for their existing mathematics programs, and they pursued the enactment of these ideas, their understandings of the reforms tended to miss the full import of reformers' proposals. Looking beneath the structures and forms of district professional development programs to examine district leaders' theories about teacher learning and change, my analysis showed that a quasi-behaviorist perspective dominated among these leaders. As discussed, the predominance of the quasi-behaviorist perspective was supported by the relations between the district leader as change agent and the classroom teacher and by the fragmentation of district leaders' responsibilities.

This analysis underscores the complexity of the task that state and national reformers face in communicating their proposals for change to district leaders. As the data suggest, stronger accountability mechanisms are unlikely to be sufficient to get local school districts to implement state instructional policies in ways that reflect their core intent. Carrots and sticks of various sorts can get district leaders to pay attention to state policies, but they cannot ensure that district leaders learn what state policy makers intended them to learn. While state policies cannot ensure that district leaders learn, they can *represent* reform ideas in ways that are more likely to enable district leaders' learning about these ideas. State and national policy makers will have to think carefully about how they might design policies that take district leaders' understandings and thinking about classroom instruction and mathematics into account—that is, their prior knowledge as learners. A key task involves figuring out how to *represent* ideas about reforming instruction so that they enable district leaders to develop function-focused understandings of the reforms. The patterns in district leaders' understandings of the mathematics reforms documented in this chapter highlight potential starting points for this task.

A second challenge for school reformers illuminated by this analysis concerns the role of district leader as teacher educator. Unless state and national reformers create opportunities for district leaders to develop conceptions of teacher learning and change that are different from the quasi-behaviorist perspective, the training paradigm that dominates school districts' approach to professional development (Little, 1993a) is likely to persist. Alternative models of professional development may help, but district leaders are likely to adapt these alternative models to fit with their existing theory about teacher learning.

NOTE

This report is based on research supported in part by the National Science Foundation under Grant No. OSR-9250061. The Consortium for Policy Research in Education (CPRE), which is supported by a grant (No. OERI-R308A60003) from the National Institute on Educational Governance, Finance, Policymaking and Management (U.S. Department of Education), and Northwestern University's School of Education and Social Policy, and Institute for Policy Research supported work on this paper. All opinions, findings, and conclusions expressed in this report are those of the author and do not necessarily reflect the views of any of the funding agencies. Various sections of this paper draw on previous work: Spillane (1999, 2000a, 2000b, in press).

CHAPTER 10

Leadership for Learning: A Theory of Action for Urban School Districts

LAUREN B. RESNICK AND THOMAS K. GLENNAN, JR.

In the national drive to raise school achievement, urban school districts pose the greatest challenges. These districts serve the vast majority of poor, minority, and immigrant children in the country. As various achievement indicators have begun to creep upward for the nation as a whole, poor and minority students have largely been bypassed, and early gains in reducing achievement gaps have not been maintained. Achievement levels are low in urban districts, even when controlling for their level of poverty. On the 1994 National Assessment of Educational Progress (NAEP) reading test, for example, only 23% of fourth-graders in high-poverty urban schools achieved at the basic level or above. This statistic compares with 46% of students in high-poverty schools in nonurban areas; in nonpoverty schools, 69% of fourth-graders were ranked at the basic level above ("Quality Counts," 1998).

Urban schools generally have a more difficult time attracting and holding well-prepared teachers. Leadership turns over rapidly; only 20% of urban superintendents have been on the job 5 years, and 29% have been in their current districts less than 1 year. Despite the fact that urban schools serve students who are more needy, urban school expenditures per pupil are close to national averages and have been increasing much less rapidly than average expenditures nationally (Council of Great City Schools, 2000; "Quality Counts," 1998).

Daunting as these statistics are, there is evidence that careful and sustained attention to the quality of instruction and the conditions of learning can make a difference to urban students. A growing number of individual schools can document successes with urban student populations. Studies have begun to uncover the institutional conditions conducive to higher-

School Districts and Instructional Renewal. Copyright © 2002 by Teachers College, Columbia University. All rights reserved. ISBN 0-8077-4266-X (pbk), ISBN 0-8077-4267-8 (cloth). Prior to photocopying items for classroom use, please contact the Copyright Clearance Center, Customer Service, 222 Rosewood Dr., Danvers, MA 01923, USA, tel. (508) 750-8400.

quality instruction and better learning. These include extensive professional development of certain types (e.g., Ball & Cohen, 1999; Briars & Resnick, 2000; Resnick & Harwell, 2000), smaller class size (Finn & Achilles, 1999), careful monitoring of student achievement, and a focus on classroom learning at all levels of a district hierarchy (Elmore & Burney, 1997a).

Evidence ranging from school case studies to large-scale quantitative studies now strongly suggests that, given high-quality learning opportunities, poor and minority students can succeed academically according to measures ranging from achievement test scores to college entrance and completion. The issue today is not whether it is possible for urban students to learn well, but rather how good teaching and, therefore, learning can become the norm rather than the exception in urban education settings. The problem, in other words, is taking powerful teaching and learning to scale in urban school districts. We believe that this cannot be done without organized support for a new form of education leadership. This will require substantial redesign of urban school districts along with more powerful external support systems to help districts in the process of redesign and leadership development.

FORCES INHIBITING HIGH PERFORMANCE
IN URBAN SCHOOL DISTRICTS

Several cultural and managerial features of urban school districts guarantee that converting them into functional agents of reform will be a considerable challenge. Thirty or more years of experience and research point to some of these features. School districts in general and urban districts in particular possess bureaucratized management structures that tend to provide fragmented direction, often reinforced by the demands of funding and regulatory agencies (Hill, 2000; Hill, Pierce, & Guthrie, 1997; Tyack, 1974; Wise, 1979).

In the past two decades, many reform initiatives have called for devolving management responsibility to the school level (Bimber, 1994; Fullan, 1991; Hill & Bonan, 1991). In practice, this often occurs without corresponding devolution of authority and without changing the theories of professionalism that shape school building leadership. Too often the result is paralyzing confusion in school governance (Hill, Campbell, & Harvey, 2000; Hill & Celio, 1998).

In many districts, efforts to reform schooling are further hampered by rules associated with collective-bargaining agreements that constrain the use of staff time and the functions of management. These rules, which may sometimes reflect past managerial abuses, can limit, shape, and derail reforms involving changes in ways of working and using staff time. Even when local unions have actively supported reform, working within collective-bargaining agreements adds significant complexity to reform efforts (McDonnell & Pascal, 1988).

Districts' Limited Capacity for Instructional Support

With most time and attention swallowed by management and political concerns, usually little central focus remains in urban school districts on what Elmore (1996) has persuasively termed the *instructional core*. Education reform in America has typically involved tinkering with bureaucratic arrangements and oversight systems while leaving details of instruction to teachers (Elmore, 1996, 2000; Tyack & Cuban, 1995). Even though the last 30 years have seen a veritable revolution in our understanding of learning and teaching (Resnick & Hall, 1998), so-called reform efforts have generally proceeded without systematic reference to this vast body of research and increasingly refined practice. One exception lies in the demands in the past 2 or 3 years for scientifically grounded instruction in reading (U.S. Department of Education, Reading Excellence Program, 2000). However, we have yet to see these demands, generally imposed by federal programs or state boards, go to scale.

Despite calls in virtually every major reform proposal of the last decade for vastly improved professional development services for teachers, most of those services have been narrow, episodic, and frequently tied to external categorical programs. The diffused control of professional development resources, coupled with frequently inept preparation and recruitment of new teachers, leads to inadequate development of professional competencies and cultures (Ball & Cohen, 1999; Miles & Guiney, 2000; National Commission on Teaching and America's Future, 1996). Meanwhile, district administrators, from principals to central office staff, spend relatively little time in classrooms and even less time in analyzing instruction with teachers. They may arrange time for teachers' meetings and professional development, but they rarely provide intellectual leadership for growth in teaching skill (Fink & Resnick, 2001).

The structure of large school districts makes it difficult for administrators to provide instructional leadership. Educators seeking career opportunities beyond the individual classroom usually have to choose between an administrative track (the "line") or a curriculum and professional development track ("school support"). Those who enter the administrative track, typically by first becoming assistant principals, become more and more distant from questions of instruction and learning. Training programs for principals typically reinforce these conventions, focusing primary attention on a myriad of administrative competencies and devoting little attention to questions of learning, curriculum, and professional development.

Various movements for teacher empowerment have further exacerbated this pattern of distancing administrative leaders from instruction and learning. Unions and others have seemed to argue that pedagogy is the professional purview of the individual teacher and that a supervisor's or a principal's intervention intrudes on the teacher's professional judgment and prerogatives. Teacher contracts are often written to protect teachers from arbitrary judgments by principals and others. This trend, combined with a traditional view that evaluation and support are two distinct functions, discourages principals from taking the lead in shaping a focused culture of instruction within their schools. Questions of instruction are most frequently left to the teacher, perhaps influenced by actions of centralized staff offices for curriculum and instruction.

Furthermore, over time those in the school support track in central offices become unfamiliar with the details and demands of day-to-day school practice. They typically struggle to be heard by teachers and principals and find that even their best-designed programs, with good evidence of effectiveness, are fully implemented by only a few supporters in the district. Briars and Resnick (2000), for example, described a highly effective district mathematics instruction and professional development system, one that raised overall achievement and shrank gaps in racial achievement, which the district allowed schools to choose to implement on a voluntary basis. Many declined, without offering evidence that an effective alternative was in place. The result was extremely variable outcomes in mathematical proficiency.

In another example, an external audit of a district's literacy program found great variation from school to school and even classroom to classroom. Despite the availability of an officially adopted textbook in every classroom, the auditors concluded that no systematic program existed in the district.

Disband Urban Districts or Modify Them?

These features of urban education systems have led some reformers to propose disbanding school districts. Voucher systems, charter school arrangements, and contract schooling all seek to free schools of the restrictions associated with many of these trends. In essence, these reformers argue that the benefits provided by school districts through effective guidance and support to schools have proven limited and, further, that the bureaucratic form of administrative management noted above has hamstrung effective decentralized leadership (Chubb & Moe, 1990b; Hill & Celio, 1998; Hill et al., 1997).

We take a counterperspective. We agree that most urban districts function poorly, but we believe that providing leadership, capacity, and coherence in the instructional core of schooling is a crucial role that effectively reorganized districts would be better positioned than any other agency to fill. A restructured urban school district, focused on instruction and learning rather than on bureaucratic administration, could meet the goals that the American public and educators share for urban school districts. The functions that we think are essential could be carried out by organizations other than districts, but we think those organizations would then function as *virtual* or *quasi* school districts. Today, some managers of chains of contract or charter schools or "whole-school design" networks carry out the functions of defining curriculum and training teachers and administrators for a geographically dispersed set of schools. Traditionally, these were—and could be again—the responsibility of functional urban school districts. We think it unlikely, however, that a vast collection of independent charter or alternative schools, not to mention private schools, could develop and maintain enough instructional expertise to raise student achievement significantly on a large scale.

DESIGN PRINCIPLES SUPPORTING HIGH PERFORMANCE IN URBAN SCHOOL DISTRICTS

Our belief in the possibility of revitalized urban school districts is supported by the research on Community School District #2 in New York City carried out by the High-Performance Learning Communities (HPLC) project at the University of Pittsburgh's Learning Research and Development (LRDC) Center and the Harvard Graduate School of Education. HPLC has documented and analyzed the work of Anthony Alvarado and Elaine Fink in leading District #2 to a new form of district organization that has produced higher achievement as a result of new forms of investment in professional development and instructional improvement (see Chapter 4, this volume, for a description of this district's schools, community, and student population).

An initial paper by Elmore and Burney (1997a) described a district organized almost entirely around instruction and learning, with principals selected and internally trained to serve as substantive instructional leaders. Since then, a series of studies analyzing the district-level, school-level, and classroom-level functioning (e.g., Elmore & Burney, 1997b; Fink & Resnick, 2001; Stein & D'Amico, in press; Chapter 4, this volume) have provided details of how the District #2 system works and how it has evolved over a 10-year period. Video documentaries (e.g., Barnett & Maloy,

1997; Barnett & Stein, 1998) have made the analyses accessible to a wide practitioner community as well as to research audiences.

Even as HPLC's research was unfolding, Resnick began to use lessons from District #2 as part of the basis for a set of design principles for urban districts that had become partners in LRDC's new Institute for Learning (IFL). Formed in 1995, the Institute enrolled a number of districts in a program of national seminars and on-site technical assistance designed to help them reorganize as *nested learning communities*; that is, organizations in which all individuals and units are expected to upgrade their capacities continuously in accord with a shared set of instructional principles and strategies. In this design, instructional leadership, coupled with reciprocal accountability between "layers" of the organization, provides professional learning opportunities specifically geared to the district's vision of instruction.

The IFL program was based on principles generated from 25 years of work in cognitive psychology (Resnick & Hall, 1998) along with the research emerging from District #2. The Institute was committed to engaging both practitioners and researchers in developing ways to apply these principles. From the beginning, the work was carried out in school settings. The staff of the IFL, its "Resident Fellows," gathered with individuals from up to a dozen school districts to reflect on the principles, the ways in which they could be incorporated into instruction, and how to develop and sustain effective leaders within school districts.

Over several years, the IFL has evolved a program for developing instructional leadership in schools and designing districts—especially in urban settings—that will support such leadership and instructional practices. As of the fall of 2001, nine urban school districts were full working partners of the Institute, which is also developing affiliated programs for clusters of smaller districts that have substantial poor and minority populations. These districts are Austin, Texas; Bridgeport, Connecticut; Columbia, South Carolina; Los Angeles, California; Kansas City, Missouri; Pittsburgh, Pennsylvania; Providence, Rhode Island; St. Paul, Minnesota; and Springfield, Massachusetts.

The experience of working with these districts, the research of LRDC and other analysts, and what was learned in studying District #2 have generated a set of design principles for a district in which effective instruction would be the norm and all students learn and reach high standards. These principles do not constitute a rigid specification of a design. Specifics of the organization and operations vary from one district to another, depending on a district's history, its size, the population it serves, and the particular characteristics of its staff. Not static, these principles evolve as the Institute and its member districts learn from their experiences.

These design principles lead to a district whose operations have the following characteristics:

1. *A commitment to an effort-based concept of intelligence and education.* District staff should act in the belief that all students can reach demanding standards, provided they are enabled to do so and are willing to work. Staff should view enabling students to reach these standards as their core function (Resnick, 1995, 1999; Resnick & Nelson-Le Gall, 1997).

2. *A focus on classroom instruction throughout the district.* Personnel at all levels in the instructional line (e.g., principals, area superintendents or supervisors, the superintendent) as well as those in instructional support offices (e.g., curriculum, professional development, mandated programs) should spend the bulk of their time and attention on instructional, as opposed to managerial, functions. Their work should be aimed at encouraging and supporting classroom instruction that is powerful in both content and pedagogy. The Institute's *Principles of Learning* (Resnick & Hall, 2002) provides one of the primary guides for this work.

3. *A culture emphasizing continuous learning and two-way accountability—the core elements of nested learning communities—throughout the system.* Commitment to continued learning on the part of all professionals in the system is a central feature of the IFL's district reform efforts. Schools need to become places of learning for teachers as well as for students, and principals have a primary responsibility for bringing this about. In these nested learning communities, principals should be accountable to teachers in the same way that teachers are accountable to students; that is, principals have a responsibility to establish effective learning opportunities for teachers. At the same time, just as students must take advantage of the learning opportunities that teachers provide if they are to achieve, so teachers must take advantage of the professional learning opportunities provided and expected in their schools. Principals and senior district administrators should be in a similar relationship of two-way accountability for continuous learning and school improvement.

4. *Continuing professional development for all staff, based in schools and linked to the instructional program for students.* Educating the full range of urban students in intellectually demanding programs will require education professionals to learn new ways of teaching and, in many cases, new content. Much of that professional development should take place in schools and frequently be embedded in the professionals' jobs. For maximum impact, professional development should be linked to the instructional program actually taught to students, rather than being generic in nature.

5. *Coherence in standards, curriculum, assessment, and professional development.* Curriculum and assessment should be aligned throughout the district

and focus on a set of clear achievement standards (usually the state's academic standards). The district should consider adopting a core instructional program in each subject-matter area around which all or most of its professional development efforts will be focused. Variations in instructional program and implementation should be carefully studied, with the most effective variants gradually incorporated into the district's core program.

Implicit in these design principles is a commitment to a shared set of beliefs in the district concerning good instructional practice, sustained communication among professionals concerned with instruction, and a shared conviction that continued learning is a professional responsibility. The principles rest on the premise that districts with these qualities will be high performing.

SUPPORTING ENACTMENT OF THE PRINCIPLES

Frameworks, strategies, and tools for engagement and assistance, offered by external agents, can help districts move toward operations that realize these principles. The principles represent what Fullan (1999) calls a "theory of education"—a coherent set of ideas concerning curricular and pedagogical practice and organizational behavior that guide instructional practice. Along with a theory of education, reformers need a "theory of change"— a set of strategies for achieving organizational behaviors and cultures that embody the theory of education (Fullan, 1999).

If the reformer is the leader of the organization being reformed, his or her theory of change should guide the actions that lead that organization toward operations consistent with his or her theory of education. External agents, such as the Institute for Learning or the New American School's District Services Program, support the reform leader's work and learning by providing strategies, services, and tools that are intended to help leaders to bring about reform. External agents are not themselves reformers, nor do they directly produce reform efforts. Rather, they help to build a district's capacity to bring about improvement in instructional practices and to engage in continuous learning.

The work of external agents should rest on a systematic set of ideas about supporting the reform leaders' *learning* of appropriate education and change theories, and also their *application* of these theories to practice. For example, the contractual agreement that IFL strikes with its partner districts creates a framework within which actions will be jointly undertaken. This agreement proposes a set of activities and policies including the following:

- *Initial and continued personal engagement of the district superintendent* and his or her senior staff in instructional improvement to convey vividly to the district staff the importance they attach to the endeavor
- *Development of the instructional leadership skills* of all first-line managers (i.e., principals and assistant principals)
- *Provision of tools and protocols* that enable principals and district staff to continually develop their instructional capabilities as well as those of teachers in the district
- *Focus on a small number of core academic skills*—normally literacy and mathematics
- *On-the-job coaching* of principals, district leaders, and teachers
- *Use of school, department, and leadership learning plans* to organize nested learning communities and the two-way accountability they imply

Specific features of the activities are negotiated with each district to reflect the community and policy environments in which they operate. We discuss these activities supporting reform below and illustrate them with IFL's current work. While not the only way to imagine support for reform leaders' work and learning, the IFL case offers one viable way of realizing this support relationship.

Engagement of the Superintendent

Profound changes sought in the culture and organization of a school district can occur only if the top district leadership understands the instructional design and provides leadership consistent with it. Without such engagement, the staff will not treat the changes in operations consistent with the design as a major priority. Membership in the IFL program, therefore, requires that superintendents and deputy superintendents be actively engaged in instructional decisions and leadership.

The superintendent's engagement begins before any agreement is formalized. Superintendents expressing interest in the IFL program are often invited to Institute meetings so they can develop a sense of what the Institute does. Through early visits by IFL staff to the district—including conversations, presentations, and visitation of schools—senior leaders come to understand the theory of education that underlies the Institute program. Without their commitment to this theory, participation in the Institute makes little sense. During this early engagement, the Institute also encourages the district to involve principals and teachers so that they have a better understanding of what will be involved if a district joins with the Institute and in order to build an internal constituency for the work.

Normally, the Institute director and staff continue personal consultations with the superintendent regarding effective ways to use IFL programs and services and to move toward implementing the design principles. All superintendents are expected to participate in a Superintendents' Think-Tank, where documents such as district strategic (or learning) plans are examined and critiqued, instructional programs and teaching are analyzed, continuous self-evaluation plans are outlined, and strategies for continuous professional development of principals and teachers are developed. Associated with the Think-Tank is a program of intervisitation among districts so that superintendents can engage in critical but collegial analyses of one another's work. The Institute thus encourages the superintendents to form and become members of a learning community of similarly committed senior district leaders.

Instructional Leadership Skills

Developing skills of instructional leadership at all levels in a district, but with particular emphasis on the building principal, is critical to bringing reform ideas to scale in the district. Universal, sustained training in instructional leadership promotes coherent language and practices throughout the district, as well as modeling learning community behaviors.

Accordingly, IFL membership agreements set up an instructional leadership program, usually involving 1½- to 2-day training sessions in the district every month or 6 weeks for all principals and, increasingly, assistant principals. In some districts, area superintendents run the meetings with assistance from Institute staff. In others, Resident Fellows from the IFL may lead these meetings. In most districts, members of central office staff concerned with curriculum or professional development are beginning to participate as leading teachers from the district.

Tools and Protocols

District leaders' learning to apply coherent theories of education and change can be enhanced by a variety of structured tools and protocols—the "curriculum materials" of the external agents' work. When designed with sufficient scaffolding to enable people without great expertise to use them effectively, these tools make high-quality professional development and guidance more readily available within districts.

These tools are heavily technology-based, developed through the Institute's NetLearn project. For example, an interactive CD-ROM provides an overview of the Institute's Principles of Learning with multiple video examples illustrating classroom implementation of the principles along with suggestions for professional study-group activities (Resnick & Hall, 2002). Separate CDs on individual principles are now in beta-test form and a CD on nested learning communities is under development. Tools such as these are designed to support a learning culture in which analysis of practice is at the heart of the improvement effort (see Ball & Cohen, 1999; Stigler & Hiebert, 1999). Future NetLearn developments include networked discussion environments intended to facilitate the learning community.

Focus on Core Academic Skills

Developing a districtwide focus on a shared set of instructional and learning goals can be facilitated by concentrating on one or two core subject areas, normally literacy and math. While the Institute does not explicitly recommend particular content programs, it encourages such a focus, providing advice if requested and helping districts incorporate the Principles of Learning into all professional development related to content areas.

On-Site Coaching and Study Groups

Professional development for educators—at any level of the organization—needs to be rooted in practice and in the communities in which educators work. Although a place exists for courses and workshops that provide some of the theory and content of instructional programs, fundamental learning of practice needs to focus on the educator's day-to-day teaching and learning work. This focus can be realized through systems of on-site coaching (in classrooms for teachers, in schools for principals) coupled with study groups in which educators analyze their own practice against examples of "best practices" and principles of effective instruction.

   All of the Institute partner districts, as well as many other districts throughout the country (see, e.g., Chapter 5, this volume), are committing to developing and supporting a corps of coaches in core subject-matter areas. The Institute offers training for literacy and math coaches in the schools through its *Content-Focused Coaching* program. Through monthly on-site training, it also provides direct coaching of principals and senior district staff who train or support principals.

Nested Learning Plans

Established practices within the district can provide a platform for undertaking the hard work of realizing a new theory of instruction and change.

For example, there is no reason why school improvement plans and district strategic plans cannot become real instruments for change, rather than the compliance and public relations documents that they now largely are. In principle, such practices can be harnessed to the reform support agenda we have been describing.

Because most schools today are required to prepare school improvement plans, the IFL is currently exploring how to shape these plans to support the Institute's nested learning community design. Renaming them "learning plans," the IFL and its partners are developing concepts and rubrics for assessing the quality of such plans. Such school-level learning plans should be associated with individual learning plans for each major department in the central office concerned with improving instruction and learning.

Meaningful learning plans, in contrast to most current improvement plans, would specify mutual commitments between actors at different levels (e.g., the principal will provide time and coaching for teachers; teachers will improve specific skills and knowledge in the course of a schoolyear) or in different departments (e.g., the literacy department will provide defined training for a school's literacy coach; the school's principal and teachers will engage with the coach in learning specified content or skills). They would also specify measurable benchmarks and accountability for achievement of the learning goals. Collectively, these individual, school, and department learning plans would "nest" with one another to become the strategic plan for the improvement of instruction and learning for the district as a whole.

LOOKING AHEAD

In this chapter, we have presented an emerging theory to guide urban school district efforts in enabling their diverse students to learn the kinds of high-level knowledge and skills called for in today's education policy environment. Both the district design principles and the theory of change we have outlined are guides to action, which districts may try to realize on their own or which can be tested and refined through collaboration between districts and external agents such as the Institute for Learning.

It is important to emphasize the term *theory*. What we have set forth here is the product of several years of joint effort of IFL staff, district staff, and independent researchers. We view this effort as an instance of *problem-solving research and development* that is desperately needed to make large-scale progress in improving the performance of complex educational systems. As argued by a recent National Academy of Education Panel, such a research-and-development (R&D) approach develops designs for system improvement and continually modifies them through experience and tests in real settings (Brown, Greeno, Lampert, Mehan, & Resnick, 1999). Such problem-solving R&D engages researchers and practitioners in developing the theory, the tools, and the cadre of leaders that will allow successful educational interventions to "travel" to additional classrooms, schools, and districts.

From the Institute for Learning's perspective, the theory of action presented here is just that—a theory to be tested, elaborated, and improved through concrete work with school districts. It recognizes that scaling up effective instruction practices to all schools within urban school districts will not be a simple matter of testing effectiveness of design elements and then "replicating" the successful ones elsewhere. The theory of education and design principles set forth in this chapter will need to be examined in interaction with one another and with associated theories of change, and this work must be done in a sufficient range and number of districts in order to understand the limiting conditions for this theory.

The accompanying challenge is to develop the leaders who possess sufficient understanding of the emerging theory of district design and change that they, quite possibly in collaboration with external agents, can create variants suitable to their particular demographic, economic, and political situations. The combination of theory, tools, and leadership capability is our vision of the means by which successful, systematically developed educational practices can travel to multiple districts across our large and diverse country.

NOTE

Preparation of this chapter was supported by a grant from the Wallace/Readers Digest Foundation (#20000050). It is based in part on a concept paper whose preparation was supported by the Spencer Foundation. The Resident and National Fellows of the Institute for Learning made important contributions to the conception and writing of both papers.

CHAPTER 11

Reforming Districts

MILBREY W. McLAUGHLIN AND JOAN E. TALBERT

Districts' dismal track record in carrying out or sustaining school reform leads some to conclude that while districts are part of the reform problem, they should not be part of the solution. Major reform initiatives such as the Coalition of Essential Schools, early Annenberg Challenge grants, and Goals 2000 cut districts out of the action on the assumption that central office incompetence was incurable and school reforms were bound to fail at the district door. Others have argued that district authority needs to be weakened, advancing radical decentralization or "consumer" choice as a school improvement strategy. We offer a different response: For better or worse, districts matter fundamentally to school reform outcomes and without effective district engagement, school-by-school reforms are bound to disappoint.

This chapter develops a picture of a "reforming district" by exploring the questions: Does district reform affect school reform? If so, how, and what do reforming districts do? Our analysis draws on 4 years of survey and case study research to examine links between district action and elements of school-level reform. To isolate patterns of action particular to reforming districts, we use survey data from districts in the San Francisco Bay Area and case accounts of three reforming districts—two in the Bay Area and San Diego City Schools.

The Bay Area districts—Highland and East Bay Unified (pseudonyms) —are middle-sized districts of 10 to 12 schools; San Diego City Schools is the state's second-largest district, with more than 170 schools. San Diego and East Bay serve students in grades K–12, while Highland is K–8. All three have diverse student populations typical of California districts, with Anglo White students comprising between one-half and less than one-third of their enrollments. Compared to state norms, San Diego City Schools

School Districts and Instructional Renewal. Copyright © 2002 by Teachers College, Columbia University. All rights reserved. ISBN 0-8077-4266-X (pbk), ISBN 0-8077-4267-8 (cloth). Prior to photocopying items for classroom use, please contact the Copyright Clearance Center, Customer Service, 222 Rosewood Dr., Danvers, MA 01923, USA, tel. (508) 750-8400.

serves a poorer, more racially and ethnically diverse student population; demographics of the two Bay Area districts are typical of that region, though Highland students are significantly poorer than average—one-third of students qualify for free or reduced-price lunches—and one-fourth are English-language Learners.

DOES DISTRICT REFORM AFFECT SCHOOL REFORM?

Existing studies demonstrate connections between district office actions and school-level reform activities (e.g., Elmore & Burney, 1997a; Spillane, 1994, 1998a; Chapter 9, this volume). However, little systematic evidence exists to suggest that district-level reform pays off at the school level. This question provides a critical starting place for our analysis of reforming districts. Absent evidence that reforming districts impact school outcomes, investigation into strategies that distinguish reforming from traditional districts is moot. Policy analysts and education reformers who have discounted districts must be convinced that schools benefit from a district's proactive involvement in school reform.

We address the effects of district-level reform from the vantage point of reforming schools. Longitudinal survey data from California Bay Area reforming schools suggest that, for better or worse, districts' actions and reform stance are strongly related over a 4-year period to their schools' progress on a range of school culture outcomes sought by reform initiatives.

How Teachers and Principals Perceive Their Districts

Teachers and principals working in Bay Area School Reform Collaborative (BASRC) schools were asked in 1998 and again in 2001 to report on their district context and on aspects of their school culture. These surveys included items that comprise a global measure of "district professionalism," or principals' and teachers' views of their district's commitment to student learning, high expectations and professional development resources for schools, and educators' pride in working in the district.

Educators' reckoning of a district's professional culture impacts their motivation, willingness, and capacity to engage a reform agenda. We have seen that, absent positive valuation of district attitudes and support, teachers become disengaged and principals struggle to create a positive school climate within a stormy district sea. In one such case, for example, teachers called the district attitudes toward them "infantalizing" and elected to "work to rule," crippling reform efforts in their school (McLaughlin & Talbert, 2001).

Additional measures of district context tap central office actions in support of school reform work: "district support for whole-school reform" (teacher survey) and "district support of inquiry-based reform" (principal survey). These measures pertain to particular reform demands made upon BASRC schools and feature the extent to which the district provided data and technical assistance enabling reforming schools to implement BASRC's required "cycle of inquiry." Our analysis of *change* from 1998 to 2001 on these district culture measures assesses the extent to which district offices increased their support of schools' reform work and professional development.

What School Culture Changes Are Linked to District Change?

Changes in district action are significantly related to elements of school culture that appear on most lists of "essentials" for successful school reform. Tables 11.1 and 11.2 summarize results of the longitudinal analyses of both teacher and principal survey data.

Primary among the school culture outcomes linked to district change are fundamental goals of school reform—raising expectations that all students can engage and succeed in rigorous, challenging work and fostering commitment to enabling all students to meet those higher standards. "All students can learn" has become a reform slogan and one that makes many teachers, especially in large comprehensive high schools, roll their eyes.

Table 11.1. School Culture Change and Change in District-Level Factors: Teacher Survey Data for BASRC Schools, 1998–2001

School Culture Change	Change in District Professionalism	Change in District Support for Whole School Reform
Commitment to all students	.49[*]	.59[**]
Norm of inquiry	.35	.41[*]
Teacher learning community	.57[**]	.79[**]
Collective problem solving	.37	.43[*]
Parent involvement	.47[*]	.53[*]

Note: Change measures are the difference between a school's mean teacher score for the 2 years (2001 – 1998). Reported are correlations between change in teachers' ratings of the district's conditions and change in their ratings of the school culture (school $N = 22$).

[*] $p < .05$, two-tailed. [**] $p < .01$, two-tailed.

Table 11.2. School Culture Change and Change in District-Level Factors: Principal Survey Data, 1998–2001

School Culture Change	Change in District Professionalism	Change in District Support for Cycle of Inquiry
High academic standards	.51**	.45**
Norm of inquiry	.32**	.34**
Teachers' instructional control	.45**	.31**
Principal reform leadership	.37**	.31**
Parent-school partnership	.24*	.32**

Note: Reported are correlations between change in principals' ratings of the district's conditions and change in their ratings of the school culture (school $N = 82$).

*$p < .05$, two-tailed. **$p < .01$, two-tailed.

Yet express obligation to all students motivates comprehensive school reform, spurring teachers to take a hard look at their practice and the needs and backgrounds of the students in their classrooms. Commitment to all students recasts the problem of poor student outcomes from one situated in students' attitudes and abilities to one based in teachers' instructional practices and comprises a necessary condition for productive school reform. Facets of the "professionalism" scale that pertain to district standards and expectations for student learning capture the link between district reform and these school culture outcomes. The "district reform support" scale includes items concerning assistance for teachers in meeting the needs of all students and help for principals in setting high standards and maintaining a focus on teaching and learning.

Other elements of school culture related to district change constitute capacity for changing school and classroom practice, and improving student outcomes. Researchers from diverse perspectives elaborate the importance of site-based inquiry, teacher community, learning, and leadership to the improvement of practice (e.g., Cochran-Smith & Lytle, 2001; Hargreaves & Fullan, 1998). Timely and reliable data on student learning outcomes and capacity to use it for self-assessment are key to school reform, yet teachers typically lack expertise or occasions to engage in data-based discussion linking their practice to student outcomes. School change on the "norms of inquiry" scale reflects important shifts in this key school culture feature.

Most accounts of school reform also point to the strength and character of teachers' school-based professional communities as key to understanding teachers' motivation and support for changing instructional practices. School-based teacher communities can be the site and source of inquiry into practice, sharing of knowledge, and collective responsibility for student achievement (e.g., McDonald et al., 1999; Newmann & Wehlage, 1995; Wagner, 2000). Our "teacher learning community" scale includes teachers' assessments of central aspects of a learning community—most especially feelings of support for trying out new ideas, trust, and mutual accountability for helping colleagues do their best; the "collective problem solving" survey scale measures teachers' judgments about their school's process for problem solving, action orientation, and the availability of useful information.

Districts clearly figure into schools' progress on inquiry and improved professional community. Central office investment in developing high-quality data useful for inquiry at the school and class level comprises an important resource for reforming schools. Some Bay Area districts made significant strides toward state-of-the-art databases including individual student performance on multiple assessments and techniques for aggregating data by student characteristics. In fact, however, Bay Area districts provided schools with widely differing levels of technical support around inquiry. Districts receiving high ratings on the "support for school reform" scales had central office staff with expertise and time to help schools set benchmarks and learn to use student data to evaluate progress toward school and district standards.

Districts also varied widely in readiness and capacity to support reforming schools, and proactive district support for whole-school change was the exception in the BASRC (Center for Research on the Context of Teaching [CRC], 2000). Yet survey data suggest that as districts increased support for school-level inquiry and focus on high standards for teaching and learning, the culture and reform competencies of the schools also increased. Further, we saw that district and school change can be reciprocal. As districts afforded reforming schools support and flexibility, they learned from the experiences of these schools and adjusted their central office practices.

The survey findings over this 4-year period reveal a strong pattern of relationships with key school culture outcomes and consistent results across school samples and respondents. They capture both declines and increases in district professionalism and reform support that fit our field-based observations of Bay Area districts and school case studies. The positive changes in district culture captured in our survey data represent efforts by some district leaders to fundamentally alter the districts' posture toward their schools and ways of supporting the improvement of teaching and learning. This 4-year experience indicates that essential *district* reform, as well as school reform, is at work when school cultures change.

WHAT DO REFORMING DISTRICTS DO?

Evidence that district reform matters for school reform begs the question of how a district reforms itself to become a dynamic, proactive agent of school reform. What does a district do to boost schools' commitment to and capacity for reform? How does it learn to support reform across diverse district schools? Our survey and case data point to particular strategic conditions of reforming districts. Most fundamental to reforming districts is focus on the system as unit of change, achieved through system communication and shared commitment to reform, strategic planning at the system level, and treatment of the central office as a learning community. Working with this systemwide perspective, district leadership and staff seek to engender and sustain (1) a clear focus on teaching and learning, (2) instructional support to schools and teachers, and (3) data-based accountability.[1] Reforming districts achieve these central office functions through varied structures and practices that have evolved over time, which are pivotal to building a system of schools.

The System as the Unit of Change

A reforming district takes *itself* as the focus for change and has a clear theory of change for the system. Focusing on the system means that all schools and all elements of the district's policy environment—the business office, human resources, the school board, the union, and the broader community—are explicitly included in the reform agenda and strategic planning. As elsewhere, reforming districts engage in curriculum change, create standards for student performance, and develop strategies for recruiting and developing teachers, but they do so with an express, deliberate view of the whole. Highland's new superintendent put it this way:

> It's not independent teacher-by-teacher that's going to make a difference, it's the systemic approach. That's what impressed me [when I first came here]: there is a district moving forward. It's not school-by-school; every school is a little different, but there's a district direction.

In a reforming district, central office administrators and staff are united around a common conception of improving education for all students, a far cry from the typical fragmented district office culture in which specialized functions have their own agenda and routines. Consider the following: In the three reforming districts we studied, the heads of district business operations could articulate the district's instructional goals and defined their units' work in those terms. This unity of purpose and attention to the whole system derives from reforming districts' approach to communication, planning, and their own learning.

System Communication and Shared Reform Commitment. Reforming districts establish clear expectations for central office–school relations and take a leadership role in developing norms of reform practice across district schools. Their theory of change implicates the system and so stands in contrast to district reform strategies that import school change models.

San Diego City Schools' theory of change is rooted in powerful ideas about learning and instruction and features investment in people throughout the system. Chancellor Alvarado and the Institute for Learning he created (Chapter 5, this volume) have made educators' learning and professional growth key to district reform. Workshops and Learning Communities for principals and extensive professional development for teachers engage district educators in research and reflection.

After the first 2 years in San Diego, Alvarado had made progress toward his expressed vision of making the district a *system of schools*. In a spring 2000 survey, virtually all principals (97%) reported that "the district holds high expectations for our school" and that "the district is committed to high standards for every student" (94%). Compared to Bay Area norms (78% and 79% on the same survey items), the district's reform leadership is striking. Further, the high percentage (82%) reporting that "district priorities are consistent with my school's priorities," compared to 61% for Bay Area principals, reveals an unusually strong coherence between system levels.

Reforming Bay Area districts also invest heavily in teachers' and principals' professional growth and learning and engage the central office staff in systemwide thinking about school reform. In East Bay Unified School, the administrative team meets at least twice weekly to address educational issues. One administrator commented: "Everyone is there—personnel, special ed, business, sometimes even maintenance . . . so everyone gets to talk about whatever they want [in terms of what's hindering each school's progress]." In both East Bay and Highland, professional development for teachers and principals is extensive and intensively focused on the district's goal of improving literacy instruction.

Evidence of cohesive district reform cultures in these Bay Area districts comes from survey data and comments that reveal high levels of agreement among principals and teachers about reform goals and their ability to address them. More than three-quarters of Highland's principals reported in a 2001 survey that (1) common beliefs and norms of practice are held throughout the district, (2) they know what is expected of them as principals, and (3) district and school priorities are consistent. Most teachers feel the district holds high expectations for their school (83%) and express high levels of efficacy (87%). Teachers' sense of the district's high expectations and their own professional efficacy permeates the district's schools—from those serving the poorest, most linguistically diverse student population to those enrolling children of more advantaged families.

In East Bay Unified, a similar picture emerges. Teachers' survey ratings of the strength of districtwide community and shared goals exceed regional norms. An elementary school teacher told us, "There is a focus, we have a common goal"; an elementary school principal said, "This is a joint venture." In the district administrator survey, both East Bay and Highland surpassed regional norms on measures of systemwide communication and distributed leadership.

Strategic Planning at the System Level. Reforming districts convene people from all levels and parts of the system to deliberate reform goals and outcomes, share knowledge of successful practices, and design strategies for change. A strategic planning process is fundamental to establishing mutual accountability among district administrators, principals, and teachers for progress on agreed-upon reform goals.

Interviews in Highland presented a consistent theme: The district plans ahead, anticipates what is coming from the state, and uses data to make decisions. In the former superintendent's words:

> "Strategic" in our district has become a very embedded concept. We're strategic in our thinking. We're strategic in our actions. We're certainly strategic in our planning . . . it's more than pushing the envelope. If the things that have been done before are not producing the results we want, then doing them better is really not necessarily going to produce the results we want. So, we've got to look at it again and rethink it. That notion of strategic has been very important in this organization. I think it's what's helped us be very successful.

She also noted that it took almost 10 years for "goal-driven, data-driven" norms and procedures to be established.

An East Bay principal revealed the sense of ownership of the system's reform goals that comes from participating in the district's planning process: "I have always felt like I had so much input into whatever the district decided. And we all agree to go in the same direction." The opportunity for principals and teachers to engage in districtwide planning is typical of Bay Area districts, where planning for reform, if any, usually excludes those who would implement the plans. A teacher in a more typical Bay Area district commented: "We've never as a district sat down as all key teachers and talked about what we do."

In San Diego, the planning process through which the district developed and adopted its systemwide reform plan, the Blueprint for Student Success, was more top-down and less inclusive than in the Bay Area reforming districts. San Diego's sheer size limited inclusive strategic planning, as did the chancellor's urgency to establish the vision of teaching and learning he brought from District #2 (Chapter 4, this volume). The implementation approach, however, lacked a system change theory applicable to a large district with union resistance to a heavy central office hand in designing and carrying out system reform.

Conceptualizing their stakeholders and boundaries broadly, both Bay Area reforming districts have developed inclusive strategic planning processes that involve parents and community members. East Bay's most recent strategic planning included district residents, business leaders, teachers, parents, administrators, classified employees, and others. The steering committee of 35 people was responsible for developing, reviewing, and revising the work of 25 broad-based focus groups. The result was a plan—including mission and vision statements, 3-year goals, core values, and objectives—intended to guide East Bay for the next 5 years.

Highland's most recent round of strategic planning—reflecting inclusive norms and structures developed over 10 years—included a teacher, parent, and principal from every school, along with community representatives, who engaged in dialogue and planning for district reform. They began with the question "How are our kids doing compared to our expectations?" and tackled it with a direct look at data.

Central Office Learning Community. Reforming districts also cultivate strong norms of inquiry within the central office, which engender systemwide commitment and capacity to change. District administrators and staff explicitly model the learning and risk taking that are essential to effective change while reforming their own practice. The central office supports professional learning and its responsiveness to schools' particular needs.

In all reforming districts, central office administrators expressed support for the risk taking entailed in school reform. An East Bay central office administrator commented: "It's OK to make mistakes . . . my philosophy is [that] the risk takers are the ones that help kids. I would rather have a principal try five things and fail on three than a principal who tries zero and fails on none." Open dialogue around student performance data supports the learning process. Several East Bay principals commented on the district's strength in terms of honesty and trust—as one said, "the free flow of information—honest, and in some cases brutal, dialogue." Another said: "I personally feel confident enough to [have open dialogue with central office administrators] without fear of retribution . . . unlike the other district where I was [where] you ruffle feathers and you're marked for life."

Beyond providing normative support for the change process, district-level inquiry into practice is essential to supporting schools' reform work. Our research points to a substantial, multifaceted learning agenda for the central office, where administrators and staff learn to track schools' progress and define specialized support needs, incorporate stakeholders' input on reform goals and engage their support, employ resources strategically and broker educators' access to knowledge resources, and respond to state policy developments in ways that preserve the district's strategic focus. Central offices are thus engaged in an ongoing process of reforming their own practice in support of system reform.

The centrality of a district office learning community in a reforming district is captured by survey responses from administrators in 60 Bay Area districts: a measure of "central office learning community" predicted a range of reform roles distinguishing more and less proactive districts. This measure assessed the extent to which district administrators are "continually learning and seeking new ideas," the district is "actively involved in school reform," and the district "uses student assessment data as the basis for changing district curriculum." Scores on this scale were strongly related to scales measuring the following elements in a district:

- Standards emphasis
- Leadership building
- Reform coordination across district schools
- Resource flexibility
- Inquiry support
- Instructional support
- Organizational support

These district actions describe a syndrome of conditions that characterize reforming districts. Not only are they highly intercorrelated, but each is strongly related to independent teacher and principal ratings of district "professionalism" (described earlier). These data suggest that an inquiry stance at the central office level is central to a district's success in system-level reform, sustaining a focus on outcome standards and an evidence-based process for improving district support of all schools' improvement.

A Clear, Unitary Focus on Teaching and Learning

Reforming districts express a single-minded system emphasis on teaching and learning. More particularly, San Diego and the Bay Area reforming districts focus intensively on literacy goals. Highland's instructional focus evolved over a period of years and reflects the strategic planning process described above. At the outset, the district identified 10 goals and 10 strategies. Over the years, the district has narrowed the focus to student achievement and set measurable targets: 100% of students meeting or exceeding district standards. Reflecting on the district's progress, a central office administrator said: "I think the biggest thing [in the progress we have made] is knowing what it is we wanted to do and then focusing on it." Similarly, in East Bay, a coherent, systemwide focus on literacy means that all teachers are working on the same instructional reform focus. A staff developer in the district commented: "This [reform] is districtwide. A teacher can't transfer to another school to get out of it."

Clarity and specificity distinguish the instructional goals expressed by reforming districts. Most districts adopt multiple goals each year, with instructional progress conceived in vague terms. One relatively high-achieving district adopted three goals this year: improvement in student outcomes, facilities upgrade, and increased subsidies for teachers' housing. While many districts specify instructional reform goals in vague terms (e.g., "all students will learn to high standards"), instructional goals in reforming districts are specific and measurable.

One consequence is relative coherence in the programs and resources brought *into* reforming districts. Central office administrators reject any undertaking that might deflect from the district's particular focus on improving teaching and learning. Early in its literacy-focused reform, for example, San Diego lost significant National Science Foundation funding for science programs—on the grounds that the district was paying insufficient attention to science. The Bay Area superintendents were equally ready to forgo funding opportunities that did not mesh with the district's reform mission and strategic plan. The Highland superintendent told us that though the district is involved in various initiatives, they were selected carefully to complement each other, not "piece by piece." An associate superintendent said, "I think that's the way we've gone after funding. You have a vision of where you're going and then you find the way to make it happen."

Clear, specific goals also guide budgeting decisions. In Highland, programs are reviewed yearly as the district struggles to balance its budget. The superintendent explained how her district differed from others:

There is sort of a mantra or dogma that programs we might bring in must be aligned to student growth, student achievement, that they must be reevaluated. That's just part of the way business is done here. I've had so many conversations in other districts about, "well, we have to keep this program because we have this person we like and it has nothing to do [with district goals] . . . " Well, [in those districts] the decision is made in the best interest of the adults.

Another result of strong instructional focus is the district's ability to maintain a coherent reform agenda in the face of numerous state initiatives and high-stakes accountability measures. Leaders in all three districts, while critical of many California education initiatives, do not worry that state pressures or policies will throw them off course. The former Highland superintendent put it this way: "Compliance has never been an issue for me . . . you just do it. It's dumb stuff, so you just get that done and you keep moving in the direction you need to move." So, for example, despite state-required SAT-9 testing, district leaders continue to use local assessments they believe are essential to meeting equity goals.

Instructional Support and Responsiveness to School Needs

Reforming districts' clear unitary focus on teaching and learning is backed by responsive instructional support. While "top-down support for bottom-up change" is common central office rhetoric, the reality is different in most districts, where schools feel distanced and believe the resources provided them do not match their needs (CRC, 2000). Most BASRC schools, for example, saw their district as an indifferent reform player, at best, because it lent a deaf ear to expressed needs or as an obstacle, at worst, because it was insensitive to site-level reform agendas.

Reforming districts invest heavily in school reform, and do so more effectively than most districts, by leading, supporting, and leveraging reform in the central office. One of first things San Diego leaders did was revamp the central office to better serve schools. Likewise, Bay Area reforming districts evolved trim central offices and established express norms of responsiveness to schools. All Highland district interviews echoed one associate superintendent's sentiment: "The whole purpose of the instructional department [is] to serve. . . . We work to make things better at the school sites. . . . I would never have left a school site if I didn't feel I was still working for schools." East Bay Unified administrators expressed the same norm of responsiveness. As one administrator put it: "I never considered my position to be a power position at all. It is a service position."

Reforming districts seek out and use cutting-edge practices, especially in professional development, where they have reallocated resources to the school site—for example, school-based literacy coaches and other supports, especially for beginning teachers—to better foster teachers' learning and instructional capacity Teachers welcome these site resources, pointing to the increased competence they feel implementing the district literacy program in ways that respond to diverse student backgrounds. In stark contrast to usual groans about district "inservice," teachers in all three cases also give district-level events high marks and feel well prepared when they attend outside conferences. The new Highland superintendent commented, "Conversations I'm hearing among teachers in workshops and trainings are of a much higher level [than other places I've worked]. It's obvious that the staff development that has taken place here has been effective."

Districts managed these high-quality professional development supports within the same fiscal constraints as other California districts, by ransacking their budgets to find the necessary funds. San Diego reallocated Title I dollars and various state funds, notably support for new teachers. Bay Area districts also used funds targeted at new teachers and aggressively sought other supports for site-based coaches.

Reforming districts attend to the professional development needs of principals. San Diego City Schools saw principals as key to their reform agenda and therefore focused on their learning even before teachers' learning. Bay Area districts developed learning opportunities for principals based on feedback from site administrators that they needed occasions to have joint access to professional learning resources. In a systemwide culture of school reform, principals are linchpins in constructing and conveying a district theory of instructional improvement.

Reforming districts use conventional district management tools in unconventional ways to support school reform. For example, Highland uses teacher evaluation to foster school-level learning and change. The district's alternative evaluation plan allows tenured teachers to design and conduct an action research project. Teachers work with their principals to formulate a research question, identify relevant data, and specify outcomes they will measure. Principals report changes in classroom practices resulting from these projects. One enthusiastic principal said: "It's improving what they're doing in the classroom because they're going to choose something that they feel that they need to do."

An effective district instructional support role relies on building teachers' trust in district administrators' commitment and ability to support their learning and change. An East Bay administrator commented: "There is a strong relationship between the district and the schools in that sites are starting to trust and realize that the district office is there to be of help to them . . . and that their opinions are important." An assistant superintendent saw the district's commitment to system goals and supporting schools' progress as key to building this trust and district reform capacity: "We always make sure that we're doing it not for our own needs and interests but for the sake of the schools and the kids."

The instructional supports reforming districts provided schools differ in both kind and degree from resources furnished to schools elsewhere. They are intensive, site-focused, of high quality, and responsive to teachers' expressed needs and evidence about student learning. Teachers and principals award them exceptionally high marks.

Data-Based Accountability

Reforming districts establish accountability for student outcomes throughout the system and with local stakeholders. In San Diego, principals are held accountable for their school's student performance, especially students in the lowest quartile. The two Bay Area districts hold schools accountable for goals established in their strategic planning processes. Here, feedback, clear channels of communication about student outcomes, and indicators of instructional progress are vital to an effective accountability system. These districts collect and examine data to set goals and identify improvement plans throughout the system—from district to the school, teacher, and individual student.

Both districts' strategic planning systems use school, district, and community data in yearly review and adjustment. The districts make assessment a priority—not only state-required standardized tests, but also locally developed performance-based assessments in reading, writing, and math. They regularly disaggregate data "to set targets" particular to subgroups of students and schools. The districts also use portfolios to allow students other opportunities to show progress. "We want to determine if the things we are providing are curing the right illness," said one superintendent. "What are the underlying causal factors?"

The districts also make efforts to provide teachers and parents with data. Highland initiated a strategy to get student data and related information to teachers' desks. Despite gripes about this new data-management system, however, teachers and principals applaud the fact that they have up-to-date information on their desktops for planning and assessment. East Bay's district assessment resource teachers commented on a growing demand for data in the district: "Our theory . . . is that we use data and student work to drive instruction. My work has almost doubled to provide resources for schools. We had a theory which now is becoming action."

Strategic planning and accompanying data-based decision making also enable districts to respond proactively to state accountability pressures, as a Highland district administrator explained:

> Usually we're a kind of district that we sense what's coming . . . and that's part of strategic planning . . . you do an internal and external scan. So you look at what the state's doing to you, what society's doing, the change in demographics. You're creating your future, you're not reacting. A lot of other districts [say], "Let's wait and see what really is going to happen." So we've usually started the process.

In both reforming Bay Area districts, educators credit strategic planning with an unusual degree of open communication. Data on programs and funds are available to all. "Nobody's hiding anything in this district," said a principal. "Nobody's trying to covet any particular program. It's really open."

San Diego reformers are still trying to develop a comprehensive system of data collection, analysis, and feedback. Its absence is an acknowledged problem, since timely data necessary to manage change are not available to educators from the central office down to schools. The result is miscommunication, anxiety over performance outcomes, and lack of information needed for resource allocation decisions. By contrast, Bay Area districts show how essential comprehensive data and effective feedback are to reform at both district and school levels, and how comfort and competence with data grow over time.

REVISITING CONVENTIONAL WISDOM
ABOUT DISTRICT REFORM

Conventional wisdom holds that districts cannot undertake or sustain serious reform. Autopsies of failed efforts offer three major obstacles to significant system change: school-level resistance to a strong central office role, personnel turnover, and the politics of local education reform (Fullan, 2001; Hess, 1999). The reforming districts featured here provide instructive exception to general beliefs about district reform.

Myth 1: Teachers and Schools Resist a Strong Central Office Role

Distinctive to reforming districts is their strategic conception of functions at different levels of the system. The central office and the schools have mutually reinforcing but different roles in defining and advancing a strong reform agenda. The central office assumes responsibility for defining goals and standards for teaching and learning, allocating resources to schools, and providing supports principals and teachers need to successfully meet district-established standards. And in reforming Bay Area districts, significant authority and responsibility are assigned to the schools. Principals and teachers are responsible for defining school-specific teaching and learning goals, allocating professional development resources, and developing strategies for evaluating their progress. School administrators understand that their professional discretion does not comprise "site-based management" because the district built overall budgets with attention to equity.

Teachers and principals appreciate this strong district role because they feel the district provides both clear standards and effective support. For example, most of Highland's principals (90%) said the district helped their school develop and maintain high standards, and helped them promote and nurture a focus on teaching and learning (70%). A principal commented that this kind of district support and responsiveness "does not happen in most places."

District support translates into teachers' positive sense of capacity. The vast majority of teachers in Highland indicate they are well prepared to create equitable learning opportunities for an increasingly diverse student population, a key challenge to California's teaching force.

Many factors contribute to these reforming districts' successes in defining distinct district and school responsibilities. For one, clear, consensual goals allow districts to assign significant authority to schools. The Bay Area districts involve teachers in decisions regarding teaching and instruction as part of their strategic planning processes. A long-time Highland central office administrator explained: "A strength [of our district] is that we've never worked top-down. We've always involved teachers and sometimes it's frustrating and it takes longer. But there's always been the intent to have ownership where it counts."

An important lesson from these districts is that it is not necessarily the *strength* of the district role that affects teachers' morale and view of the district, but rather *what* that role is and *how* it is carried out. Bay Area reforming districts, where the district role has been developed over more than a decade, show that when teachers feel they are involved and treated fairly, the typical "them/us" tensions dissolve. For example, one district's teacher union president said "the classroom is supported fairly well as opposed to monies going into the central office and never seeing the light of day again." The community generally shares this view of central office priorities. A parent commented: "It's a district that cares about making sure that the schools are OK before taking care of the district office."

In contrast to conventional wisdom that teachers will resent a strong district presence in their practice, Highland teacher survey responses show extremely high teacher ratings of professional and instructional authority. Eighty-one percent say the "district is committed to high standards for every student," and 79% are "proud to tell others I work for this district"; most say they take an active role in schoolwide decision making and feel encouraged and supported by colleagues to experiment with their teaching.

The Bay Area districts also provide exception to the assertion that strong districts squelch school-level innovation and responsiveness. Proponents of charter schools and choice models base their position in part on the cookie-cutter management style that has characterized most districts, where anything other than a "one size fits all" treatment risks contentious community political fallout. A systemwide strategy, in this tradition, weakens individual schools' reform work. Bay Area reforming districts provide instructive exception to this conclusion. Their strategic planning processes provide data and a broad-based buy-in that permits targeting resources differentially to schools, based on demonstrated need. Once the money gets to the schools, however, principals and teachers have the greatest say in what to spend it on.

Cookie-cutter district policies also raise issues of student equity. Educators and community members in reforming districts know student equity does not mean equal treatment. The former Highland superintendent commented: "Fair isn't the equal treatment of unequals. Fair is trying to support people at the level that they need support." Infighting rarely resulted from this policy:

> I think we built a caring community because we looked at each other's data, never to embarrass anybody. There were times when one school would want to allocate some of their money to another school because they needed it more.

This explicit district role in advancing and protecting equity suggests that decentralization reforms that maximize school-level control may be, in fact, fundamentally undemocratic from a school system perspective.

The Bay Area reforming districts move debate about district role beyond centralization/decentralization dichotomies to appropriate distribution of responsibilities and functions among levels. The salient issue tackled in reforming districts is being tactical about what decisions are made where and how responsibilities follow.

Myth 2: Turnover and Change Will Sink Reform Efforts

Leadership turnover can derail district efforts to establish and sustain a consistent reform agenda; boards' tendency to search for a school leader with a different style or goals (often in response to disappointment over the departing superintendent) adds to "churn" in district-level goals and norms. Bay Area reforming districts suggest ways of dealing with the potentially destabilizing consequences of leadership change. When the visionary Highland superintendent responsible for instituting the strategic planning process left, core district norms and functions proceeded as they had in the past because the superintendent had taken care to integrate them throughout the system, using among other things the planning process. A central office administrator said:

> She's built a team and a structure and a vision that will outlive her
> . . . we all know where we're going. We might slow down a little . . .
> [but] there's so much in place that now's the time to implement it
> and drive it deeper. I'm sure that it won't look exactly the same
> because everyone has a unique style in how they do things, but I
> think the direction and the vision and the planning that's been put
> into place won't miss a beat because it's in motion. There's a strong
> commitment to the way we're moving with data and technology
> and instruction.

The transition was smooth, even in the context of other leadership changes. Despite gaining a new superintendent, two new assistant superintendents, and several other position changes within the district office, Highland's programs and policies supporting teachers and priorities for systems change stayed on track, and even moved forward. In both Bay Area districts, turnover in top leadership did not trigger significant change in district goals or norms because, over time, planning processes and inclusive communication strategies had made them part of the "water supply."

Myth 3: Local Politics Will Defeat a Serious Reform Agenda

The strong, clear statements of purpose and priority found in these reforming districts counter the view that superintendents can advance only general objectives unlikely to offend anyone. Conventional wisdom advises broad goals with something for everyone, especially in districts serving a diverse student population. Superintendents and their boards, observers assert, have strong incentives to choose flashy, inoffensive reform strategies—initiatives that "maximize political impact and minimize potential adverse reaction" (Hess, 1999, p. 123).

Yet leaders in each reforming district advanced unambiguous goals and priorities. Strong boards, carefully built and tended for more than a decade to provide consistent direction and allied backing, enabled Bay Area superintendents to navigate local political waters and project a strong district role. Survey data from Bay Area district administrators underscore the point: District office investment in reform, technical support, and networking were all significantly associated with school board support. The former Highland superintendent sees board relations as the sine qua non of a reforming district:

> The number-one thing resides in the relationship between the board and the superintendent. I would never have been able to move in the directions that I've moved if I didn't have those people along with me. I've worked hard at not just educating the board on a variety of issues, but I worked very hard on who was on my board.

The result was a cohesive board that functioned smoothly with little political posturing.

Strategic planning can also help maintain strong board support by building a base and buy-in for implementing plans and, as an associate superintendent said, bringing "resources to [the plan] because the board is always very conscious about parent input and the base of decision making."

San Diego's leaders enjoy no such support with a bitterly divided 3–2 board. Their political base initially derived from the business community, its reform agenda developed out of dissatisfaction with prior leadership (Hightower, 2001; Chapter 5, this volume), and its mandate was for fundamental change. But the fragility of the San Diego initiative lies in a split board that ultimately may decide to fire the superintendent and discard the reform. In this regard, San Diego reformers suffer from the absence of the data and communication structures that Bay Area reforming districts used to build strong support within the board and the community.

LESSONS AND CONCLUSIONS

The experience and evolution of district-level reform in these cases teach some unsurprising lessons—that system change takes time and that a supportive school board is critical to system learning and risk taking. That said, together these three districts add important perspective to what we know about reforming districts.

A strategic conception of roles and functions features critically in district reform. Moreover, a strong district role makes an essential contribution to school reform when it provides both the clear goals and necessary supports to school staff. Our analysis suggests that a weakened central office cannot advance school reform that is equitable or sustainable.

As self-conscious "learning organizations," these districts invest in learning throughout the system—in the central office, schools, and units such as the business office that are traditionally excluded from instructionally focused professional development. Bay Area districts' commitment to strategic planning enables them to avoid "competency traps" (March, 1994); annual reviews of programs and resource allocation ask tough questions about progress against district goals and needed changes. Their organizational culture makes "self-correction a norm and not a war" (Sarason, 1991, p. 129).

Finally, the experience of San Diego and Bay Area educators reinforces districts' responsibility for attending to equity goals. Only a systemwide can create and nourish a system of schools where opportunities and resources are both site-specific and reflective of district goals for all students.

NOTES

This chapter reflects the work of the entire Center for the Study of Teaching and Policy team, most especially that of Amy Hightower, Julie Marsh, and Marjorie Wechsler, whose case analyses figure prominently here.

1. Correlations of district scores on the "central office learning community" scale with survey measures of each of these district roles are, respectively: .28, .42, .45 (statistically significant at .05 and .01 levels). Scale definitions and more extensive statistical data are available on request.

The District Role in Instructional Renewal: Making Sense and Taking Action

The chapters in this volume raise possibilities that beg to be pursued by educators and scholars. We offer these ideas as starting points for conversation among all who care about forging viable district roles in instructional renewal. In this concluding chapter, we make several observations, first, about what can be learned from these cases, and, second, about challenges and opportunities for further action and inquiry.

LESSONS FROM THE RESEARCH IN THIS VOLUME

The research reported in this volume needs to be carefully interpreted lest we invest it with more meaning than it rightfully possesses. Because the districts described in this book are unusual cases, we first need to consider whether they are aberrations, arrangements too hard to achieve or sustain in the vast majority of districts across the country. Consider, for example, the stable district leadership over long periods of time in New York's Community School District #2 or New Haven, California (Chapters 4 and 6), and strong board support in the two Bay Area districts (Chapter 11). It is tempting to dismiss these districts' achievements because superintendents typically do not last long and boards are often split and volatile, especially in large urban settings. But to do so begs questions about the ways in which superintendent and board stability might be a *result* of coherent renewal strategies as much as a prerequisite to them. Furthermore, such a dismissal cuts short deeper thinking about precisely what district leaders and boards are doing in the cases in question and what their counterparts in other settings might do differently.

While districts typically do not assume the roles described here, these tendencies do not represent a priori constraints on the district's participation in instructional renewal. Rather, they suggest matters of habit, tradition, or conventional wisdom. As we see it, the districts examined here have begun to demonstrate ways of doing business that are as instructive as they are unusual. Accordingly, what they are doing can be the source of new *learning*—admittedly, hard learning, but nonetheless within reach of many.

The district work that lies ahead implies analysis, conceptualization, and persistent experimentation. Cases such as these challenge educators and observers to articulate underlying design principles, develop frameworks representing these principles at work in a variety of settings, and invent new realizations of the principles. To that end, a careful reading of these cases offers, first, a vocabulary of generative concepts, and second, the beginnings of several robust, testable frameworks.

Creating a Vocabulary of Generative Concepts

This book presents a complementary set of concepts that hold promise for fashioning powerful district approaches to instructional renewal. These concepts have not arisen independently of one another. Rather, they represent a mutually informing set of ideas with common intellectual roots, in some instances, originating with the authors in this volume, in other instances, elsewhere in the literature.

Six sets of concepts form a reinforcing storyline about the district's role in instructional renewal:

- District leaders as learners, teachers, and teacher educators
- District as "nested learning community" and "learning laboratory"
- District as source of instructional focus
- District as channel for subject-specific learning
- District as context for a culture of inquiry and professional accountability
- District as partner engaged with community and professional organizations

District Leaders as Learners, Teachers, and Teacher Educators. A persistent theme in these chapters is that district leaders are both learners and teachers. They are engaged in *learning* about the meaning and substance of renewal initiatives, whether these originate at state level (Chapter 9) or locally (Chapter 10). Simultaneously, central office leaders and administrators act as *teacher* (Chapter 9) and *teacher educator* (Chapters 6 and 8), especially for staff newly entering the profession but also for veteran staff (Chapter 4). Drawing on what they understand and believe about teaching practice, district-level staff communicate reform messages, provoke conversations, and create opportunities for teachers to engage in learning (Chapters 3, 8, and 10).

As learners and teachers, district and school leaders make assumptions about learning and teaching (Chapter 9), derived in part from their own knowledge but also from structural features of administrators' work, which typically is fragmented, and the relationship between administrators and teachers, which typically is distant and episodic. These assumptions may or may not match the forms of instructional practice that reformers espouse, thereby providing a target for the district's professional learning agenda.

District as "Nested Learning Community" and "Learning Laboratory." The district has the capacity to create a mutually reinforcing set of venues, experiences, and incentives supporting the professional learning that lies at the core of instructional renewal. Framed by Resnick and Glennan (Chapter 10) as a set of "nested learning communities" (classroom nested within school, nested within district) and by Hightower (Chapter 5) as "an infrastructure" supporting professional learning, the district is creating an environment within structures and routines at *all* levels of the system that makes professional learning an inescapable norm. As community participants, central office administrators, school principals, and teachers engage in dialogue about teachers' work and the quality of students' learning experiences, these communities go beyond the boundaries of a single school to represent districtwide communities of practice. These communities embrace considerable variation in expertise and perspective, which the districts can exploit as an instructional resource rather than treating as a liability or impediment (Chapter 4).

District as a Source of Instructional Focus. In addition to creating a supportive infrastructure, districts can focus the work and learning of these communities. Cases in this volume show district central offices projecting a clear, sustained focus on selected aspects of the curriculum and teaching practice (Chapters 5 and 10), thereby directing attention toward the technical work of schools (Chapter 11). Given the complexity of these districts, the high degree of focus is striking—and noticeable by its absence under conditions of district "policy flux" (Chapter 7). Through system-level planning and strong district-level leadership—which does not necessarily engender school-level resistance—districts can promote a focus on instructional improvement that is widely shared among participants and can be sustained over time, even across periods of leadership turnover (Chapter 11).

District as Channel for Subject-Specific Learning. The work in this volume suggests that instructional renewal benefits from professional learning within particular subject areas and that district choices can maximize the channels for subject-specific learning (Chapter 8). These channels (e.g., through curriculum, mentoring, professional development, participation in external networks) reflect the particulars of a given subject matter, rather than forms of practice that are standardized across subject matters (Chapters 4 and 8).

Most of the districts considered in this book have chosen to focus on literacy instruction, and some have taken aim at mathematics teaching. While the nature of the channel varies with the subject matter, the underlying principle is constant: Advancing teachers' actual practice implies a rich, ongoing conversation about the particulars of subject matter and its manifestations in classroom activities and student work.

District as Context for a Culture of Inquiry and Professional Accountability. The instructional learning that both teachers and administrators do in the districts studied in this volume often takes place through inquiry into practice, prompted by data regarding individual students' work, performance patterns across classrooms and schools, and other aspects of school or district functioning (Chapters 3, 10, and 11). Data of several kinds ground educators' conversations about improvement of practice and place all participants in the role of *inquirer*—that is, in a position of asking and answering questions about practice, rather than rendering judgment on performance.

The resulting culture of inquiry provides a constructive context for districts to assert and maintain *professional* accountability. For example, in contrast to Chicago's sudden press for accountability, perceived by educators as punitive and restrictive (Chapter 7), the use of data for decision making about instructional or school improvement in other districts provides a basis for constructive scrutiny of professional work (Chapters 3 and 11). Furthermore, explicit in some chapters (e.g., Chapters 3 and 10) and implicit in others is the two-way flow of information—both to the district or other constituents and back to the teacher in various forms of feedback.

District as Partner Engaged with Community and Professional Organizations. Various authors underscore the ways in which the district's capacity to learn, lead, and educate is enhanced by partnerships with external organizations, such as professional development providers (Chapter 7), national learning networks (Chapter 10), or regional reform networks (Chapter 11). These partnerships not only expand the capacity of the district but also extend the concept of "district" to include a particular community and professional context. Conceived in this way, new avenues arise for districts to develop more consequential approaches to instructional renewal.

The district's outreach to community or professional organizations involves more than reaching for resources. As several authors point out, the district's pursuit of instructional renewal relies on public trust (Chapter 1) and takes place in the context of a relationship with communities (Chapter 2). What districts do to cultivate that trust—for example, by proactively engaging community interests (Chapter 11), fostering a sense of the common good, or mediating between professional innovations and public interests (Chapter 1)—becomes an essential part of the district's instructional renewal story. In this regard, district leaders' conceptions of the community—as obstacle or social resource—have much to do with the potential for districts to enable instructional renewal (Chapter 2).

Building Powerful, Testable Frameworks

Concepts such as these frame courses of action that might help districts make more potent contributions to instructional renewal. Several chapters (Chapters 10 and 11) offer frameworks explicitly, others do it more implicitly, by describing such systems (Chapters 5 and 6) or examining features such as systemic supports for professional learning (Chapter 4).

Powerful, testable frameworks regarding the district in instructional renewal have at least four attributes. First, they take the district *system* as the primary unit of change (Chapters 5 and 11) and make the quality of teaching a prominent focus of the system renewal (e.g., Chapter 6). The chapters offer various takes on the primary attributes of such a system, and how district leaders and others might take steps in that direction. More than one framework might be imagined; indeed, Massell and Goertz (Chapter 3) identified several dominant strategies in their study of several dozen cases.

Second, powerful frameworks consider not only multiple routes by which district-level actions and structures can reach teaching and learning but also the coherence among these routes. As such, the frameworks we are calling for address the "whole-cloth" character of the environment in which teaching and learning take place as much as any single feature of that environment.

Third, for *all* actors, the frameworks highlight the means and nature of engagement in professional learning that is intimately connected to the agenda for student learning. Renewal is not possible without learning, and the agenda for learning must be commensurate with the intellectual ambitions of the renewal vision(s) operative within a particular context.

Fourth, powerful frameworks are rendered with sufficient concreteness and conceptual specification to be "tried out" and studied in a variety of circumstances. This specificity serves equally the scholar and the practicing district leader bent on developing more effective strategies for instructional renewal.

OPPORTUNITIES AND CHALLENGES CONFRONTING
DISTRICTWIDE INSTRUCTIONAL RENEWAL

Make no mistake: Achieving a constructive and proactive district role in instructional renewal is not a simple matter. The experiences examined in this volume imply that many obstacles stand in the way, starting with the sheer weight of organizational traditions and histories, which in larger districts relegate lines of improvement activity to different units within a bureaucratized hierarchy. And given the tendency toward organizing the district's work in ways that disconnect administrative functions from each other and from instruction (Chapters 5 and 9), the creation of a coherent renewal strategy is unlikely to be part of most district officials' working repertoires.

Four Critical Challenges

Even when district staff understand and seek coherence, forging coherent strategies, enacting them, and realizing their potential equitably across a complex district's classrooms is daunting. In addition to an inevitable "implementation gap," four critical challenges arise in the unfolding interaction between district actions and classroom practice: (1) managing the politics of instructional renewal; (2) accommodating variability among schools, classrooms, and teachers; (3) balancing school and district authority over teaching conditions; and (4) making renewal strategies appropriately sensitive to subject matter.

Managing the Politics of Instructional Renewal. Instructional renewal strategies touch many people's interests, which are varied and often in contention with one another within a pluralistic, democratic society. Recent battles over approaches to reading instruction, the content of social studies curriculum, or the degree of emphasis to be placed on basic skills development in mathematics teaching underscore the fact that people often hold fundamentally conflicting conceptions of both content and pedagogy. Therefore, an instructional renewal strategy that purports to touch many aspects of teacher development and teachers' work is bound to surface such conflicts, especially in the public debate where such conflicts often erupt.

Viewed as a political course of action, instructional renewal strategies may be understood as a means of managing such conflicts (Malen & Knapp, 1997), in which leaders, policy makers, and other participants maneuver adroitly, gather political intelligence, build coalitions, gather political and symbolic resources, and exercise power in a fluid political field. Compounded by the racial politics that characterize many high-poverty settings, the challenge to groups guiding the renewal of instruction is considerable.

At a minimum, renewal strategies are only likely to survive if leaders develop a politically sustainable "cover story" that generates confidence and willingness to suspend doubt while changes are being made. The cases presented in this volume raise the possibility that, in districts both large and small, such conflicts can be managed without sacrificing forcefulness, direction, or a targeted allocation of resources—attributes of a renewal strategy that can be so easily lost in compromise (Chapter 11).

Accommodating Variable Capacity Among Schools, Classrooms, and Teachers. Whatever the instructional renewal strategy espouses, these expectations for teachers' work and student performance encounter enormous variability in the capacity of schools, classrooms, and teachers to realize these expectations. As several chapters in this volume assert (Chapters 2 and 3), the knowledge, skills, and beliefs of teachers and district leaders about learning, schooling, and teacher development are highly varied. As existing case research suggests, this variability greatly influences how much and whether teachers realize ambitious reforms in the classroom (e.g., *Educational Evaluation and Policy Analysis*, 1990; Spillane & Jennings, 1997).

Renewal initiatives can approach this variability in one of two ways: by insisting that all classrooms and schools "measure up" to the same standard, without regard for their differences in capacity, or by differentiating the way in which schools (or classrooms) are treated, depending on some initial indications of capacity. New York District #2 offers one example of what such a differentiated strategy might look like (Elmore & Burney, 1997b); and within such a strategy, variability itself can become a learning resource, as noted earlier (Chapter 4). Without this or some other means of addressing variability, renewal strategies risk a high failure rate, cynicism and low morale, lower public trust, and reduced learning opportunities for students.

There also are costs to addressing variability proactively. For example, school professionals, unions, and others may perceive differential treatment as unfair. But that may be a necessary cost of trying to achieve instructional renewal on a systemwide basis, rather than in pockets of excellence, as is so often the case. Addressing equity—a major district responsibility (Chapters 1 and 11)—often means *unequal* treatment.

Balancing School and District Authority over Teaching Conditions. In enacting a proactive instructional renewal strategy, district policy makers inevitably face questions of where to centralize authority within the system—at the central office, in some districtwide entity, or in the schools. The lines of least resistance are for the district to "tell teachers what to do," through mandates, prescriptive regulation, monitoring, and sanctions, but the pros and cons of doing so are well established (see Porter, 1989; Chapter 1, this volume), as are the dangers of relying too single-mindedly on "democratic localism" (Chapters 1 and 11).

Some balance must be struck between centralization and decentralization, between exerting pressure on teachers to change their practice and granting them room to experiment with, or define the direction of, the changes, if ambitious goals for instructional renewal are to be realized (Knapp & Associates, 1995). As McLaughlin and Talbert (Chapter 11) argue, the issue has less to do with the strength of the district's presence in instructional renewal and more with *what* it assumes responsibility for and *how*. It is thus possible that districts can be simultaneously assertive and empowering, strong and supportive, and that dichotomous thinking about centralization and decentralizing tendencies is not useful for identifying the district's role in instructional renewal.

Making Instructional Renewal Appropriately Sensitive to Subject Matter. Many renewal strategies are conceived without thought to teachers' subject-matter contexts, as is often the case with compensation policies, professional standards, and workplace enhancement initiatives. Even professional development activities may be framed with all teachers in mind or without reference to particular subject matter (Chapters 1, 3, and 6), as in workshops focused on generic classroom management techniques, student discipline, the dimensions of multicultural education, or the health problems of early adolescent children (Chapter 8). As useful as exploring these topics may be, it may not help teachers address central questions about what to teach, how to engage students, how to give critical feedback or assess student work, and the like.

More to the point, without paying attention to the *differences* in subject-matter contexts, renewal strategies may simply ignore, to their peril, teachers' likely response to these strategies (Grossman & Stodolsky, 1994). For example, a text-based curriculum reform may work well in a subject area such as mathematics, which by tradition is heavily dependent on texts, but poorly in language arts or social studies, where textbooks are not typically viewed as central features of the curricular landscape. Generically construed strategies may also miss the mark in more subtle ways, as in mentoring policies for new teachers. Though clearly an improvement over the frequent sink-

or-swim approach to new teacher induction, arrangements that do not provide new teachers with access to a mentor with expertise *in the particular subject area with which they are struggling* deprive the teachers of the support for which they are desperately looking (Chapter 8). District strategies can forestall this kind of problem by continually considering how teachers will be found, hired, compensated, and supported for work in particular subject areas, given the unique features of teaching and learning in those disciplines.

This coin has two sides, however: The district environment for teaching touches many aspects of teachers' working lives, only some of which are defined by a subject-matter context (or, in the case of most elementary teachers, multiple subject-matter contexts). The simultaneous arrival of different, teaching-related reforms raises other kinds of questions about the impact of a policy environment on classroom teachers' working lives that would be overlooked when one considers the influence of teaching policy one subject at a time. For example, the question of overload due to simultaneous new expectations or incompatibility among multiple policies is unlikely to be considered when examining renewal strategy effects with a particular subject-matter lens, as are the politics of managing the competing interests of subject-defined groups (e.g., high school departments). While negotiating a balance between subject-specific and generic considerations is difficult, district leaders have more to consider in enhancing teachers' work and careers than can be anticipated by subject-matter considerations alone.

Leadership and Inquiry in Pursuit of Instructional Renewal

The politics of renewal, variability across schools and classrooms, the tension between district and school authority, and the ramifications of subject-matter contexts are critical issues with which district leaders grapple as they fashion strategies aimed at instructional renewal. Each issue raises important questions for further research at the same time that it poses conundrums for district leadership and policy design. On the one hand, for example, we do not yet fully understand the subject-specific ramifications of the many strands in a district policy environment, yet on the other, we have much to discover about how teachers navigate a reform environment in which many conditions related to their work and careers are changing at once.

Districts will not stop experimenting with instructional renewal strategies while researchers explore these matters. But scholars and district leaders would do well to take note of teachers' work, and even to join forces in pursuit of districtwide instructional renewal. There is urgent work to be done and much to be discovered, as educational leaders, observers, and teachers themselves share with one another and outside audiences what they are learning as these local experiments proceed.

References

Anderson, C., & Smith, E. (1987). Teaching science. In V. R. Koehler (Ed.), *Educators' handbook: A research perspective* (pp. 80–111). New York: Longman.

Annenberg Institute for School Reform, Brown University. Retrieved September 30, 2001, from http://www.annenberginstitute.org/dtf/framework.html.

Argyris, C., & Schön, D. (1974). *Theory in practice: Increasing professional effectiveness*. San Francisco: Jossey-Bass.

Ball, D. L., & Cohen, D. K. (1996). Reform by the book: What is or might be the role of curriculum materials in teacher learning and instructional reform. *Educational Researcher, 25*(9), 6–8.

Ball, D. L., & Cohen, D. K. (1999). Developing practice, developing practitioners: Toward a practice-based theory of professional education. In L. Darling-Hammond & G. Sykes (Eds.), *Teaching as a learning profession* (pp. 3–31). San Francisco: Jossey-Bass.

Barnett, D., & Malloy, K. (1997). *Building a learning community: A portrait of a public school district* [video]. (Available from High-Performance Learning Community Project, Learning Research and Development Center, University of Pittsburgh, 3939 O'Hara Street, Pittsburgh, PA 15260).

Barnett, D., & Stein, M. K. (1998). *Building a learning community: Professional development* [video]. (Available from High-Performance Learning Community Project, Learning Research and Development Center, University of Pittsburgh, 3939 O'Hara Street, Pittsburgh, PA 15260).

Bereiter, C., Brown, A., Campione, J., Carruthers, I., Case, R., Hirshberg, J., Adams, M. J., McKeough, A., Pressley, M., Roit, M., Scardamalia, M., & Treadway, G. H., Jr. (2000). Open court phonics (grades K–6 reading and writing program). Columbus, OH: SRA/McGraw-Hill.

Berliner, D. (1986). In pursuit of the expert pedagogue. *Educational Researcher, 15*, 5–13.

Berman, P., & McLaughlin, M. W. (1977). *Federal programs supporting educational change: Vol. 7. Factors affecting implementation and continuation*. Santa Monica, CA: RAND.

Bimber, B. (1994). *The decentralization mirage: Comparing decisionmaking arrangements in four high schools*. Santa Monica, CA: RAND.

Blodgett, J. H. (1897). Education. In *Report on population of the United States at the eleventh census: 1890*. Washington, DC: U.S. Government Printing Office.

Bodilly, S. J. (1998). *Lessons from New American Schools' scale-up phase: Prospects for bringing designs to multiple schools*. Santa Monica, CA: RAND.

Bransford, J., Brown, A., & Cocking, R. R. (1999). *How people learn: Brain, mind and experience and school.* Washington, DC: National Research Council.

Briars, D., & Resnick, L. B. (2000). *Standards, assessments, and what else? The essential elements of standards-based school improvements* (CSE Tech. Report No. 528). Los Angeles: University of California, National Center for Research on Evaluation, Standards, and Student Testing (CRESST).

Brown, A. L., Greeno, J. G., Lampert, M., Mehan, H., & Resnick, L. B. (1999, March). *Recommendations regarding research priorities: An advisory report to the National Education Research Policy and Priorities Board.* New York: National Academy of Education.

Brown, J. S., Collins, A., & Duguid, P. (1989). Situated cognition and the culture of learning. *Educational Researcher, 18*(1), 32–42.

Bryk, A. S., Lee, V. E., & Holland, P. B. (1993). *Catholic schools and the common good.* Cambridge, MA: Harvard University Press.

Bryk, A. S., Sebring, P. B., Kerbow, K., Rollow, S., & Easton, J. Q. (1998). *Charting Chicago school reform: Democratic localism as a level for change.* Boulder, CO: Westview Press.

Burch, P. (2000). *Moving from the margins to the mainstream: Teaching and learning reform in local policy context.* Unpublished doctoral dissertation, Stanford University, Stanford, CA.

Center for Research on the Context of Teaching (CRC). (2000). *Assessing results: The Bay Area School Reform Collaborative, year four.* Stanford, CA: Author. Stanford University.

Chancellor, W. E. (1915). *Our schools: Their administration and supervision.* Boston: Heath.

Chicago Merchants' Club. (1906). *Public schools and their administration: Addresses delivered at the fifty-ninth meeting of the Merchants' Club of Chicago.* Chicago: Author.

Chicago Public Schools. (1994). *Pathways to achievement: Self-analysis guide.* Chicago: Author.

Chrispeels, J. H. (1997). Educational policy implementation in a shifting political climate: The California experience. *American Educational Research Journal, 34,* 453–481.

Chubb, J. E., & Moe, T. M. (1990a). America's public schools: Choice *is* a panacea. *Brookings Review, 8* (3), 4–12.

Chubb, J. E., & Moe, T. M. (1990b). *Politics, markets, and America's schools.* Washington, DC: Brookings Institution.

Classified partner notes Ed. Center dysfunction. (1999, May 19). *The Advocate* (San Diego Education Association), p. 1.

Cochran-Smith, M., & Lytle, S. L. (2001). Beyond certainty: Taking an inquiry stance on practice. In A. Lieberman & L. Miller (Eds.), *Teachers caught in the action: Professional development that matters* (pp. 45–58). New York: Teachers College Press.

Cohen, D. K. (1988). Teaching practice: Plus ca change. In P. W. Jackson (Ed.), *Contributing to educational change: Perspectives on research and practice* (pp. 27–84). Berkeley, CA: McCutchan.

Cohen, D. K. (1990). A revolution in one classroom: The case of Mrs. Oublier. *Educational Evaluation and Policy Analysis, 12,* 327–345.

Cohen, D. K. (1995). What is the system in systemic reform? *Educational Researcher,* 24(9), 11–18.

Cohen, D. K. (1997, March). *Policy, cognition, and instruction.* Paper distributed at Center for Policy Research in Education/Learning Research Development Center Conference, Pittsburgh, PA.

Cohen, D., & Ball, D. (1997). *Where macro and micro perspectives meet: Resources and teacher policy.* Ann Arbor: University of Michigan Press.

Cohen, D. K., & Barnes, C. A. (1993). Pedagogy and policy. In D. K. Cohen, M. W. McLaughlin, & J. E. Talbert (Eds.), *Teaching for understanding: Challenges for policy and practice* (pp. 207–239). San Francisco: Jossey-Bass.

Cohen, D. K., & Hill, H. C. (1998). *State policy and classroom performance: Mathematics reform in California* (CPRE Policy Brief). Philadelphia, PA: University of Pennsylvania, Consortium for Policy Research in Education.

Cohen, D. K., & Spillane, J. P. (1993). Policy and practice: The relations between governance and instruction. In S. H. Fuhrman (Ed.), *Designing coherent education policy: Improving the system* (pp. 35–95). San Francisco: Jossey-Bass.

Cohen, D., Spillane, J., Jennings, N., & Grants, S. (1998). *Reading policy.* Unpublished manuscript, University of Michigan, Ann Arbor, MI.

Columbia Group. (1997). *Teachers teaching in the Southeast.* Raleigh, NE: Author.

Community School District #2. (1999). *The District #2 Balanced Literacy Program 1999: A handbook for teachers.* New York: Author.

Confrey, J. (1990). A review of the research on student conceptions in mathematics, science, and programming. In C. Cazden (Ed.), *Review of research in education* (Vol. 16, pp. 3–55). Washington, DC: American Educational Research Association.

Consortium on Chicago School Research. (1993). *A view from the elementary schools: The state of reform in Chicago.* Chicago: Author.

Consortium on Chicago School Research. (1995). *Charting reform: Chicago teachers take stock.* Chicago: Author.

Consortium on Chicago School Research. (1996). *Charting reform in Chicago: The students speak.* Chicago: Author.

Council of Great City Schools. (2000, March). *Ten-year trends in urban education: 1987–1997.* Washington, DC: Author.

Cross-City Campaign for Urban School Reform. Retrieved March 6, 2001, from <http://www.crosscity.org/pubs/flashfacts.htm.

Cubberley, E. P. (1914). *Rural life and education: A study of the rural-school problem.* Boston: Houghton Mifflin.

Cubberley, E. P. (1915). Organization of public education. *NEA addresses and proceedings, 1915,* 91–97.

Cubberley, E. P. (1916). *Public school administration: A statement of the fundamental principles underlying the organization and administration of public education.* Boston: Houghton Mifflin.

D'Amico, L., Harwell, M., Stein, M. K., & van den Heuvel, J. R. (2001, April). *Examining the implementation and effectiveness of a district-wide instructional improvement effort.* Paper presented at the Annual Meeting of the American Educational Research Association, Seattle, WA.

Danzberger, J. P. (1987). School boards: Forgotten players on the educational team. *Phi Delta Kappan, 69,* 53–59.

Darling-Hammond, L. (1997a). *Doing what matters most: Investing in quality teaching.* New York: National Commission on Teaching and America's Future.

Darling-Hammond, L. (1997b). *The right to learn: A blueprint for creating schools that work.* San Francisco: Jossey-Bass.

Darling-Hammond, L., & McLaughlin, M. W. (1999). Investing in teaching as a learning profession: Policy problems and prospects. In L. Darling-Hammond & G. Sykes (Eds.), *Teaching as the learning profession: Handbook of policy and practice* (pp. 376–411). San Francisco: Jossey-Bass.

Darling-Hammond, L., & Sykes, G. (Eds.). (1999). *Teaching as the learning profession: Handbook of policy and practice.* San Francisco: Jossey-Bass.

David, J. (1978). *Local uses of Title I evaluations.* Washington, DC: Office of the Assistant Secretary for Planning and Evaluation, Department of Health, Education and Welfare.

David, J. L. (1990). Restructuring in progress: Lessons from pioneering districts. In R. F. Elmore & Associates (Eds.), *Restructuring schools: The next generation of education reform* (pp. 209–250). San Francisco: Jossey-Bass.

Educational Evaluation and Policy Analysis, 12 (3). (1990). [Issue on implementation of California Mathematics Framework].

Ellis, W. S. (1900). School board organization. *NEA addresses and proceedings, 1900,* 631–634.

Elmore, R. F. (1993). The role of local school districts in instructional improvement. In S. H. Fuhrman (Ed.), *Designing coherent education policy: Improving the system* (pp. 96–124). San Francisco: Jossey-Bass.

Elmore, R. F. (1996). Getting to scale with good educational practice. *Harvard Educational Review, 66*(1), 1–26.

Elmore, R. F. (1997). Accountability in local school districts: Learning to do the right things. *Advances in Educational Administration, 5,* 59–82.

Elmore, R. F. (2000). *Building a new structure for school leadership.* Paper prepared for the Albert Shanker Institute, Washington, DC.

Elmore, R. F., & Burney, D. (1997a). *Investing in teacher learning: Staff development and instructional improvement in Community School District #2, New York City.* New York: National Commission on Teaching and America's Future and the Consortium for Policy Research in Education.

Elmore, R. F., & Burney, D. (1997b). *School variation and systemic instructional improvement in Community School District 32, New York City.* Pittsburgh, PA: High Performance Learning Communities Project, Learning Research and Development Center, University of Pittsburgh.

Elmore, R. F., & Burney, D. (1999). Investing in teacher learning: Staff development and instructional improvement. In L. Darling-Hammong & G. Sykes (Eds.), *Teaching as the learning profession: Handbook of policy and practice* (pp. 263–291). San Francisco: Jossey-Bass.

Evans, P. M., & Mohr, N. (1999). Professional development for principals: Seven core beliefs. *Phi Delta Kappan, 80*(7), 530–532.

Exton, E. (1965, June). Will local school boards flourish or fade in the great society? *American School Board Journal, 150,* 7–8, 66–67.

Fink, E., & Resnick, L. B. (1999). *Developing principals as instructional leaders.* Pittsburgh, PA: High Performance Learning Communities Project, Learning Research and Development Center, University of Pittsburgh.

Fink, E., & Resnick, L. B. (2001). Developing principals as instructional leaders. *Phi Delta Kappan, 82,* 578–606.

Finn, C. (1991). *We must take charge: Our schools and our future.* New York: Free Press.

Finn, J. D., & Achilles, C. M. (1999). Tennessee's class size study: Findings, implications, and misconceptions. *Educational Evaluation and Policy Analysis, 20*(2), 97–109.

Firestone, W. A. (1989a). Educational policy as an ecology of games. *Educational Researcher, 18*(7), 18–24.

Firestone, W. A. (1989b). Using reform: Conceptualizing district initiative. *Educational Evaluation and Policy Analysis, 11,* 151–164.

Firestone, W. A., & Fairman, J. C. (1998). *The district role in state assessment policy: An exploratory study.* Paper presented at the annual meeting of the American Educational Research Association, San Diego, CA.

Florian, J., Hange, J., & Copeland, G. (2000). *The phantom mandate: District capacity for reform.* Paper presented at the annual meeting of the American Educational Research Association, New Orleans, LA.

Fountas, I. C., & Pinnell, G. S. (1995). *Guided reading: Good first teaching for all children.* Portsmouth, NH: Heinemann.

Fuhrman, S. H., & Elmore, R. F. (1990). Understanding local control in the wake of state education reform. *Educational Evaluation and Policy Analysis, 12,* 82–96.

Fullan, M. (1991). *The new meaning of educational change.* New York: Teachers College Press.

Fullan, M. (1994). Coordinating top-down and bottom-up strategies for educational reform. In R. F. Elmore & S. H. Fuhrman (Eds.), *The governance of curriculum* (pp. 186–202). Alexandria, VA: Association for Supervision and Curriculum Development.

Fullan, M. G. (1997). *What's worth fighting for in the principalship.* New York: Teachers College Press.

Fullan, M. (1999). *Change forces: The sequel.* Philadelphia: Falmer.

Fullan, M. (2000). The return of large-scale reform. *Journal of Educational Change, 1,* 5–28.

Fullan, M. (2001). *The new meaning of educational change* (3rd ed.). New York: Teachers College Press.

Fuller, F. F. (1969). Concerns of teachers: A developmental conceptualization. *American Educational Research Journal, 6,* 207–226.

Fuller, W. E. (1982). *The old country school: The story of rural education in the middle west.* Chicago: University of Chicago Press.

Fuller, W. E. (1994). *One room schools of the middle west.* Lawrence: University Press of Kansas.

Gagne, R. (1965). *The conditions of learning.* New York: Holt, Rinehart, & Winston.

Gearhart, M., Harding, N., Saxe, G., & Troper, J. (1997). *Shared commitment, varied understandings: Elementary mathematics teachers' interpretations of reform-minded practices.* Los Angeles: UCLA, Center for Research on Evaluation, Standards, and Student Testing. Unpublished manuscript.

Goertz, M. E., Floden, R. E., & O'Day, J. (1995). *Studies of education reform: Systemic reform.* New Brunswick, NJ: Consortium for Policy Research in Education (CPRE), Rutgers University.

Goertz, M., Massell, D., & Chun, T. (1998). *District response to state accountability systems.* Paper presented at the annual meeting of the Association for Public Policy Analysis and Management (APPAM), New York.

Goldring, E. B., & Hallinger, P. (1992). *District control contexts and school organizational processes.* Paper presented at the annual meeting of the American Educational Research Association, San Francisco.

Goldsmith, L. T., & Schifter, D. (1993). *Characteristics of a model for the development of mathematics teaching.* Newton, MA: Education Development Center.

Greeno, J., Collins, A., & Resnick, L. (1996). Cognition and learning. In D. C. Berliner & R. C. Calfee (Eds.). *Handbook of educational psychology* (pp. 15–46). New York: Macmillan.

Greeno, J., Riley, M, & Gelman, R. (1984). Conceptual competence and children's counting. *Cognitive Psychology, 16,* 94–143.

Grossman, P. L., Smagorinsky, P., & Valencia, S. (1999). Appropriating tools for teaching English: A theoretical framework for research on learning to teach. *American Journal of Education, 108,* 1–29.

Grossman, P., & Stodolsky, S. (1994). Considerations of content and the circumstances of secondary school teaching. *Review of Research in Education, 20,* 179–221.

Grossman, P. L., Valencia, S. W., Evans, K., Thompson, C., Martin, S., & Place, N. (2000). Transitions into teaching: Learning to teach writing in teacher education and beyond. *Journal of Literacy Research, 32,* 631–662.

Gulliford, A. (1986). *America's country schools.* Washington, DC: Preservation Press.

Guskey, T. R. (2000). *Evaluating professional development.* Thousand Oaks, CA: Corwin Press.

Guthrie, J. W., & Sanders, T. (2001, January 7). Who will lead the public schools? *New York Times,* p. 46.

Hannaway, J., & Kimball, K. (1997). *Reports on reform from the field: District and state survey results.* Washington, DC: U.S. Department of Education.

Hargreaves, A., & Fullan, M. (1998). *What's worth fighting for out there.* New York: Teachers College Press.

Harris, W. T. (1892, February). City school supervision. *Educational Review, 3,* 168–169.

Harwell, M., D'Amico, L., Stein, M. K., & Gatti, G. G. (2000). *The effects of teachers' professional development on student achievement in Community School District #2.* Paper presented at the annual meeting of the American Educational Research Association, New Orleans, LA.

Hess, A. J. (1995). *Restructuring urban schools: A Chicago perspective.* New York: Teachers College Press.

Hess, F. M. (1999). *Spinning wheels: The politics of urban school reform.* Washington, DC: Brookings Institution Press.

Hightower, A. M. (2001). *San Diego's big boom: District bureaucracy meets culture of learning.* Unpublished doctoral dissertation, Stanford University, Stanford, CA.

Hill, P. T. (1999). Supplying effective public schools in big cities. *Brookings Papers on Education Policy, 1999.*

Hill, P. T. (2000). The federal role in education. *Brookings Papers on Education Policy, 2000,* 1–40.

Hill, P., & Bonan, J. (1991). *Decentralization and accountability in public education.* Santa Monica, CA: RAND.

Hill, P. T., Campbell, C., & Harvey, J. (2000). *It takes a city: Getting serious about urban school reform.* Washington, DC: Brookings Institution Press.

Hill, P. T., & Celio, M. B. (1998). *Fixing urban schools.* Washington, DC: Brookings Institution Press.

Hill, P. T., Pierce, L. C., & Guthrie, J. W. (1997). *Reinventing public education: How contracting can transform America's schools.* Chicago: University of Chicago Press.

Huberman, M. (1993). The model of an independent artisan in teacher's professional relations. In J. Little & M. McLaughlin (Eds.), *Teachers' work* (pp. 11–50). New York: Teachers College Press.

Hutchins, E. (1995). *Cognition in the wild.* Cambridge, MA: MIT Press.

Jackson, P. (1986). *The practice of teaching.* New York: Teachers College Press.

Judd, C. H. (1934). School boards as an obstruction to good. *The Nation's Schools, 13,* 1–15.

Kagan, D. M. (1992). Professional growth among preservice and beginning teachers. *Review of Educational Research, 62,* 129–169.

Katz, M. B., Fine, M., & Simon, E. (1997). Poking around: Outsiders' view of Chicago school reform. *Teachers College Record, 99,* 117–137.

Kirp, D., & Driver, C. E. (1995). The aspirations of systemic reform meet the realities of localism. *Educational Administration Quarterly, 31,* 589–612.

Knapp, M. S., & Associates. (1995). *Teaching for meaning in high-poverty classrooms.* New York: Teachers College Press.

Knapp, M. S., Bamburg, J. D., Ferguson, M. C., & Hill, P. T. (1998). Converging reforms and the working lives of frontline professional in schools. *Educational Policy, 12*(4), 397–418.

Knapp, M. S., & McLaughlin, M. W. (1999, April). *The district role in the renewal of teaching: Framing the conversation and the research.* Paper presented at the annual meeting of the American Educational Research Association, Montreal, Canada.

Kozol, J. (1991). *Savage inequalities: Children in America's schools.* New York: Crown.

Lampert, M. (1992). Practices and problems in teaching authentic mathematics. In F. Oser, A. Dick, & J. L. Patry (Eds.), *Effective and responsible teaching: The new synthesis* (pp. 295–313). San Francisco: Jossey-Bass.

Lanzara, G. F. (1998). Self-destructive processes in institution building and some modest countervailing mechanisms. *European Journal of Political Research, 33,* 1–39.

Lave, J. (1988). Situating learning in communities of practice. In L. Resnick, S. Levine, & L. Teasley (Eds.), *Perspectives of socially shared cognition* (pp. 63–82). Cambridge, MA: MIT Press.

Leinhardt, G. (1985). *Getting to know: Tracing students' mathematical knowledge from intuition to competence.* Pittsburgh: Learning Research and Development Center, University of Pittsburgh.

Lieberman, M. (1960). *The future of public education.* Chicago: University of Chicago Press.

Lin, A. (1998, October). *To cope is also to act: Understanding variation across street-level bureaucracies.* Paper presented at the twentieth annual research conference of the Association for Public Policy Analysis and Management, New York.

Lindblom, C. E. (1980). *The policy-making process* (2nd ed.). Englewood Cliffs, NJ: Prentice-Hall.

Lipsky, M. (1980). *Street-level bureaucracy: Dilemmas of the individual in public services.* New York: Russell Sage Foundation.

Little, J. W. (1993a). Teachers' professional development in a climate of educational reform. *Educational Evaluation and Policy Analysis, 15*(2), 129–151.

Little, J. W. (1993b). *Teachers' professional development in a climate of educational reform* (CPRE Policy Brief). New Brunswick, NJ: Consortium for Policy Research in Education, Rutgers University,.

Little, J. W. (1999). Organizing schools for teacher learning. In L. Darling-Hammond & G. Sykes (Eds.), *Teaching as the learning profession: Handbook of policy and practice* (pp. 376–411). San Francisco: Jossey-Bass.

Lortie, D. (1975). *Schoolteacher.* Chicago: University of Chicago Press.

Loucks-Horsley, S. (1995). Professional development in the learner-centered school. *Theory into Practice, 34,* 265–271.

Loucks-Horsley, S., Hewson, P., Love, N., & Stiles, K. (1998). *Designing professional development for teachers of science and mathematics.* Thousand Oaks, CA: Corwin.

Magee, M., & Leopold, L. S. (1998, September 1). New superintendent, many other changes welcome 139,000. *San Diego Union-Tribune,* p. B1.

Malen, B., & Knapp, M. S. (1997). Rethinking the multiple perspectives approach to education policy analysis: Implications for policy-practice connections. *Journal of Education Policy, 12*(5), 419–445.

Mann, H. (1891). Duties of school committees. In *Educational writings of Horace Mann* (pp. 245–246). Boston: Lee & Shepard Publishers.

March, J. G. (1994) A *primer on decision making: How decisions happen.* New York: Free Press.

Marsh, D. D., & McCabe, L. L. (1998). *School restructuring: From state policy to district superintendents.* Paper presented at the annual meeting of the American Education Research Association, San Diego, CA.

Marsh, J. A. (2000). *Connecting districts to the policy dialogue: A review of literature on the relationship of districts with states, schools, and communities.* Seattle, WA: Center for the Study of Teaching and Policy (CTP), University of Washington.

Martin, D. (1987, April). What critics won't see: If school boards vanished, we'd have to reinvent them. *The American School Board Journal, 174*(4), 29–30.

Massell, D. (2001). The theory and practice of using data to build capacity: State and local strategies and their effects. In S. H. Fuhrman (Ed.), *From the capitol to the classroom: Standards-based reform in the states: One hundredth yearbook of the National Society for the Study of Education, Part II* (pp. 148–169). Chicago, IL: The University of Chicago Press.

Massell, D., & Goertz, M. (1999). *Local strategies for building capacity: The district role in supporting instructional reform.* Paper presented at the annual meeting of the American Education Research Association, Montreal, Canada.

McDiarmid, G. W. (1999). *Still missing after all these years: Understanding the paucity of subject-matter professional development in Kentucky.* Retrieved from http: //www.pfks.org.

McDonald, J. P., Hatch, T., Kirby, E., Ames, N., Haynes, N. M., & Joyner, E. T. (1999). *School reform behind the scenes.* New York: Teachers College Press.

McDonnell, L. M., & Elmore, R. F. (1987). Getting the job done: Alternative policy instruments. *Educational Evaluation and Policy Analysis, 9,* 135–152.

McDonnell, L., & Pascal, A. (Eds.). (1988). *Teachers unions and educational reform.* Santa Monica, CA: RAND.

McLaughlin, M. W. (1987). Learning from experience: Lessons from policy implementation. *Educational Evaluation and Policy Analysis, 9,* 171–178.

McLaughlin, M. W. (1992). How district communities do and do not foster teacher pride. *Education Leadership, 50,* 33–35.

McLaughlin, M. W., & Oberman, I. (1996). *Teacher learning: New policies, new practices.* New York: Teachers College Press.

McLaughlin, M. W., & Talbert, J. E. (1993). *Contexts that matter for teaching and learning: Strategic opportunities for meeting the nation's goals.* Stanford, CA: Stanford University, Center for Research on the Context of Secondary School Teaching.

McLaughlin, M. W., & Talbert, J. E. (2001). *Professional communities and the work of high school teaching.* Chicago: University of Chicago Press.

Mehan, H., & Grimes, S. (1999). *Measuring the achievement gap in San Diego City Schools.* San Diego: University of California, San Diego.

Mehan, H., Quartz, K., & Stein, M. K. (1999). *Co-constructing San Diego's Institute for Learning.* Paper prepared for the Spencer Foundation, Pittsburgh, PA.

Metz, M. H. (1990). Real school: A universal drama amid disparate experience. In D. E. Mitchell & M. E. Goertz (Eds.), *Educational politics for the new century* (pp. 75–91). New York: Falmer.

Meyer, J. W. (1980). *The impact of centralization of funding and control of state and local educational governance.* Stanford, CA: Institute for Research on Educational Finance and Governance, Stanford University.

Meyer, J. W., Scott, W. R., & Strang, D. (1994). Centralization, fragmentation, and school district complexity. In W. R. Scott, J. W. Meyer, & Associates (Eds.), *Institutional environments and organizations* (pp. 160–178). Thousand Oaks, CA: Sage.

Miles, K. H.,& Guiney, E. (2000). School districts' new role. *Education Week, 19*(40), 30, 32–33.

Murphy, J., & Hallinger, P. (1986). The superintendent as instructional leader: Findings from effective school districts. *The Journal of Educational Administration, 24,* 213–236.

Murphy, J., & Hallinger, P. (1988). Characteristics of instructionally effective school districts. *Journal of Educational Research, 81,* 175–181.

National Board for Professional Teaching Standards (NBPTS). (1989). *Toward high and rigorous standards for the teaching profession: Initial policies and perspectives of the National Board for Professional Teaching Standards.* Washington, DC: Author.

National Commission on Teaching and America's Future. (1996). *What matters most: Teaching for America's future.* New York: Author.

National Council of Teachers of Mathematics (NCTM). (1989). *Curriculum and evaluation standards for school mathematics.* Reston, VA: Author.

National Council of Teachers of Mathematics (NCTM). (1991). *Professional standards for teaching mathematics.* Reston, VA: Author.

National Council of Teachers of Mathematics (NCTM) (2000). *Principles and standards for school mathematics.* Reston, VA: Author.

Nelson, B. S. (1999). *Building new knowledge by thinking: How administrators can learn what they need to know about mathematics education reform.* Newton, MA: Center for the Development of Teaching, Education Development Center, Inc.

New Zealand Ministry of Education. (1996). *Reading for life: The learner as a reader.* Wellington, New Zealand: Learning Media Limited.

Newell, A., & Simon, H. (1972). *Human problem-solving.* Englewood Cliffs, NJ: Prentice-Hall.

Newmann, F. M., & Wehlage, G. (Eds.). (1995). *Successful school restructuring: A report to the public and educators by the Center on Organization and Restructuring of Schools.* Madison, WI: University of Wisconsin.

O'Connell, M. (1991). *School reform Chicago style: How citizens organized to change public policy.* Chicago: Center for Neighborhood Technology.

O'Day, J. A., & Smith, M. S. (1993). Systemic school reform and educational opportunity. In S. Fuhrman (Ed.), *Designing coherent educational policy: Improving the system* (pp. 250–312). San Francisco: Jossey-Bass.

Pearse, C. G. (1903). Comment. In *NEA addresses and proceedings* (p. 162). Minneapolis: NEA.

Pinnell, G. S., Fountas, I. C., Giacobbe, M. E., & Fountas, A. C. (1998). *Word matters: Teaching phonics and spelling in the reading/writing classroom.* Portsmouth, NH: Heinemann.

Porter, A. (1989). External standards and good teaching: The pros and cons of telling teachers what to do. *Educational Evaluation and Policy Analysis, 11,* 343–356.

Price, J. N., Ball, D. L., & Luks, S. (1995). *Marshaling resources for reform: District administrators and the case of mathematics.* East Lansing, MI: National Center for Research on Teacher Learning.

Purkey, S. C., & Smith, M. S. (1985). School reform: The district policy implications of the effective schools literature. *Elementary School Journal, 85*(3), 353–389.

Quality counts '98: The urban challenge. (1998). *Education Week, 17,* 3–270.

Reller, T. L. (1935). *The development of the city superintendency of schools in the United States.* Philadelphia: Author.

Resnick, L. (1991). Shared cognition: Thinking as social practice. In L. Resnick, J. Levine, & S. Teasley (Eds.), *Perspectives on socially shared cognition* (pp. 1–20). Washington, DC: American Psychological Association.

Resnick, L. B. (1995). From aptitude to effort: A new foundation for our schools. *Daedalus, 124,* 55–62.

Resnick, L. B. (1999, June 16). Making America smarter. *Education Week,* pp. 38–40.

Resnick, L. B., & Hall, M. W. (1998). Learning organizations for sustainable education reform. *Daedalus, 127,* 89–118.

Resnick, L. B., & Hall, M. W. (2002, March 18). *Principles of learning for effort-based education.* Manuscript in preparation, Institute for Learning, Learning Research and Development Center, University of Pittsburgh.

Resnick, L. B., & Harwell, M. (2000, August*). Instructional variation and student achievement in a standards-based education district* (CSE Tech. Report No. 522). Los Angeles: University of California, National Center for Research on Evaluation, Standards, and Student Testing.

Resnick, L. B., & Nelson-Le Gall, S. (1997). Socializing intelligence. In L. Smith, J. Dockrell, & P. Tomlinson (Eds.), *Piaget, Vygotsky and beyond* (pp. 145–158). London/New York: Routledge.

Rosenholtz, S. J. (1989). *Teachers' workplace: The social organization of schools.* White Plains, NY: Longman.

Rowan, B. (2000). *Reinventing organizational studies in education: A pressing need for the 21st century.* Paper presented at the American Educational Association of Researchers Annual Meeting, New Orleans, LA.

Rowan, B., Edelstein, R., & Leal, A. (1985). *Pathways to excellence: What school districts are doing to improve instruction.* San Francisco: Far West Laboratory for Educational Research and Development.

San Diego City Schools (2000, March 14). *Blueprint for student success in a standards-based system.* San Diego, CA: Author.

Sarason, S. (1991). *The predictable failure of school reform.* San Francisco: Jossey-Bass.

Saxe, G., Gearhart, M., Franke, M., Howard, S., & Crockett, M. (1999). Teachers' shifting assessment practice in the context of educational reform in mathematics. *Teaching and Teacher Education, 15,* 85–105.

Scholes, R. (1995). An overview of pacesetter English. *English Journal, 84*(1), 69–75.

Schultz, S. K. (1973). *The culture factory: Boston public schools, 1789–1860.* New York: Oxford University Press.

Scott, W. R. (1995). *Institutions and organizations.* Thousand Oaks, CA: Sage Publications.

Shaw, A. M. (1904, October). The public schools of a boss-ridden city. *World's Work, 7,* 5405–5414.

Sheldon, G. W. (1991). *The political philosophy of Thomas Jefferson.* Baltimore: Johns Hopkins University Press.

Siljestrom, P. (1853). *The educational institutions of the United States: Their character and organization* (pp. 11, 39–42). London: Chapman.

Snowball, D., & Bolton, F. (1999). *Spelling K–8: Planning and teaching.* Portland, ME: Stenhouse.

Spillane, J. P. (1994). How districts mediate between state policy and teachers' practice. In R. F. Elmore & S. H. Fuhrman (Eds.), *The governance of curriculum* (pp. 167–185). Alexandria, VA: Association for Supervision and Curriculum Development.

Spillane, J. P. (1996). School districts matter: Local educational authorities and state instructional policy. *Educational Policy and Analysis, 10*(1), 63–87.

Spillane, J. P. (1998a). A cognitive perspective on the LEA's role in implementing instructional policy: Accounting for local variability. *Educational Administration Quarterly, 34*(1), 31–57.

Spillane, J. P. (1998b). State policy and the non-monolithic nature of the local school district: Organizational and professional considerations. *American Educational Research Journal, 35*(1), 33–63.

Spillane, J. P. (1999). External reform initiatives and teachers' efforts to reconstruct their practice: The mediating role of teachers' zones of enactment. *Journal of Curriculum Studies, 31*(2), 143–175.

Spillane, J. P. (2000a). Cognition and policy implementation: District policy-makers and the reform of mathematics education. *Cognition and Instruction, 18*(2), 141–179.

Spillane, J. P. (2000b). [Untitled (CPRE occasional paper no. OP-05)]. Philadelphia: University of Pennsylvania, Graduate School of Education, Consortium for Policy Research in Education.

Spillane, J. P. (2000c). *District leaders' perceptions of teacher learning.* Philadelphia: Consortium for Policy Research in Education (CPRE).

Spillane, J. (in press). The change theories of local change agents: The pedagogy of district policies and programs. *Teachers College Record.*

Spillane, J., & Callahan, K. (2000). Science standards: What district policy-makers make of the hoopla. *Journal of Research on Science Teaching, 37*(5) 401–425.

Spillane, J. P., & Jennings, N. E. (1997). Aligned instructional policy and ambitious pedagogy: Exploring instructional reform from the classroom perspective. *Teachers College Record, 98*, 449–481.

Spillane, J., & Reimer, T. (2001). *Policy implementation: A cognitive model.* Manuscript submitted for publication, Northwestern University, Evanston, IL.

Spillane, J. P., & Thompson, C. L. (1997). Reconstructing conceptions of local capacity: The local education agency's capacity for ambitious instructional reform. *Education Evaluation and Policy Analysis, 19*(2), 185–203.

Spillane, J. P., Thompson, C. L., Lubienski, C., Jita, L., & Reimann, C. B. (1995). *The local government policy system affecting mathematics and science education in Michigan: Lessons from nine school districts.* Unpublished manuscript, Michigan State University, East Lansing.

Spillane, J. P., & Zeuli, J. S. (1999). Reform and mathematics teaching: Exploring patterns of practice in the context of national and state reforms. *Educational Evaluation and Policy Analysis, 21*(1), 1–27.

Stein, M. K., & D'Amico, L. (in press). Inquiry at the crossroads of policy and learning: A study of a district-wide literacy initiative. *Teachers College Record.*

Stein, M. K., D'Amico, L., & Israel, N. (1999, April). *Observations, conversations, and negotiations: Administrator support of literacy practices in New York City's Com-*

munity School District #2. Paper presented at the annual meeting of the American Educational Research Association, Montreal, Canada.

Stigler, J. W., & Hiebert, J. (1999). *The teaching gap: Best ideas from the world's teachers for improving education in the classroom.* New York: Free Press.

Strayer, G. D. (1930, September). Progress in city school administration during the past twenty-five years. *School and Society, 32,* 375–378.

Swan, W. W. (1998). *Local school system implementation of state policy actions for educational reform.* Paper presented at the annual meeting of the American Educational Research Association, San Diego.

Terman, L. M. (1919). *Intelligence of school children.* Boston: Houghton Mifflin.

Thompson, C. L., Spillane, J. P., & Cohen, D. K. (1994). *The state policy system affecting science and mathematics education in Michigan.* Unpublished manuscript, Michigan Statewide Systemic Initiative Policy and Program Review Component, Michigan State University, East Lansing.

Thompson, C. L., & Zeuli, J. S. (1999). The frame and the tapestry: Standards-based reform and professional development. In L. Darling-Hammond & G. Sykes (Eds.), *Teaching as the learning profession: Handbook of policy and practice* (pp. 341–375). San Francisco: Jossey-Bass.

Turner, L. C. (1940, June). School-board minutes of one hundred years ago. *American School Board Journal, 100* (6), 18, 91.

Tyack, D. B. (1974). *The one best system: A history of American urban education.* Cambridge, MA: Harvard University Press.

Tyack, D. B. (1993). School governance in the United States: Historical puzzles and anomalies. In J. Hannaway & M. Carnoy (Eds.), *Decentralization and school improvement: Can we fulfill the promise?* (pp.1–32). San Francisco: Jossey-Bass.

Tyack, D. B., & Cuban, L. (1995). *Tinkering toward utopia: Reflections on a century of public school reform.* Cambridge, MA: Harvard University Press.

Tyack, D., & Hansot, E. (1982). *Managers of virtue: Public school leadership in America, 1820–1980.* New York: Basic Books.

U.S. Department of Education. (1997). *Digest of educational statistics.* Washington, DC: Author.

U.S. Department of Education. (1999). *Teacher quality: A report on the preparation and qualifications of public school teachers.* Washington, DC: National Center for Education Statistics.

U.S. Department of Education. (2000, April 14). *Reading Excellence Act State Competitive Grant Program: Non-regulatory guidance for state applicants.* Washington, DC: Author.

Vigil, D. W., & Carstens, L. J. (1998). *The San Diego high school cluster case.* Pittsburgh, PA: Pew Forum on Standards-Based Reform.

Wagner, T. (2000). *How schools change: Lessons from three communities revisited* (2nd ed.). New York: Routledge Falmer.

Wallace–Reader's Digest Funds. (2001). *Request for proposal: Learning from the Wallace–Reader's Digest Funds' efforts to strengthen educational leadership.* New York: Author.

Wechsler, M. E. (2001). *A district community of practice: Understanding the relationship between a supportive district and its schools.* Unpublished doctoral dissertation, Stanford University, Stanford, CA.

Wechsler, M. E., & Friedrich, L. D. (1997). The role of mediating organizations for school reform: Independent agents or district dependents? *Journal of Education Policy, 12*(5), 401.

Weick, K. E. (1976). Educational organizations as loosely coupled systems. *Administrative Science Quarterly, 21*, 1–19.

Weick, K. E. (1979). *The social psychology of organizing* (2nd ed.). Reading, MA: Addison-Wesley.

Wenger, E. (1998). *Communities of practice: Learning, meaning and identity.* Cambridge, UK: Cambridge University Press.

Will, G. F. (1995, March 20). Presidential minimalism. *Newsweek,* p. 72.

Wilson, S. M., & Floden, R. (2001). Hedging bets: Standards-based reform in classrooms. In S. H. Fuhrman (Ed.), *One-Hundredth Yearbook of the National Society for the Study of Education: Part II. From the Capitol to the classroom: Standards-based reform in the states* (pp. 193–216). Chicago: University of Chicago Press.

Wise, A. E. (1979). *Legislated learning: The bureaucratization of the American classroom.* Berkeley: University of California Press.

Yanow, D. (1996). *How does a policy mean? Interpreting policy and organizational actions.* Washington, DC: Georgetown University Press.

About the Editors and the Contributors

Patricia Ellen Burch currently serves as the principal investigator of a three-district study of central office–school interaction. Prior to receiving her Ph.D. from the Stanford University School of Education, she worked as a program developer and as a policy analyst. Her research focuses on policy implementation and distributed leadership.

Laura D'Amico is a Research Associate at Simon Fraser University. Her research focuses on the support systems necessary to implement educational reform, including assessment infrastructures, learning technologies, and professional development systems for teachers and principals.

Thomas K. Glennan, Jr. is Senior Advisor for Education Policy at RAND. He directed the initial stages of RAND's New American Schools Development Corporation evaluation and has worked closely with the Institute for Learning at the University of Pittsburgh to develop a program of research and evaluation related to the Institute program. Dr. Glennan was the first director of the National Institute of Education.

Margaret E. Goertz is a professor of education policy and a co-director of the Consortium for Policy Research in Education (CPRE) at the Graduate School of Education, University of Pennsylvania. Her research focuses on education finance, education policy, and intergovernmental relations, paying particular attention to fiscal and programmatic equity and students with special needs.

Pam Grossman is Professor and Co-Chair of Curriculum and Teacher Education at Stanford University. Her research interests include teacher learning, the relationship between teacher knowledge and teacher education, and the teaching and learning of English.

Amy M. Hightower (Editor) is a Research Scientist at Stanford University's Center for the Study of Teaching and Policy. Her research focuses on organizational learning, education policy, and governance structures, with particular emphasis on the role of school districts in reform.

Michael S. Knapp (Editor), a Professor of Educational Leadership and Policy Studies at the University of Washington, directs the Center for the

Study of Teaching and Policy. His research and teaching concentrate on educational policy making and reform, with emphasis on the influence of policy and leadership on classroom practice and school improvement.

Julie A. Marsh (Editor) is a Researcher at the Center for the Study of Teaching and Policy at Stanford University. Her research focuses on deliberative democracy, policy implementation, and district–community partnerships.

Diane Massell is a senior research associate at the Consortium for Policy Research in Education (CPRE) at the University of Michigan's School of Education. Her research focuses on education policy; she is currently focusing on standards-based reform and comprehensive schoolwide improvement programs.

Milbrey W. McLaughlin (Editor) is the David Jacks Professor of Education and Public Policy at Stanford University. She is Executive Director of the John W. Gardner Center for Youth and Their Communities and Co-Director of the Center for Research on the Contexts of Teaching, and is affiliated with the Center for the Study of Teaching and Policy. Her research focuses on community youth development and school reform.

Lauren B. Resnick is Professor of Psychology at the University of Pittsburgh, where she directs the Learning Research and Development Center. She founded and directs the Institute for Learning, which works with urban school districts to develop and implement strategies for effort-based education of diverse student populations. Dr. Resnick is past president of the American Educational Research Association.

Jon Snyder is the Dean of the Graduate School of Education at Bank Street College and Senior Researcher for the National Commission on Teaching and America's Future. His practice and research focus on conditions that support teacher learning and the relationships between teacher learning and student learning.

James P. Spillane is Associate Professor of Education and Social Policy, and a Faculty Fellow at the Institute for Policy Research, at Northwestern University. His work explores policy implementation at state, district, school, and classroom levels, focusing on intergovernmental relations and policy–practice relations. He is associate editor of *Educational Evaluation and Policy Analysis*.

Mary Kay Stein is a Research Scientist at the Learning Research and Development Center and an Associate Professor of Administrative and Policy Studies at the University of Pittsburgh. Her research focuses on educational change, teacher learning, and school leadership within specific subject areas.

Joan E. Talbert is Senior Research Scholar and Co-Director of the Center for Research on the Context of Teaching (CRC) at Stanford University. She studies ways in which teachers' work and professional careers are shaped by organizational, policy, and collegial contexts.

Clarissa S. Thompson is a graduate student in Curriculum and Instruction at the University of Washington, specializing in English Education and Teacher Education. Her research focuses on the pedagogy of teacher education and how beginning teachers learn to teach English/language arts. She was formerly a high school English teacher.

David Tyack is the Vida Jacks Professor of Education and Professor of History Emeritus at Stanford University. He is author of *The One Best System* and co-author (with Larry Cuban) of *Tinkering Toward Utopia*.

Sheila W. Valencia is Professor of Curriculum and Instruction, and Chair of the Language, Literacy and Culture program at the University of Washington, Seattle. Her research interests focus on reading and writing instruction, and the role that assessment, policy, and teacher development play in promoting effective literacy classroom practice.

Index